American

Civilization

An introduction

SECOND EDITION

■ David Mauk and John Oakland

First published 1995
Second edition first published 1997
by Routledge
11 New Fetter Lane, London EC4P 4EE

Simultaneously published in the USA
and Canada
by Routledge
29 West 35th Street, New York,
NY 10001

Typeset in Sabon and Futura by
Florencetype Ltd, Stoodleigh, Devon

Printed and bound in Great Britain by
Biddles Ltd, Guildford and King's Lynn

*British Library Cataloguing in
Publication Data*
A catalogue record for this book is
available from the British Library

*Library of Congress Cataloguing in
Publication Data*
Mauk, David, 1945–
   American civilization: an
introduction / David Mauk and John
Oakland. – 2nd ed.
   p. cm.
   Includes bibliographical references
and index.
   ISBN 0–415–16523–7
   1. United States – Civilization.
2. United States – Civilization – Study
and teaching – Foreign countries.
I. Oakland, John. II. Title.
E169.1.M45   1997
973–dc21   97–240
CIP

ISBN 0–415–16523–7

Contents

Plates

Figures

Tables

xiii

Preface and acknowledgements

This book deals mainly with central institutional features of American (US) civilization such as the political and governmental systems, the legal structure, the economy, social services, education, the media and religion. But chapters on the country and the people are also included in order to provide a wider background and to emphasize the geographical and human diversity of the US.

Methodologically, the book combines descriptive and analytical approaches within a historical context and provides information on recent developments in the US. It is intended to allow students to develop their own responses to American society and to encourage discussion.

A book of this type is necessarily indebted for many of its ideas, facts and statistics to a wide range of reference sources, too numerous to mention individually here, but to which a general acknowledgement is made (see Bibliography and Suggested Further Reading).

Introduction

MANY IMAGES HAVE BEEN ATTRIBUTED to the US, both historically and at present. People inside and outside the country have varied, and often conflicting, views about it. Some of these perspectives are based on observable and quantifiable facts. Others may be conditioned by ideology and rhetoric.

American self-images sometimes betray an exalted and isolationist view of the nation's alleged 'exceptionalism' (its unique mission in the world, idealistic values and sense of destiny). Non-American opinions are frequently driven by prejudice, envy, ignorance, or a bias towards other systems.

In order to understand the contemporary US and appreciate how it has developed historically, some conditioning factors need to be emphasized. Among these are the treatment of Native Americans; the effects of large-scale immigration into the country; the westward expansion of the nation; the War for Independence from Britain (1775–83) and the Civil War to end Black slavery (1861–5);

1

the principles (like human dignity and rights to freedom, justice and opportunity) of the new nation contained in the Declaration of Independence (1776) and the US Constitution (1787); associated ideologies of egalitarianism, individualism and utopianism; and the later developments of corporate capitalism, government regulation and bureaucracy which have arguably undermined individual autonomy.

These historical features have created three major cultures in the US, which may conflict with each other and operate on levels of idealism and pragmatism. The first is an ethnic culture based on Native-American civilization, Black slavery and immigration, which attempts to express human diversity. The second is a political culture which tries to unite the people under ideal versions of 'Americanness', such as egalitarianism, morality and patriotism. The third is an economic and consumer culture driven by corporate and individual competition which encourages the consumption of goods and services. But a number of subcultures (such as youth culture and an underclass of disadvantaged people) may be alienated from the main cultures.

In terms of ethnic culture, the initial bases of US society, in addition to existing Native-American communities, were largely British. Over half of the population until 1776 came from British Isles stock. These people assimilated other early European settlers into a White, Anglo-American, Protestant dominant culture. They were responsible for promoting many of the political, social, constitutional and religious institutions of the new nation. Their values continued to influence the society into the twentieth century.

Northwestern Europe supplied over two-thirds of US immigration for most of the nineteenth century. There were also many Asian immigrants in this period. At the end of that century there was a shift towards newcomers from southern and eastern Europe. The twentieth century saw a great variety of other nationalities from all over the world immigrating to the US. In the 1980s and 1990s, the largest groups of immigrants have come from Asia, the Caribbean and Latin America.

The effects of immigration and the importation of Black slaves on the culture of the US have been substantial, in terms both of the total figures involved and the high number of very different groups from world-wide origins. This background of large-scale immigration, slavery and Native-American experiences is different from that of other nations, arguably defines American history as special and provides the US with a distinct identity. Immigrants have considerably affected public life at different times in US history. But they have also experienced difficulties of integration due to language problems or differences in cultural practices. There have been conflicts and racial tensions between settled groups and waves of immigrants into the US, which have sometimes erupted into violence. These factors reveal a nativism (discrimination towards newcomers by the existing population) and racism in many areas of American life, frequently in institutionalized form, which have continued to the present. Ethnic diversity has therefore brought advantages and disadvantages, but it has also reduced the dominance of the original Anglo-American culture, which has had to take account of a growing pluralism in society.

Many diverse cultural groups have thus had to both coexist and struggle for individual expression. They must today somehow live together in spite of tensions between them. But there is always the possibility of political and social instability in this multicultural situation. Critics continue to debate whether these conflicts (arising out of social pluralism) should be seen as distinctively American or are also applicable to other nations.

Tensions resulting from ethnic diversity have also partly shaped and affected the nature of American politics and created a particular political culture. Responses to pluralism have often resulted in consensus politics based on political and judicial compromise. US politics are not normally therefore as polarized or radical as in some other nations. But differences between political policies for dealing with majority and minority rights continue to play a central role.

American politics often tend to be more concerned with local, special and regional interests than national matters.

Politicians in Washington, DC, try to promote their own local constituency legislation as a response to local and regional pressures (including ethnic and minority matters). Such concerns often persuade American voters to vote simultaneously for political representatives from different parties.

The pressure to produce consensual national politics is also due to the central place of the Constitution in American life; to the restrictions that the Constitution places upon politics; and to the fact that many Americans believe in minimal government. The Constitution has to be interpreted, and the governmental system of checks and balances sometimes results in stalemate. But these features do help to solidify the society, and idealized versions of 'America' constructed through its political institutions can minimize conflict.

They also illustrate the degree of abstraction that is involved in defining the US and Americanism. The notion of what constitutes 'America' has had to be revised over time. This process reflects both a materialistic/practical reality and an idealistic/abstract hope. Racial differences have demonstrably presented the greatest barriers to national unity. Consequently, for some critics, the American political system consists of both hard-nosed manipulation of group interests and exaggerated rhetoric.

The third major culture comprises the economic system and consumerism. The US social and economic cultures are also both materialistic/practical and idealistic/abstract. A competitive economic philosophy is connected to a belief in individualism. People have to fight for their economic and social survival. But this emphasis disguises the contradictory structures of economic cooperation (which has always been present in American society) and corporate domination of economic life.

The ethnic, political and economic cultures influence and are reflected in other aspects of American life such as the law, the health care system and religious institutions. They also condition questions of national identity. Major problems for the US historically have been how to balance the need for national unity with ethnic diversity and avoid the dangers of fragmentation. An emphasis has often been placed on 'Americanization', or the attempted assimilation of different ethnic groups into a shared, mainly Anglo-American-based identity. The ethnic blending suggested by the metaphor of the 'melting-pot' has frequently referred instead to pressures to assimilate into this dominant culture. Whatever the degree of attempted incorporation, Americans have historically tried to construct a sense of national identity and unity by binding the ethnically diverse population to significant images or symbols of 'Americanness', such as the flag, the Declaration of Independence, the Liberty Bell, Abraham Lincoln's Emancipation Proclamation and Gettysburg Address, 'the Star-Spangled Banner' and the Constitution. These are meant to provide a collection of common cultural assumptions which promote loyalty to shared notions of what 'America' and 'Americanness' might be. Their representative qualities attempt to avoid the potentially divisive elements of economic, class or racial differences.

Certain values have also been traditionally associated with these symbols, such as individualism, utopianism, self-reliance, egalitarianism, liberty, anti-statism (distrust of government), populism (grassroots activism) and an American sense of destiny. They stem largely from the ideas of the European Enlightenment, which influenced the framers of the Declaration of Independence and the US Constitution. Thus, there are layers of idealism and abstraction in American life which coexist, and may clash, with reality. Yet this situation is not unique. It echoes the experience of other countries, particularly those that are unions, federations or collections of different peoples with contrasting roots and traditions, which feel the need to erect distinctive national identities.

Some critics try to explain the US and national identity by 'American attitudes'. Features like restlessness, escape from restraints, change, action, mobility, quests for new experiences, self-improvement and a belief in potential are supposedly typical American traits. They are often attributed to the legacy of immigrant and frontier experiences and an American belief in progress, both individually and for the larger society. Americans allegedly refuse to accept a fixed fate or settled location, but seek new jobs, new horizons and new beginnings in a hunt for self-fulfilment and self-definition.

Yet many Americans also seek roots and stability. Similarly, while the alleged informality of American life is supposedly founded on individualism, egalitarianism and a historical rejection of European habits, many Americans respect and desire formalities, order and hierarchy.

Americans may stress their individualism, distrust of big business and government and their desire to be free. But communalism and group endeavours are also a feature of US life. Individuals additionally have to cope with corporate, political and social bureaucracy, employment environments and economic and social hierarchies with their power bases. Indeed, American literature is full of characters' romantic attempts to be free and their frequent failures when faced with the realities of society and their individual conditions.

One cannot therefore define a single and simple set of values and attitudes which are shared by all Americans. Diversity and individual differences, whether from personal, social, religious or economic circumstances, limit possibilities and can result in contradictions or tensions rather than unified beliefs. Arguably, the supposedly American values and attitudes are universal characteristics and are not exceptional in themselves or distinctively American.

But the degree to which they are propagated in US society is nevertheless significant. They are attractive and valid for many people. A key feature of American life, therefore, is how individuals manage to combine traditional ideals with the actual realities of society and cope with the resulting oppositions. Underneath the surface idealism is an essential American pragmatism, a need to apply ideas to real situations and a respect for practical solutions to problems.

In recent decades, debates on national identity have centred on questions of unity (or Americanization) as against diversity (or ethnic pluralism). These reflect an American historical pattern which has shifted between reform/liberal and consolidation/conservative periods of development. In the 1950s, ethnic differences and issues seemed to be declining, but have revived since the 1960s. Arguments have vacillated between the adequacy of old values of Americanism (often represented by conservatives) and ethnic or minority group interests (supported by liberals). Critics suggest that the American ideal of *e pluribus unum* (out of many one) is an abstract concept which does not reflect reality. On the other hand, emphases on ethnicity and difference have arguably weakened the possibility of achieving a set of values that could represent a distinctive 'American Way of Life'. Some critics feel that American society is at risk because of the very diversity of competing cultures and interest groups.

But from the late 1970s through to the 1990s, there has been a reaction against liberal 1960s' policies and affirmative action programmes for minority groups. Conservatives assert what they consider to be traditional American values. These debates have further increased anxieties about national identity and where the country is headed. The conflicts over supposedly fundamental American values continue at present in many areas of national life, ranging from abortion and educational issues to political and economic questions.

Such concerns have led critics to argue that the US should be regarded as a 'mosaic', 'salad bowl', 'pizza' or even 'stew mix', rather than a 'melting-pot'. The old 'melting-pot' metaphor of America, which implied ultimate cultural unity, has been largely rejected. But the metaphors of salads and stews nevertheless suggest that variety and difference should somehow be incorporated into a larger 'American' whole.

The metaphors, however, do indicate a certain acceptance of cultural and ethnic pluralism. Heterogeneity has continued despite pressures and arguments in support of homogenization. Critics argue that degrees of separateness and assimilation vary between groups and that absolute integration is both undesirable and impossible. But this can lead to hybrid cultural identities or the breakdown of strong national links.

Arguably, the tension is between absolute pluralism, on the one hand, and an acceptance of pluralism under an umbrella American identity, on the other. The latter solution has to be achieved within defining institutional structures which allow the facts of pluralism to exist. Varying degrees of assimilation could then be achieved in specific areas, while forms of differentiation would be recognized as valid.

The three major cultures have produced a composite Americanism. They have also partly influenced an international culture, for good or bad. They are expressed, for example, through Hollywood films, television and radio, newspapers and magazines, music and art, professional and amateur sport, patterns of consumption, well-known chain stores and brand names, and corporate and financial institutions.

But the major US cultures are not static. They have evolved and may gradually absorb and refashion other existing cultures, as they have done in the past. On the other hand, pressures for change may modify the major cultures themselves. Even though these are driven by the increasingly multinational forces of consumerism, they must remain responsive to political and minority pressures of many kinds.

This book first considers the land itself and its cultural regions. It then looks at the indigenous peoples, the settler and immigration experience, women and minorities. The rest of the book examines those institutional structures (and restraints), within which the majority of the American population have to operate. The historical development and modern roles of some central institutions, together with the values that underlie them, are described and analysed.

Institutions are organizations which have been gradually constructed over varying periods of time and reflect a variety of values and practices. Some of the US's institutional structures are particular to America and others reflect similarities with other nations. All have been developed over the past 400 years to cope with, and adapt to, an increasingly complex, diverse and dynamic society. They take many different forms and sizes, operate on national, state and local levels, and may be public or private in character.

The larger elements, such as federal and state governments, are involved with national, state, or public business. But there is a wide range of smaller units on both the public and private levels

of social activity, such as sports, local communities, neighbourhoods, religion, the theatre and various expressions of racial and
ethnic identity, which are often institutionalized. They may take
on more individualistic forms than the larger public institutions.
For some critics, it is the localized life and behaviour of
Americans at the community level which typically define their
society, rather than centralized federal institutions. However,
the national and larger public frameworks do serve as a cement
which holds local activities and people together. They also give
an umbrella sense of American identity and 'Americanness'.
Consequently, the US, like other countries, gains its identity from
a mixture of the local and the national, which inform and influence each other.

The American 'way of life' is partly defined by how citizens
function within and respond to local and national institutions,
whether positively or negatively. The large number and variety of
such institutions mean that there are many different 'ways of life'
and all contribute to the diversity and particular characteristics
of American society.

Institutions are not remote abstractions; they affect individuals directly in their daily lives. Despite their diversity, Americans
do have shared concerns which result from institutional life.
They can identify what are for them the major problems facing
the country and which affect most people in varying degrees.
Public opinion polls report on these concerns and show how
respondents are sensitive to changing conditions over time (see
Figure 0.1).

This book also stresses the historical context of US institutions and suggests that the contemporary situation can only be
adequately understood by reference to the past. Institutions are
adaptable, provide frameworks for new situations and their
present roles may be different from their original functions. They
have changed and evolved over time as they have been influenced
not only by elite and government policies, but also by grassroots
impulses and reactions. This process of change and adaptation
continues in the present and reflects current anxieties and concerns
in American life.

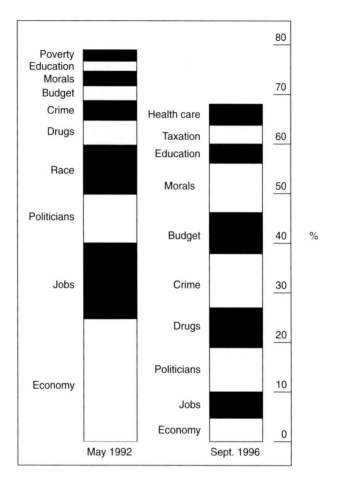

FIGURE 0.1 Top ten problems facing the US, 1992–6
(*The Economist/The American Institute, 1996*)

Institutional structures at various levels contribute to a culture of varied and conflicting habits and ideals, as well as being practical organizations for realizing them. The book therefore attempts to present a range of critical viewpoints on the society and its institutions in an attempt to describe what may, or may not, be regarded as distinctively American.

■ **Examine and explain the following terms:**

slavery	individualism	rhetoric
populism	ethnic	anti-statism
diversity	consensus	corporate
grassroots	culture(s)	consumerism
'America'	frontier	'salad bowl'
utopianism	pluralism	assimilation
multicultural	egalitarianism	'Americanization'

■ **Write short essays on the following topics:**

1   What are some of the characteristics that you would associate with the American people and their society? Why?

2   Try to define the term 'institution' and examine its possible usages.

The country

WITH A TOTAL AREA OF 3,615,122 square miles (9,363,123 square kilometres) the United States is exceeded in size only by Russia, Canada and China. The forty-eight contiguous states lie between the Atlantic and Pacific Oceans, Canada and Mexico. The two states that share no boundaries with the rest of the nation, Alaska and Hawaii, are located in the far northwest corner of the continent and the middle of the Pacific Ocean, respectively. Widely separated possessions in the Caribbean and the Pacific add another 11,000 square miles (17,600 kilometres) to American territory.

The most pronounced feature of the country, however, is not size but variety. Its natural environment varies from the arctic to the tropical, from rainforest to desert, from vast plains to cliffs and mountain peaks. The exploitation of its natural resources has depleted reserves, caused extensive pollution and shown a wastefulness that today results in a dependence on resources from other nations. Still, the country's own natural riches remain the main support of its economic life, which is the world's most diversified and presents pockets of both poverty and great affluence.

Physical features

Approached from the Atlantic Ocean or the Gulf of Mexico, the contiguous states' first major land formation is the Atlantic Plain, a nearly flat coastal lowland which runs from New England to the middle of the Texas–Mexico border. During the last ice age, glaciers pressed most of the Plain beneath the sea as far south as New York City, leaving only a narrow coastal strip. South of New York, the Plain gradually widens, but large fjords and bays break it up. Along the Gulf coast the Plain is at its widest and includes all or large parts of the Southern states from Florida to Texas.

PLATE 1.1 Manhattan Island, New York *(D. Scott/Barnaby's Picture Library)*

Most of the Atlantic Plain has poor soil, but exceptions are found in its southern fertile citrus-growing region and the Cotton Belt. The Plain's most important natural wealth is the oil and natural gas deposits along the Gulf coast, where much of the nation's crude oil and one-eighth of the world's natural gas reserves are located.

Inland from the Atlantic Plain the land rises to the Piedmont. This is a gently rolling, well-drained plateau, narrow in the north and broader in the south, which stretches from New York State to Alabama. The Piedmont is quite fertile, often reporting agricultural yields that are among the nation's highest. Along the eastern edge of the Piedmont is the fall line, where rivers running into the Atlantic produce waterfalls. When water power was used for grain and textile mills, important cities grew up along the fall line.

On its western side, the Piedmont rises further to the foothills of the Appalachians, a belt of old and much eroded mountains that runs from the Canadian border to Alabama and so separates the Eastern Seaboard from the interior. The Appalachians are actually a complex system containing several mountain ranges. These are separated from the Central Lowland by the Appalachian Plateau and a strip of land called the Ridge and Valley country. One of the main routes through the Appalachians, the Great Valley, extends for almost the whole length of the Appalachians. West of the Mississippi, the Ouachita Mountains and Ozark Plateau are much like the Ridge and Valley country.

Although the Appalachians and their related upland sub-regions contain a great variety of minerals, only iron, marble, granite and coal are found in large enough quantities for long-term exploitation. The coal deposits in Pennsylvania and West Virginia, in the area popularly called Appalachia, are among the world's largest. For decades these areas provided soft bituminous coal for the development of industry along the Great Lakes and hard anthracite coal for heating homes across the nation. Today, the coal-mining districts of Appalachia are among the nation's most economically depressed areas because 'cleaner' gas and oil have replaced coal.

To the west of the Appalachians and associated highlands lies the Central Lowland. This vast area stretches from upper New York State to central Texas and north to Canada. It resembles a huge, irregular bowl that is rimmed by the Great Lakes and various highlands. One of these, the iron-rich Mesabi Range west of the Lakes, has ores that complemented the coal of the Appalachians in the establishment of industry in lakeshore and Central Lowland cities.

Despite its popular reputation, the landscape of the Lowland is not entirely flat, although rough terrain and heights are rare. Ancient glaciers left enormous amounts of debris, creating the

THE UNITED STATES OF AMERICA

VT = VERMONT
NH = NEW HAMPSHIRE
MA = MASSACHUSETTS
RI = RHODE ISLAND
CT = CONNECTICUT
NJ = NEW JERSEY
DE = DELAWARE
MD = MARYLAND

FIGURE 1.1 The United States of America

glacial moraine (rocky territory with a complex pattern of lakes and drainage channels). The moraine runs along a line just north of the Ohio and Missouri Rivers. To the north of the moraine, the Lowland has a table-like flatness, except near major rivers, where there are low, rounded hills.

The landscape's appearance also varies because of differences in rainfall and temperature. Annual rainfall decreases towards the west, resulting first in a change from country where forests are well mixed with fields to the prairies, where trees are rare. Farther west, high prairie grass gives way to short grass at the 20-inch annual rainfall line where the Great Plains begin. As one goes south, the long, severe winters of the Upper Midwest change by degrees to the brief, snowless winters in the Gulf states.

The major natural resources of the Central Lowland are its soil and fossil fuels. Often called the nation's breadbasket, or the world's granary, the Lowland is extremely fertile. Coal deposits are found in Illinois and western Kentucky, and the fields of oil and gas in Texas, Oklahoma, and Kansas were the nation's most important domestic supply of these fuels until reserves in Alaska were tapped.

Covering the whole distance between Canada and Mexico, the Great Plains are a band of semi-arid territory almost 500 miles (800 kilometres) wide. Built up from materials that rivers carried down the Rocky Mountains, the Plains rise so gradually towards the west that large parts of the region appear to be utterly flat. Most of the Plains, however, are broadly rolling, and parts of the northern plains are cut up into spectacular gorge and ridge country called 'badlands'.

The short, deep-rooted buffalo grass of the Plains makes them excellent for cattle ranching and sheep-raising. Better farming machinery and the use of hardy strains of winter wheat have turned parts of the Plains into high-yield farm country. The mineral wealth of the Plains, mainly low-grade brown coal, lies near the surface, and in some areas has been extracted through environmentally damaging strip-mining.

From the western edge of the Great Plains to the Pacific Coast, fully one-third of the continental United States is occupied

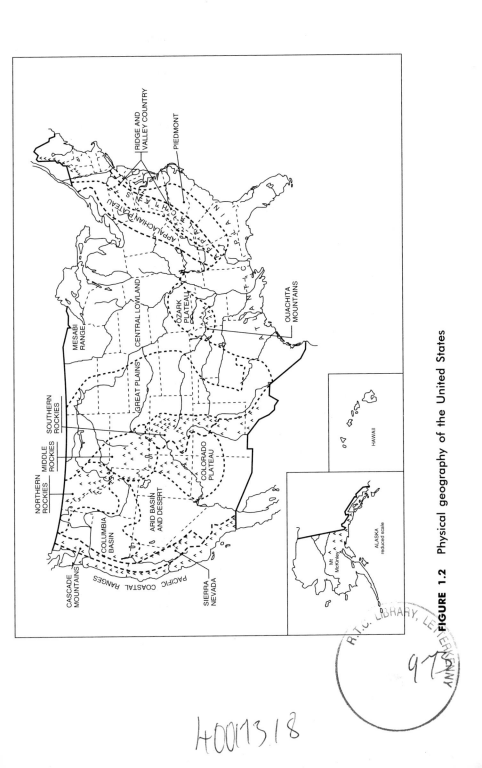

FIGURE 1.2 Physical geography of the United States

CASCADE MOUNTAINS

NORTHERN ROCKIES
MIDDLE ROCKIES
SOUTHERN ROCKIES

MESABI RANGE

GREAT PLAINS

CENTRAL LOWLAND

OZARK PLATEAU

RIDGE AND VALLEY COUNTRY

PIEDMONT

OUACHITA MOUNTAINS

COLUMBIA BASIN

ARID BASIN AND DESERT

COLORADO PLATEAU

PACIFIC COASTAL RANGES

SIERRA NEVADA

APPALACHIAN PLATEAU

HAWAII

ALASKA
reduced scale

Mt McKinley

H0017318

by the Cordillera mountain chains and the basins and plateaus that lie between them. The Cordillera consist of two main branches, the Rockies on the East and the Pacific ranges on the west. Nestled against the Southern Rockies' western slopes is the Colorado Plateau. Through ancient volcanic action and erosion, the Plateau became a maze of buttes, mesas, cliffs and canyons, the most famous of which is the Grand Canyon. Surrounding the Plateau are the desert sections of the Southwest.

Valleys and plains rather than mountains occupy much of the Middle Rockies. Here the Wyoming Basin has provided a path for routes through the mountains, from the Oregon Trail that pioneers followed in covered wagons to the interstate highways that today's trucking fleets ply. The Northern Rockies contain varied mountain landscapes and include the largest wilderness area in the contiguous United States. The Columbia Basin, between the Northern Rockies and the northern Coastal Ranges, is etched by the Snake and Columbia Rivers, which have gouged out a series of remarkable canyons.

The western arm of the Cordillera consists of two lines of mountains with a series of valleys between them. The Sierra Nevada and Cascade Mountains, farther in from the coast, contain the highest peaks in the contiguous states, including Mt Whitney and the volcanoes, Mt St Helens and Mt Ranier. The inland valleys have attracted much of the West Coast's population and economic activity. The lowland around Washington's Puget Sound, the Willamette Valley of Oregon, and California's Central Valley are the only lowland plains of significant size near the coast. All the valleys are blessed with rich soils, and the more southerly valleys have proven relatively easy to irrigate. Since the advent of railroad refrigeration cars, these valleys have been important fruit and vegetable gardens for the entire nation.

The Pacific Coastal Ranges, the line of hills and low mountains between the valleys and the coast, include several topographic sections. The California Coastal Ranges contain major

---

PLATE 1.2 Field of furrow, Arizona *(Day Williams/Barnaby's Picture Library)*

earthquake faults, including the notorious San Andreas Fault, which caused the 1906 quake that levelled San Francisco.

In Alaska the Cordillera divides into three parts and includes North America's highest peak, Mt McKinley (20,320 ft, 6,194 m). Largely ecologically fragile tundra, the state's interior is comprised of broken plateaus, although parts of the Yukon and Fraser valleys are fairly flat. The state's southern, coastal 'tail' and the islands ringing the Gulf of Alaska have a moist, temperate climate because of warming ocean currents. Mountain peaks and fjords separate these narrow lowlands.

The American Cordillera have been the source of much more mineral wealth than the Appalachian system. The western mountains are world-famous for fabulous veins of precious metals: the Sierra gold in California, the gold of the Yukon, the Comstock and other silver lodes of western Nevada. More recently, basic industrial metals like copper and lead, and more unusual metals used in alloys have been mined. Fuels are found in most of the nearby basins with especially large occurrences of oil and gas in California and Wyoming. The Colorado Plateau contains deposits of uranium, oil shale and bituminous coal. To extract the oil and coal at a profit, according to mining companies, open-pit and strip mining are necessary. Conservationists, on the other hand, argue that this kind of mining has already devastated parts of the Plateau as thoroughly as it earlier destroyed areas of the Great Plains and the coal-mining county of Appalachia.

The natural riches of Hawaii are vegetable rather than mineral and come from its rich volcanic soil and unique ocean climate. The state's five major islands and many islets contain almost a million acres (200,000 ha) of commercial forest and twice as much land suitable for tropical farming. Trade winds give the islands a temperate climate. The volcanic mountains catch much of the rain on the windward side so that the leeward side has only moderate rainfall.

Coastlines and river systems

Among the most important physical features and resources of the United States are its coastlines, harbours, ocean currents and extraordinary network of lakes and rivers. The rather shallow waters of the Continental Shelf off the North Atlantic coast known as the Great Banks contain many kinds of fish and attracted fishermen from Europe even before its settlers established their first colonies in the New World. Despite violent seastorms, a rocky coastline and few good natural harbours, New England has always provided livelihoods for fishermen, seafarers and shipbuilders. The Mid-Atlantic coast from New York to Maryland has a more temperate climate because of the Florida Current. Fine harbours, fjords and large estuaries made the sites of New York City, Philadelphia and Baltimore excellent locations for centres of trade, providing both natural highways and major sources of seafood.

The great Eastern water systems are those that drain the Central Lowland: the Mississippi with its major tributaries (the Ohio, the Tennessee, and the Missouri) and the Great Lakes–St Lawrence system. The Mississippi system is one of the world's great inland water networks, carrying enormous amounts of freight from New Orleans north to Minneapolis and as far east as Pittsburgh. Western tributaries of the Mississippi are mostly unfit for navigation but, since the middle of this century, the Missouri has carried considerable barge traffic as a result of dams, locks and dredging.

Because canals connect it to the Mississippi system, the Great Lakes–St Lawrence system functions as the second half of one vast network of inland waterways. By far the biggest group of freshwater lakes in the world, the Great Lakes carry more shipping than any other inland lake group. The fertile farmland surrounding the lakes and the iron, lumber and fossil fuels transportable to their shores supported the phenomenally rapid urbanization and industrialization of the Midwest in the last century. The opening of the St Lawrence Seaway in 1959 made the lake ports major international seaports by bypassing the obstacles to ocean-going freighters in the St Lawrence with huge locks.

Between the Rockies and the Pacific Coast, America's waterways are so strongly influenced by limited rainfall and scant mountain run-off that only three large river systems, the Columbia, the Colorado, and the San Joaquin–Sacramento, reach the sea. They do not support shipping, but the West's largest rivers have brought prosperity to many areas by providing hydro-electric power and water for irrigation. The gorges of the Columbia and Colorado are suitable for damming. The Columbia, once a wild White river, now runs down through a step-like series of dams and calm lakes, turning the arid plateaux of Washington state into vegetable gardens and supplying electrical power to several states. The Colorado serves the same purposes on a smaller scale. Proposals for its further development have met stiff opposition on the ground that more dam construction would destroy the spectacular beauty of the Grand Canyon and the river's other canyon lands.

Conservation and recreational areas

Although the country's population is now about 260 million, most of these people are concentrated in relatively small areas. Some parts of the country are not suitable for urbanization because of climate or difficult topography. Others have been set aside as recreational areas or plant and wildlife preserves. These and other factors give the United States a great variety of national, state, and local parks and open spaces.

Along the East Coast, there are many beaches, bird sanctuaries, and wilderness areas, most of them of limited size but of great diversity. Intermittently along the whole length of the Atlantic Plain there are offshore barrier islands that provide a marine playground more than 1,000 miles long. The entire state of Florida is a magnet for holidaymakers, due to its sub-tropical climate, beaches, natural attractions like the Everglades National Park, and man-made amusements like Disneyland and Epcot Center. The Appalachian Mountains have long offered an escape to cooler upland forests where holiday camps and resort hotels present a wide range of entertainments. In the Central Lowland, the Great Lakes, the many smaller lakes formed by the glacial moraine, and the reservoirs created by hydro-electric dams on the Tennessee River system support vacation industries.

In the US, conservation of natural beauty and resources through national parks gained acceptance in the late 1800s, with vocal support from President Theodore Roosevelt, among others. Yellowstone National Park, the first nature preserve created by Congress, was put under federal control as early as 1872. In 1916 Congress established the National Park Service and gave it the somewhat paradoxical double duty of making the areas entrusted to it accessible for industry and public enjoyment, and of preserving them for future generations.

Today, the Park Service administers over 200 different sites, including national parks, monuments, memorials, cemeteries, historical parks, and recreational areas, whose combined territory exceeds 40,000 sq miles (104,000 km) of land and water. There are national parks in all parts of the country, but the largest and most famous, such as the Yellowstone and Grand Canyon National Parks, are located between the canyon, foothill, and 'badlands' areas of the Rockies and the Pacific.

In practice, government protection of the parks has meant controlled development, because the federal Department of the Interior and its Land Management Bureau have long granted licences or leases allowing private economic interests to use the parks' resources at low cost. According to federal law, the government must balance the interests of developers, vacationers, environmentalists, and Native Americans. Some observers say this ideal of 'multiple use' may have worked when the West was under-populated, but that today it satisfies no-one and could lead to the loss of irreplaceable resources.

Climate

Arctic and tropical climates are limited to high mountaintops, inland Alaska, Hawaii, and the southern tip of Florida. The middle latitudes are, however, known for wide variations in temperature and rainfall, and the great size of North America reinforces these differences. In general, the more distant a place is from an ocean, the more likely it is to have a 'continental' climate with temperature extremes in the summer and winter. Near the centre of the continent in North Dakota temperatures have varied from a summer high of 121°F (49°C) to a winter low of −60°F (−51°C).

Most climates in America are distinctly continental because, with the general eastward movement of air across the country, the Cordillera mountain system effectively limits the moderating influence of the Pacific to a narrow margin along the West Coast. Thus, San Francisco experiences only a small differential between winter and summer temperatures. But coastal cities in the Northeast, such as Boston, have the continental range of temperatures that extend from the Cascades and Sierra Nevada all the way to the East Coast. Because of the prevailing easterly direction of weather systems across the country, the Atlantic Ocean has only a weak moderating influence.

Rainfall

Pacific rainfall is confined to the coastal strip by the Cordillera. The low coastal ranges catch some rain and the higher inland mountains take so much more that the region between the mountains and the Great Plains is arid or semi-arid. Farther east rainfall increases because warm, moist air moves up over the nation's midsection from the Gulf of Mexico, producing more rainfall in the US than that coming from the Pacific and Atlantic Oceans combined. This rain often comes in cloudbursts, hailstorms, tornadoes and blizzards, with rapid temperature drops and rises, as cold continental Canadian air collides with warm, humid air masses from the Gulf of Mexico.

The seasons

Largely because of the movement of the contrasting Gulf and Canadian weather systems, winter and summer east of the Rockies are very different. In the winter, dry frigid Canadian air moves south, spreading cold, sparkling weather to the interior plains and lowlands and causing storms at its southern edge. In summer that stormy edge migrates much farther north as Gulf air invades the continent and a hot, soggy blanket of humid weather eliminates much of the temperature difference between the North and South.

Along the Pacific, seasonal changes follow another pattern. Winter weather in the Pacific Northwest is typically overcast and drizzly as a result of warm, moist air that moves south from the Alaskan coast. This kind of winter weather now and then reaches southern California, but that area is a climatic refuge in winter because of its mild temperatures (on average, between 45 and 64°F, or 7 and 18°C) and long periods of sunny weather. In summer, the Pacific Northwest is covered by mild air from the subtropical Pacific, and, except in the mountains, is nearly rainless. Farther south summer means dry, hot air and blistering temperatures.

Autumn ('Fall') in the Northeast and Upper Midwest is marked by mild days, frosty nights, and the brilliantly coloured leaves of trees set against crystal-clear skies. Spring here brings temperate weather and a profusion of flowering trees and bushes. But fall and spring are also the seasons when the Gulf and Canadian air masses lurch most violently together, spawning the hurricane season along the Gulf and Atlantic Coasts in the fall and more tornadoes in the Mississippi Valley in the spring than occur anywhere else on Earth.

The regions: cultural geography

The definitions and boundaries of American regions vary according to the uses they are put to and the people making the divisions. While debating about regional classifications, most cultural geographers agree that more than one meaningful division of a country into regions is possible; that cultural regions defined as groups of American states give only approximate borders because cultural boundaries rarely coincide with political units; and that individual Indian cultures, geographic areas and states often show a unique mixture of traits that makes their inclusion in regional cultures inaccurate at best.

Native-American cultural regions

In the mid-1500s, when Europeans began permanent settlement there already existed a multitude of distinctive Native-American cultures. The estimated 10 million Indians in North America then lived in cultures that had developed several hundred mutually incomprehensible languages and widely varying social structures including both male- and female-dominated societies, rigid caste systems and classless democratic family bands, and very peaceful as well as very warlike traditions. It no longer seems likely that all of these cultures developed from a single background in migration from Siberia to Alaska during the last ice age. Recent archeological finds indicate that humans inhabited the continent long before then and may also have crossed the Atlantic and the Pacific Oceans to Central and South America and spread north from there. Any survey overview of cultural regions in such a diversity of groups cannot avoid simplifying differences and focusing on broad similarities.

This discussion of Native-American cultural geography divides the present-day US into regions according to the major foods and economies around which cultures developed. In the Eastern half of the country were two woodland areas now known as the Northeastern and Southeastern Maize regions. Here a variety of native cultures depended on different combinations of hunting, fishing, farming and gathering. These are called maize cultures because maize or corn (as it is called in the US) provided the most important staple of the Indians' diet. The Southeastern Maize Region had the more extensive and highly developed agriculture allowed by a longer growing season. In the East as a whole, most housing was constructed of wood, bark and thatch. Women and children usually farmed while men hunted and fished. Well-known cultural groups in these eastern regions were the

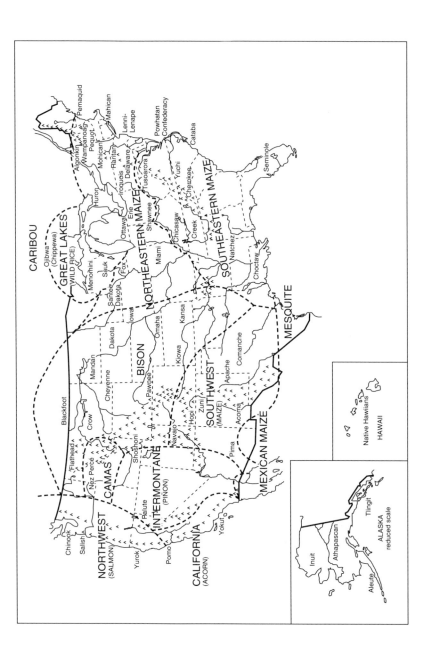

FIGURE 1.3 Native-American cultural regions

Iroquois, Huron, Mohican, Delaware and Shawnee in the North and the Powhatan, Creek, Cherokee, Seminole and Natchez in the South.

The Indian cultural area in the prairies and Great Plains is commonly known as the Plains or Bison Region. For thousands of years the native population of this area was sparse compared with other parts of the continent. People lived along waterways and scratched out a living through riverbank farming, small-game hunting and gathering. Lacking any other means of transportation, these peoples went on a communal buffalo (bison) hunt once a year on foot. Then, sometime between 1700 and 1750 they discovered how to use the horses that reached them from Spanish-controlled areas to the south, and Native-American Plains culture was transformed. The population grew because the food supply increased dramatically when bison were hunted on horseback. Learning of this, some tribes, such as the famous Dakota or Sioux, migrated from nearly woodlands in present-day Minnesota to the open steppes farther west. Many Plains peoples exchanged their sedentary agricultural customs for the nomadic culture of year-round buffalo hunters, discarding sod lodges for the portable *tipi* and evolving a patriarchial society dominated by a warrior hunting-class. The groups transformed by the arrival of the horse (the Blackfoot, Crow, Cheyenne and Dakota) are among the best-known of Indians, largely because of their fierce resistance to White settlement on their hunting grounds. Ironically, United States' policy towards these peoples when they were defeated militarily was to force them to give up the nomadic culture the White man's horse had made possible.

The Indian cultural region usually called the Southwest includes the arid inland area of present-day western Texas and Oklahoma, Colorado, Arizona, New Mexico, Nevada and Utah. It once encompassed a wide diversity of native cultures, nomadic hunters and gatherers as well as farmers, but most of its people relied on advanced forms of agriculture, including extensive irrigation systems. Several different farming peoples are often

PLATE 1.3 Grand Canyon, Arizona *(Rex Features)*

lumped together as 'Puebloes' after the two- to three-floor adobe or stone buildings they lived in. Actually, Hopi, Zuni, and Acoma Indians, among others, lived in such dwellings, but there was no culture called the Pueblo. These cultures varied significantly but shared the customs of tracing ancestry through the female line, of having men do the farming while women owned the fields, and of making a range of sophisticated, richly decorated pottery. Two famous native cultures of the Southwest, the Navaho and Apache, were latecomers to the region, hunters and gatherers who migrated south from the Canadian Great Plains between AD 1000 and 1500. Their society transformed as they adopted farming customs of the pueblo-dwelling peoples. The Navaho later learned sheep-raising, peach-growing and silver-working from the Spanish, while some Apache groups took up aspects of nomadic Plains cultures, such as the *tipi* and hunting buffalo on horseback, and copied cattle-raising from Spaniards and Americans.

The California–Intermontane Indian cultural area included the barren Basin and Range territory on three sides of the Colorado Plateau and most of present-day California. The nomadic hunters and gatherers that lived in this harshest of American climates are often considered materially the poorest of the continent's native cultures. On the other hand, their loosely organized family bands are often praised for their democratic political traditions and peaceful way of life.

The plentiful nature available to the coastal cultures from northern California to southern Alaska made them a stark contrast to highland cultures of the nearby inland areas. One of the most advanced groups of related cultures north of the Mexican border, the Northwest peoples lived in coastal villages similar to small city states that were politically and culturally independent. Well supplied with wild food plants and game animals both large and small, the Chinook, Tsimshian, Kwakiutl, Haida, Tlingit and other peoples in this region did not have to farm. Fishing for salmon represented these cultures' primary economic activity, but saltwater fishing and whaling were also important. The Northwest coastal cultures exploited the region's forests to make long sea-going canoes and massive wooden lodges, decorating these, as well as household items and the totem poles for which they are famous, with a high order of symbolic woodcarving. These peoples of plenty are also well known for the *potlatch*, several days of feasting during which a leading family gave its guests extravagant gifts. The family's wealth was demonstrated by the richness of its generosity, and the guests' degree of satisfaction determined their hosts' prestige in the community. The Northwest coastal peoples were also among the few non-agricultural societies to practise slavery, which was common among Native-American farming cultures.

The various Inuit groups (including the Aleuts) are the native peoples of the Western Arctic culture region that coincides with the state of Alaska, the Aleutian Islands, and nearby coast of Siberia. Inuit, which means 'people', is the word those commonly called Eskimos use for themselves. The Inuit were late arrivals on the continent and were Mongoloid peoples who wanted to distinguish themselves racially from all Native-Americans living farther south. The coastal peoples are highly skilled sea hunters, while their inland cultures are based on hunting big game. The stereotype of the Eskimo as a nomadic sea hunter living in an igloo actually comes from the Inuit culture of far north central Canada. By tradition, the Inuit of Alaska are settled villagers who build underground sod-walled houses. Fast and efficient transportation by dog sled in winter and kayak in summer for thousands of years made it possible for them to live in one place and still hunt in a wide enough radius to supply themselves with food.

The indigenous culture of Hawaii was developed by immigrants from the Marquesas Islands and Tahiti from about AD 400. In addition to gathering food plants from Hawaii's tropical forests, the islanders developed elaborate farming methods, including the terracing of mountainsides and construction of irrigation systems for watering crops in these fields. Experts at open-sea fishing from their outrigger canoes, the Hawaiians also provided themselves with seafood by building semi-circular fish ponds on the shores of their islands. The priesthood, aristocracy, and royal family owned most of the land, which was divided into strips (*ahupuaa*) that extended from some distance under coastal waters to a mountain top, so that its owner could meet all his needs. The common people lived in small areas (*kuleanas*) where they had limited rights to fish, water, wood, wild foods, and farming. The integrated religious–class system of Hawaiian culture became oppressive during the last period before European influence as the priesthood and aristocracy used laws and religious taboos to control the lives of commoners and of women in particular.

Attitudes towards land and land ownership in Native-American cultures varied. The Hawaiian custom of individual and class ownership of land was unusual in native cultures on the mainland, where group possession and communal use of land were most common. Almost all native groups had a concept of possessing their own territory, an area that was theirs by virtue of long residence and whose boundaries they defended or extended as circumstances demanded. Generalizations that picture all native cultures as idealized societies in which land had only spiritual value, nature was revered, and pollution prevented are invariably wrong because they romanticize and oversimplify the realities of life in North America before European settlement.

Land use for hunting, gathering, fishing and farming was the cornerstone of Native-American life. The Indians were aware of their dependence on the land for survival, and this knowledge led most native cultures to deify or revere nature. On the other hand, recent study shows that not all indigenous peoples lived in harmony with nature. Some cultures exploited their environment until it became too depleted to support life. Others over-hunted until some animals became extinct. If resources became scarce, groups moved to meet their basic needs. Sometimes these moves could be made within a cultural region without the conflict that trespassing on another culture's territory brought. But more often conflict with surrounding cultures resulted from migration to a new area.

Cultural regions in the contemporary US

Today's cultural regions derive primarily from varying mixtures of European antecedents, with Indian elements, at their most noticeable, representing one of several ethnic ingredients. The main American regions (the Northeast, the South, the Midwest, the West and their primary subdivisions) retain a powerful hold on the popular imagination and remain much-used concepts for understanding subdivisions of American culture and society. Still, America's regions tend to be less distinct than regions in older, more demographically stable countries. The European settlement of North America is relatively recent and the high mobility of the American population heightens the homogenizing effects of the mass media, popular culture, modern transportation systems, and the increasing centralization of the economy and government.

In the 1960s and 1970s, cultural geographers also stressed the rapid pace of urbanization and its standardizing effects. Since the 1980s, however, one widely noted aspect of post-industrial America has been an opposing trend towards decentralization and heterogeneity. Paradoxically, the most recent developments in transportation and communication technology have permitted business, government and cultural institutions to follow the population fleeing the old industrial cities and to spread out in suburban and small-town settings, where Americans seem to emphasize their diversity more than their similarity. Among the contemporary factors that reveal the nation's increasing cultural regionalism are attitudes towards environmental protection, energy use, sexual orientation and abortion.

The Northeast

At the end of the twentieth century, the Northeast seems to be one regional unit, especially when viewed from the perspective of other sections of the country. Stretching from Maine south through Maryland and west to the border of Ohio, the whole section is known as densely populated, highly urban, and troubled economically because of declining older industries, accumulated social problems, and rising taxes. In fact, the Northeast is still arguably the nation's economic and cultural centre and two regions (New England and the Mid-Atlantic) rather than one.

New England itself is often divided into two parts: a northern zone including Maine, Vermont and most of New Hampshire; and a southern zone made up of Massachusetts, Connecticut and Rhode Island. Southern New England has long had a cultural importance out of proportion to its size, natural resources and population. Of the two areas earliest settled from Britain, Massachusetts received the largest influx of colonists. It rapidly developed stable institutions, cohesive communities, and a rate of population growth that allowed it to strongly influence the settlement and culture of the rest of New England, the Mid-Atlantic, the Upper Midwest and the Pacific Northwest during the eighteenth and nineteenth centuries.

Americans trace several aspects of the nation's Anglo-American core culture to southern New England. The original settlers' goal of founding a model religious community that would inspire reform in England was generalized to 'American exceptionalism', a belief that the nation has a special mission and ability to set a good example for the rest of the world. According to traditional views, the region also bequeathed to the country belief in the so-called Puritan work ethic, the faith that hard work and good morals are rewarded in this world and the next. In the mid-nineteenth century, New England authors such as Ralph Waldo Emerson expressed central values of the region in a secular form that for over a hundred years was taught in US schools as the foundation of the entire nation's culture. In the schools' popularized version, the American creed was an optimistic individualism expressed in introspective self-reliance and self-improvement, thrift, hard work and a belief in progress.

In the 1800s, New England Yankees became famous first as fishermen and travelling peddlers, then as clipper-ship builders and sailors, and finally as mill owners, industrialists and factory workers. The presence of the fall line near the coast provided a source of cheap water power close to trade routes. Later,

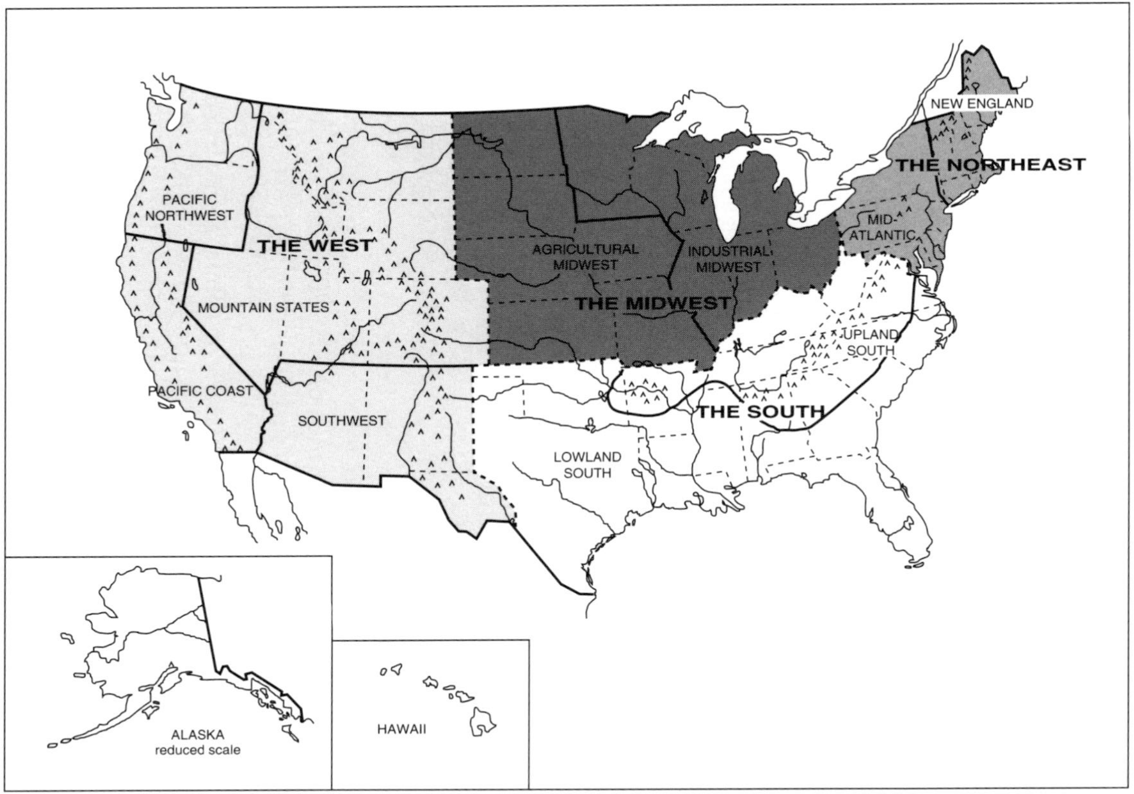

FIGURE 1.4 Contemporary regions of the United States

when industry converted to steam and then electricity, the region welcomed European immigrants as cheap labour, imported fuels, and, most recently, constructed nuclear power plants. But manufacturing jobs continue to be lost to parts of the country that are richer in the natural resources essential to modern industry.

One of New England's greatest strengths in its economic competition with other regions is its long tradition of support for education, which dates from the seventeenth century. It is still thought of as containing the nation's greatest concentration of high quality institutions of higher education and research. New England today is a leader in innovative business methods, publishing, and the design and production of high-technology weaponry, aircraft, engines, tools and computers. In addition, the region's tourist industry has grown both because of its scenic qualities and its status as a repository of the nation's history from the site of the first shots in the Revolutionary War to the homes of classic American authors and restored colonial and industrial towns. The northern zone of the region, with its woodland mountain areas, has developed a lucrative industry providing summer cottages and second homes for people who want an escape from congested East Coast cities.

In its early period New England represented a devotion to preserving a homogeneous society based on a shared religious ethic. The Mid-Atlantic region, from its founding, showed a Euro-American diversity. The original vision of America as a pluralistic mix of religions, ethnic groups and races developed here before the end of the colonial period. With a larger, more varied population, better soil and a greater share of natural resources, the Mid-Atlantic surpassed New England in trade and manufactures during the 1700s.

During the next century, the exploitation of the Mid-Atlantic's geographic advantages for trade and transportation helped it grow into the nation's commercial–industrial hub. Its harbours became the nation's premier port cities, and the nearness of the fall line to the coast provided cheap water power. But here were also passages through the Appalachian Mountains.

Successive technologies overlaid the mainly north–south grain of the land with east–west transportation networks through these openings and secured the economic supremacy of the Mid-Atlantic. First roads, then canals and later railroads opened western New York, Pennsylvania and the Great Lakes states to settlement and directed the transport of that region's products to the coastal cities of the Mid-Atlantic.

The Erie Canal, joining Lake Erie with New York City, is the most famous of these man-made routes. The Canal reduced the cost of shipping a ton of freight from Buffalo to New York from 19 cents to 0.8 cents in 1825. In the decade after the Canal's opening, the traditional pattern of inland transportation down the Ohio and Mississippi Rivers to New Orleans began a permanent shift towards New York, which became and has remained the nation's largest and wealthiest city.

By the late nineteenth century, transportation and trade networks had welded together New England, the Mid-Atlantic and the big cities of the Great Lakes and inland rivers. This was the urban, industrial core of the US, an economic region that attracted people to the jobs in its wide variety of heavy 'smoke-stack' industries. Although it includes some extensive agricultural areas, the distinguishing aspect of the core is the size and close-ness of its racially and ethnically mixed industrial cities. Though they contain many groups, however, in popular opinion today Boston is Irish, Buffalo is Polish, and New York City is Jewish, Italian, Black, Asian and Caribbean.

By the 1970s, the migration of older, heavy industries to foreign nations with cheaper labour costs and the movement of newer 'high-tech' companies to the South and Southwest resulted in the core being rechristened the 'Rust Belt'. Like New England, this region has had to rely on its centres of higher education, such as Columbia, Princeton and its large state university systems to develop new jobs. It has had to diversify its economy and recruit employers with tax breaks and social services. But the economic tug-of-war between the regions continues, and the South and West are still attracting more jobs and people than the urban core and the Midwest.

The South

Traditionally, this region is defined as the eleven states that left the US to form the Confederacy during the Civil War: Virginia, North and South Carolina, Georgia, Florida, Alabama, Mississippi, Louisiana, Tennessee, Arkansas and Texas. In addition, the South arguably contains the 'border states' of West Virginia, Kentucky, Missouri and Oklahoma (and some would add Maryland to that list).

Far from homogeneous, the South has two principal sub-regions, the Lowland (or Deep) South on the Coastal Plain and the Upland South in the Piedmont, Southern Appalachians, and Ozarks. The Lowland South includes the Creole and Cajun areas of Louisiana, the Caribbean-African-influenced Sea Islands off the Atlantic Coast, and the climates and subcultures in Tennessee, Arkansas and Texas. Today the urban South and the states of Florida and Texas have lost much of their traditional character because of their rapid economic transformation, the migration of people from other parts of the nation, and large-scale immigration from Spanish-speaking countries and Asia.

The distinctiveness of the southern Lowland developed with the earliest settlement along the Atlantic Coastal Plain. The first colonists were almost entirely Englishmen who came for economic rather than religious or political reasons. They did not find the gold and silver Spanish discoveries had made them dream about. But the climate and soil soon proved suitable for the production and export of cash crops such as tobacco, rice, sugar and cotton, that required much manual labour but offered huge profits. Landholdings larger than the family farm (called plantations) became the rule and resulted in dispersed settlements with few and small urban centres. To meet the need for field workers, plantation owners at first imported indentured servants (people who sold themselves into virtual slavery for four to seven years to pay for their passage to North America). By the late 1600s, Africans sold into permanent slavery had replaced indentured servants as the source of plantation labour. Black slavery existed in all the American colonies, but became the main source of manual workers only on the Southern Coastal Plain where the landscape and climate permitted a plantation economy.

The 1783 Treaty of Paris that recognized American independence also granted the new nation all the land east of the Mississippi and led to debate in the South over the future of slavery. As late as the 1830s, a proposal to end slavery failed by only one vote in the Virginia legislature. But cheap fertile lowlands to the west and rising returns from cotton growing encouraged expansion of the plantation-slavery economy. Because it was practised without crop rotation, plantation agriculture exhausted the soil and so depended on a supply of unspoiled land farther west. The invention of Eli Whitney's cotton gin made extracting cotton fibres from the plant much easier and more profitable. Even more important were the high prices for raw cotton paid by the Northern and British textile mills that were the backbone of the early Industrial Revolution. Industrial demand made cotton the 'king' of cash crops and confirmed the regional contrasts between the industrializing Northeast and the expanding agricultural and slave South that led to the Civil War.

The need to justify slavery before 1861 and the shared memories of secession, war, defeat and occupation by Union armies until 1877 reinforced Southerners' regional ties. Although slavery ended with the War, cotton remained the region's main cash crop into the 1930s, and most Blacks remained financially dependent on their former masters, who rented them parcels of land and gave them wages as field hands. Events as varied as the migration of Blacks to Northern cities and the Civil Rights Movement, the mechanization of cotton growing, and the damage done to cotton crops by boll weevils have caused the reorganization of the rural Southern economy. Agriculture is still important but today its products are much more varied and include citrus fruits, nuts, poultry and beef, as well as tobacco and cotton. Industry has also moved into the countryside to take advantage of low energy and labour costs and to develop natural resources, such as iron ore, bauxite, oil, gas and vast pine forests.

The last twenty-five years have witnessed a rapidly urbanizing and industrializing South that forms the eastern part of the

'Sunbelt'. From Atlanta, Georgia, to Dallas and Houston, Texas, the region has expanding financial, high-tech, and media industries in growing population centres. Since the court-ordered school integration, Civil Rights laws and voter registration drives of the 1960s and 1970s, the socio-political landscape of the region has been revolutionized. The important roles Blacks are playing in public life and their support for the Democratic Party have driven most conservative Whites to the Republicans, making the South a two-party region for the first time since the 1870s. Recently Blacks' migration out of the region has been reversed. Still, recent surveys indicate that Southerners remain less educated, more religious, more conservative and more homogeneously old-stock American than the population of the other regions.

The Midwest

The Midwest includes the states bordering the Great Lakes and the first two tiers of states west of the Mississippi River from Missouri and Kansas north to Canada. Because the Great Lakes states contain many large manufacturing centres, they are usually termed the Industrial Midwest, even though they are also important farm states. The two western tiers of states (which include roughly half of the Great Plains), in similar fashion, are called the Agricultural Midwest, despite the industry in such cities as St Louis, Kansas City, and Minneapolis. The names of the sub-regions do accurately indicate the primary emphasis of each, but in the national consciousness, the Midwest exists as one coherent region: the American heartland of family farms and small towns, perhaps naïvely provincial and optimistic but still the moral and social centre that mediates between the extremes of the nation's other regions.

The Great Lakes states were the northern part of the territory the new nation acquired through the Treaty of 1783. All the early routes of western migration through the Appalachians met in this territory, making it the first place where the cultures of New England, the Mid-Atlantic and the Lowland South combined. Traditional Midwestern agriculture, crop rotation supporting hog- and cattle-raising, developed here from central European practices adapted to American conditions by German immigrants in the Mid-Atlantic colonies. By 1860, the Great Lakes Midwest was well integrated into the markets of the Northeast. During the Civil War it gained a proud sense of its own identity from having sacrificed more than its share of men and wealth for the preservation of the Union.

After the Civil War, the settlement of the trans-Mississippi Agricultural Midwest was completed. The prairies and Great Plains resisted conversion to farmland until the introduction of steel-plated ploughs. In this century, motorized farm machinery and new strains of winter wheat have turned these areas into some of the most productive farmland in the world. But this same technology has made the American ideal of the independent small farmer nearly obsolete, as large 'agribusinesses' capture markets and replace the family farm.

During the 1980s, the region's industrial cities made great strides towards economic and environmental recovery, despite persistent problems with the unemployment, slums and general urban blight that follow in the wake of deindustrialization. Today Detroit can boast of its glamorous downtown convention centre and a strongly resurgent automobile industry. Cleveland, once infamous for the explosion of its polluted Cuyahoga River, now benefits from the successful cleansing of the river and Lake Erie. These two cities exemplify the many urban areas in the region that have reaffirmed their vitality, now primarily as business, research, cultural and service centres. The national hub of the commodities market, an important international seaport, and the home of widely diversified industry and cultural institutions, Chicago remains the region's premier city.

The political traditions of the region show a mixture of pragmatic caution and organized protest. While the Midwest has the reputation of being conservative, it was the birthplace of the Republican Party, which opposed the spread of slavery and nominated Lincoln for the presidency. Later, the Agricultural Midwest was home to the Populist and Farmer-Labor Parties, which protested against the economic domination of the Northeast, and a centre of the Progressive Movement, which strove to make American governments more honest, efficient, and democratic. Midwestern states, such as Minnesota and Wisconsin, have since then been leaders in social and environmental reform.

Until recently, Midwesterners had a reputation for being reluctant to become involved in foreign affairs. The region's Senators and Congressmen were among the staunchest supporters of isolationism before the First and Second World Wars. But, as Midwestern agriculture has become dependent on exports since the 1950s, growing numbers of its politicians have become proponents of US engagement in international institutions. On the other hand, its cities and universities were especially prominent in the opposition to US involvement in the Vietnam War.

The West

'The West' has a place in the American mind as a myth, a popular set of values, and as a region of the country. It represents possibility, freedom, self-reliance, the future. As a region, it is made up of three major parts: the Southwest, the Mountain States, and the Pacific Coast. But even these have subdivisions that make the boundaries of the West and its parts a matter for discussion.

The Southwest consists of New Mexico, Arizona, and the parts of surrounding states from Texas to southern California that have a similar climate and culture. Seized during the Mexican–American War of 1848, this area has the unique mixture of very old and unusually strong Spanish-Mexican and Native-American communities and a blend of people from many parts of the country, who began arriving in large numbers after 1945.

Cattle and sheep ranching remain important for the economy, but dams on the major rivers and deep wells have transformed deserts into irrigated farmlands and metropolitan areas, such as Phoenix and Albuquerque. The warm, dry climate has proven especially beneficial to people with respiratory ailments and has also attracted electronics, aerospace and armaments companies. While the mining and petroleum industries are important sources of jobs and capital, the Southwest's diverse cultures and stunning national parks have long made tourism a major support of local economies.

Although it is the largest landowner in the Southwest, the federal government even more clearly dominates the economy of the *Mountain States* of Nevada, Utah, Colorado, Wyoming, Montana and Idaho. The importance of its decisions concerning the leasing of federal lands to private groups and its military testing sites, airfields and training and research centres becomes obvious when one learns that the government owns over four-fifths of Nevada, two-thirds of Utah, and vast areas of the sub-region's other states. The traditional independence of long-time residents is increasingly frustrated by their lack of control over local resources. Newcomers from other regions, environmentalists, business people, Native-American groups, and government officials have now joined the debate on how resources should be used. The population density is low but appears to be growing so rapidly that some Westerners think in-migration and development are nearing their acceptable limits.

Mining the mountains' vast mineral riches provided the basis for migration to the sub-region and continues to be a mainstay of its economy. Gold and silver strikes led to the boom towns that became Denver, Virginia City and Butte. The mines brought the outside investment, the transportation infrastructure and the business that laid the financial foundation for urban areas. Agriculture here depends on ranching and forestry, because other forms of farming require irrigation, and water rights have become as precious as rare metals. Las Vegas and Reno found wealth through the gambling and entertainment industries. Denver has grown into an important centre of finance for mining, energy firms, light manufactures and the cattle business. Salt Lake City is the heart of the Great Basin Mormon area that is more homogeneous than any other cultural area in the US. Today the area prospers on expertise in computer software and technology as well as on mining and irrigated agriculture. Tourism is important throughout the Mountain States because of the natural splendours of its wilderness areas.

The European settlement of the Pacific Coast began with the establishment of Spanish missions in California in the 1700s and included Russian and British domination of the Pacific Northwest before the US gained sovereignty over the area in the 1840s. The coastal territories attracted sizeable populations and qualified as states before the interior West because of the 1849 Gold Rush and reports of the lush greenness of the Oregon and Washington valleys. The San Francisco area was the first to experience rapid development because it was the port of entry for the Gold Rush Forty-Niners. By the 1870s it was an industrializing metropolis that produced finished goods which successfully competed with imports from the East.

Today the city is the hub of a larger area that includes Berkeley and its famous university, Oakland with its many industries, the Silicon Valley complex of computer firms, Stanford University, and the Napa Valley wine district. Los Angeles has experienced rapid population growth ever since it became the end stop of a transcontinental railroad in 1885. The LA metropolis, a sprawling conglomeration of cities connected by a maze of remarkably designed highways, is home to the Hollywood film and media conglomerates as well as major energy, defence and aerospace companies. The population mix of California's two largest urban areas includes every major racial and ethnic group in the nation but especially large Asian and Latino elements. Politically, southern California has the reputation for being conservative while the northern part of the state is known for its support for liberal causes.

In the Pacific Northwest the population and culture show less Latino and more New England and northwest European influence, while Asian-American groups are as well established as farther south. During the last thirty years, so many people and businesses have relocated in Washington and Oregon that state authorities have attempted to limit growth. Their avowed goal is to preserve the environment and quality of life through a mixed economy based on agriculture, forestry and tourism, as well as on heavy and high-technology industries.

Resource and land management are also major issues in Hawaii and Alaska, as they are in the continental West. Hawaii's government instituted a detailed land-use system soon after it became a state in 1959. The law provided areas for commercial, industrial and residential building and simultaneously protected farmland, nature reserves and tourist areas. Sugar and pineapples are the most important products of Hawaii's highly mechanized agribusinesses today, and tourism and US airforce and naval bases supply other major sources of income.

In the nineteenth century, settlers from the mainland recruited large numbers of Asians to work on plantations. But after 1900, when the islands became a US territory, these contract labour arrangements became illegal, and high immigration has resulted from better knowledge of the islands' attractions and easier transportation in the age of aviation. Today, the people are highly urban and have a make-up that is unique in the nation. The majority (roughly three-fifths) is Asian-American, with people of Japanese extraction comprising the largest nationality group. Whites make up the largest minority (somewhat more than a third), followed by smaller groups of Latinos, African Americans, and native Polynesians.

The federal, state, and Native-American tribal governments own over 99 per cent of Alaska. Much of its history has involved struggles between resource-hungry developers, who lease land from government and create jobs for local residents, and conservationists, who lobby public authorities to restrict land use because they view Alaska as the last chance to preserve an American wilderness. Until Alaska won statehood in 1959, settlers and natives there subsisted primarily through fishing, hunting, and logging. Except for the short-lived Klondike Gold Rush of 1898, the area seemed destined to prove right the sceptics who said the country had bought a ridiculously expensive Russian icebox containing only sealskins and salmon in 1867.

During the 1950s and 1960s, Alaska received a wave of immigrants who wanted to escape the congestion and pollution in the forty-eight contiguous states. But at the end of the 1960s, oil strikes off the state's northern coast increased interest in developing this 'empty' land. The negotiations over how the environment should be preserved and the profits from the oil shared were the most critical in Alaska's history. The huge amounts of land and money Native-Americans received in compensation gave them an entirely new status. The state profited so much that it replaced its income taxes with an annual oil dividend of about $1,000 per resident. To safeguard wildlife and the tundra, the Trans-Alaska pipeline was insulated and lifted several feet above ground.

But the results of oil development have been mixed. The population grew rapidly, reaching over half a million by 1990, but though the per capita income for Alaskans is the highest in the nation, so is the state's unemployment rate. Much of Alaska's employment boom was temporary. In 1989 the supertanker *Exxon Valdez* went aground and spilled millions of gallons of oil on Alaska's coasts. The demands for a clean-up united environmentalists, the fishing and tourist industries, Native-American organizations and ordinary citizens.

Changing public attitudes: where do we go from here?

Not only Europeans and Americans but also Native Americans have made great changes in the natural environment. Still, it is true that the Indians were less destructive of nature and made less radical alterations in the landscape. Native cultures generally used the land extensively and in a semi-permanent fashion. Europeans and Americans, on the other hand, with rapidly growing populations, practised intensive farming methods and developed technologies that resulted in much more drastic transformations of the environment. For example, Native-Americans developed a vast transportation network of trails and portages and built swift watercraft for trade and travel. But the effects of these activities were minimal compared with the environmental impact of later Americans' expressways and airports and the concrete, energy and metal industries necessary to create these transportation systems.

Few Americans would consider giving up modern lifestyles and technology. Many have understood that the quality of life in

TABLE 1.1 Public opinion on government spending on the environment

Country	%
West Germany	61
Hungary	36
Italy	26
Norway	25
Australia	17
United States	16
Britain	15
Northern Ireland	14

Source: Jowell et al. (1993) International Social Attitudes, the 10th BSA Report
Note: Percentage in each country calling for 'much more' public spending on the environment

the future means reconciling environmental and pro-development interests to manage the nation's natural resources wisely. But in 1990 an international survey showed that Americans gave a relatively low priority to public spending on the environment (especially if it might mean raised taxes). Only in Britain and Northern Ireland did the poll find a lower percentage of citizens who wanted 'much more' spending on environmental problems (see Table 1.1).

EXERCISES

■ Examine and explain the following terms:

Atlantic Plain	Eastern Maize Regions
Piedmont	Southwest
fall line	Plains or Bison Region
Appalachians	Northwest coastal cultures
Appalachia	Inuit
Central Lowland	Hawaiians
glacial moraine	attitudes towards land
Great Plains	Northeast
Cordillera	urban industrial core
Colorado Plateau	South
California's Central Valley	cash crops
Pacific Coastal Ranges	Midwest
Mississippi system	West
Great Lakes–St Lawrence	land-use system
system	National Park Service
Trans-Alaska pipeline	'continental' climate

■ Write short essays on the following topics:

1   Give an overview of the main physical features of the geography of the US, describing the country's most important natural resources and commenting on the environmental cost of their use.

2   Compare and contrast Native-American cultural geography and contemporary American cultural geography, discussing possible causes for the differences you find.

3   Discuss conservation efforts in the US to preserve natural resources, wilderness areas and historic areas.

Chapter 2

The people: settlement and immigration

Mother of exiles

A central aspect of US history is the story of migration. Believing in the American Dream of creating a better life for themselves and their children, many tens of millions of people have come to live in the United States. They thus changed their homelands, America, and their family histories forever. They strengthened the nation's commitment to the Dream and to its ideal of being an exception, a refuge for the poor and oppressed, a nation of nations. What other nation claims to have and is universally recognized for a national dream, and at that, one that invites all the world to come and take part?

Much of Americans' (and the immigrants') core idealism, pride, and naïveté is embodied in Emma Lazarus's sonnet 'The New Colossus' (1886), which is displayed inside the base of the Statue of Liberty. There is some truth to the Dream. Settled peoples have been able to climb a 'ladder of ethnic succession' as new waves of immigrants arrive. For most of the foreign-born, life in the US has meant an improvement on their situation in the 'old country', the realization of modest hopes for land or home ownership, for example. Later generations have enjoyed more significant socio-economic progress, though 'rags to riches' careers are rare indeed.

But the newcomers have also contributed to America's history of social disorder. The constant meeting, conflict and mixing of cultures has fuelled widespread discrimination, economic exploitation, violent anti-foreign movements and a never-ending debate over equality, opportunity and national identity. In a country whose history began with the meeting of Native Americans and European colonists and continued through the importation of African slaves and several waves of immigrants, there has never been a single national culture.

The New Colossus

Not like the brazen giant of
      Greek fame,
With conquering limbs astride
      from land to land;
Here at our sea-washed, sunset
      gates shall stand
A mighty woman with a torch,
      whose flame
Is the imprisoned lightning, and
      her name
Mother of exiles. From her
      beacon hand
Glows world-wide welcome: her
      mild eyes command
The air-bridged harbor that twin
      cities frame.
'Keep ancient lands, your
      storied pomp!' cries she
With silent lips. 'Give me your
      tired, your poor,
Your huddled masses yearning to
      breathe free,
The wretched refuse of your
      teeming shore.
Send these, the homeless,
      tempest-tost, to me,
I lift my lamp beside the golden
      door!'
                    Emma Lazarus (1886)

PLATE 2.1   The Statue of Liberty and 'The New Colossus'
(Heather McCallum)

Students of the US continue to search for a metaphor that captures the character of American society. Is it best understood as a melting pot; or a salad with clearly identifiable ingredients; or a stew whose ingredients are mixed in the sauce of a common civic culture's habits and ideals; or a mosaic with many discrete pieces; or an orchestra to which each ethnic group adds its characteristic instrument? Ordinary Americans disagree over what the ultimate goal should be, the assimilation, even homogenization, of newcomers or the acceptance of a permanently pluralistic society.

Early encounters between Europeans and Native Americans

When the first European explorers and settlers encountered Native Americans in the late 1400s, a long history of mutual incomprehension and conflict began. These encounters amounted to a collision of worlds. Contacts between the Americas and the other continents were so rare before this time that plants, animals, diseases and human societies had evolved into different forms in the 'new' and the 'old' worlds. Europeans and Native Americans caught diseases from each other. Europeans had developed a greater immunity to a broad range of illnesses, and survived the first contacts better, though well over half died from difficulties in adjusting to the new environment for most of the seventeenth century. The Native Americans fared far worse: epidemics annihilated entire native cultures. Demographers estimate that North America's pre-Columbian population of 10 million shrank to between 2 and 3 million. The exchange of plants and animals had effects that were as far-reaching. Horses, donkeys, sheep, pigs and cows were alien creatures to Native Americans. Potatoes, maize, squash, pumpkins and tobacco were discoveries to Europeans. The potato transformed the diet of many Europeans and played a key role in the great population growth that brought millions of European immigrants to the US in the 1800s.

European societies were so diverse that Spaniards and Englishmen could hardly imagine living in the same place in peace.

PLATE 2.2 Umatilla Indian woman and child, Oregon
(David W. Corson/A. Devaney)

Some Native-American cultures viewed other indigenous peoples
with a dislike no less intense. Yet, each continent's diversity of
cultures were related, even quite similar in broad outline, when
compared with cultures from the other continent. Thus, all
Europeans tended to look alike to Native Americans, and most
Europeans seemed incapable of seeing Native Americans as
anything but a single people.

Native Americans shared perceptions that were sharply at
odds with those Europeans held at the time. Native Americans
were pantheists and they believed that the divine was in all things

and that human beings were no more important than any other part of the world. They expressed the essential differences between creatures through polytheism, the belief in several or many gods, one appropriate to each quality or kind of creature.

Europeans, on the other hand, viewed man as the highest creation of a single, orderly God who made all things fit a detailed system of categories and sub-categories. In this scheme, called the Great Chain of Being, only angels and human beings had souls and rational intelligence; Whites were more highly favoured by God than brown, red or Black people; men ranked higher than women; and every person had a place in a social class. The vast differences in these two visions of the divine and the world led to equally contrasting attitudes towards nature, the purpose of society, the individual's role in society, work, time and land.

To the European, changing nature from a wilderness to a garden was one of society's chief aims. Man did God's work by revealing the divine order in the world and exploiting the good things God had given him. God provided woman to be his help-meet in this. Given such an important task, people lived good lives only if they utilized their talents. This work ethic in turn supported a competitive individualism, the belief that self-interested individuals best serve society. The more successful the individual was in reaching goals, the more society profited and the more God's favour was evident. In this framework, it was natural that time and land were viewed as commodities to be measured, bought and sold as part of the individual's pursuit of success.

Native Americans had no myth of a lost Garden of Eden that had to be recreated by taming the environment. Their pantheism led them to see nature as sacred, as something to be revered or accepted rather than changed. Their alterations of the environment were usually limited to gathering, hunting, or growing enough food for survival. Although their cultures traded with each other, they were not based on production for export, and so gave less encouragement to the accumulation of material wealth. Theirs was a communal life in which material goods as well as individual talents belonged to the group and were valued for its preservation.

PLATE 2.3 Inuit family *(A. Devaney)*

To Europeans, Native Americans seemed lazy and wasteful of nature's potential. The natives neither kept appointments nor respected deeds of sale for land. Viewing time as fluid, they had only vague concepts of the past and the future, and so seemed utterly unreliable. Because they viewed nature as a great mother, they could not comprehend how pieces of her could be sold and owned by individuals. From the first European settlement until today, the main focus in conflicts between these continental culture systems has been land ownership. Wars over land began within a few years of the Europeans' arrival, and continued for nearly 300 years.

The founders

The people who established the colonies that later became the US are considered founders rather than immigrants because they created the customs, laws, and institutions to which later arrivals (the first *immigrants*) had to adjust.

The Spanish occupied coastal Florida and founded St Augustine in 1565. In the Southwest and California they first tried to exterminate or enslave the natives, but later they evolved a policy of converting them to Christianity and setting them to farming, and sheep herding. Expelling natives who rejected this new way of life, they faced border attacks from Navajos, Apaches, Utes and Commanches for over 200 years.

The English established their first permanent settlement at Jamestown, Virginia in 1607. But the English monarch had no desire to establish direct rule over distant colonies. Instead, the Crown legalized joint stock companies that assumed responsibility for colonization and sent settlers to America to make a profit as quickly as possible. Virginia's early residents were so preoccupied with the search for gold and a passage through the continent to Asian markets that the colony floundered until tobacco provided a profitable export.

Even so, settlers were difficult to recruit until the company offered free land to investors and settlers. Then the colony expanded rapidly, although most newcomers wanted to be tobacco plantation owners, not field workers. Because of the scarcity of plantation labour, in 1619 the first Black slaves were imported. Supported by tobacco profits, Virginia imported 1,500 free labourers a year by the 1680s and had a population of about 75,000 Whites and 10,000 African slaves by 1700.

In the 1630s Lord Baltimore established Maryland to the north of Virginia as a haven for Catholics, England's most persecuted minority. The leadership of the colony remained Catholic for some time, but its economy and population soon resembled Virginia's. In the 1660s, several influential English aristocrats financed the settlements that grew into Georgia and the Carolinas, as commercial investments and experiments in social organization. Within a generation, these colonies too resembled Virginia, although their cash crops were rice and indigo.

To escape religious oppression and the corrupting influence of English society, the Pilgrims, a small group of radical Protestant separatists from the Church of England landed in Plymouth, Massachusetts, and founded the first of the northern English colonies in 1620. The Puritans, who founded the much larger Massachusetts Bay Colony in 1630, wanted to purify the Church of England, not separate from it. Mostly well-educated middle-class people, they decided to emigrate in part because a depression threatened their economic situation. They also felt both church and state were becoming repressive in England. In America they believed they could create a 'city on a hill' to show how English society could be reformed. To that end, they organized themselves into a joint stock company and managed the migration of over 20,000 believers to Massachusetts by the early 1640s.

By the late 1600s, the Bay colony had expanded to the coast of present-day Maine, swallowed up Plymouth, and spawned the colony of Connecticut. Flourishing through agriculture and forestry, the New England colonies also became the shippers and merchants for all British America. Because of their intolerance towards dissenters, the Puritans' New England became the most homogeneous region in the colonies.

The founding of the Middle Colonies (New York, New Jersey, and Pennsylvania) was different. The earliest European communities here were not English but Dutch and Swedish. They were trading posts in the fur trade with the natives that almost accidentally grew into colonies. New Netherlands, along the Hudson River and New York Bay, and New Sweden, along the

Delaware River, recruited soldiers, farmers, craftsmen, clergymen and their families to meet the needs of the company employees who traded with the natives. New Sweden lasted only from 1638 to 1655, when the Dutch annexed it, but a Swedish ethnic community persisted in the area into the next century. New Netherlands itself fell to the English fleet in 1664. The Dutch, however, stubbornly maintained their culture in rural New York and New Jersey for over 200 years. Another legacy of the Dutch was the precedent set by their toleration of many ethnic, racial, and religious groups in New Amsterdam. Before it became New York, the city had White, Red, Brown and Black inhabitants. It had institutions for Catholics, Jews and Protestants, and a diversity that resulted in eighteen different languages being spoken. Although the dominant culture in colonial New York and New Jersey became English by the end of the century, the English colonial authorities continued the tolerant traditions of the Dutch in the city.

Pennsylvania's founders were Quakers who flocked to the colony after Charles II granted the area to William Penn in 1681 as a refuge for members of the sect. Again, official English tolerance took the form of allowing persecuted minorities to emigrate to the New World. Penn's publicizing of cheap land and religious freedom resulted in the migration of some 12,000 people to the colony before 1690. Penn's toleration also attracted many Europeans and produced a population whose diversity was matched only by New York's.

The first wave of immigration: 1680–1776

The founders had come for economic gain and religious freedom. But their descendants gave the first large wave of European newcomers a warm welcome only if they were willing to conform to Anglo-American culture and supply needed labour. The reception that immigrants received varied according to location and the individual's qualities, from the extremes of largely hostile New England, to the more tolerant, diverse Middle Colonies.

Everywhere, people who were willing to provide a protective buffer against the natives along the frontier were valued.

Although conditions in their homelands also played a decisive role, this first wave was possible only because the English government adopted a new policy after 1660. Convinced by mercantile economic theory that a nation's wealth lay in its people, the Crown opposed emigration from England and Wales but encouraged it from other nations. In 1662, King Charles II licensed the Royal African Slave Company as the sole supplier of slaves to English colonies, and during the next century about 140,000 Africans arrived after surviving appalling conditions and brutal treatment on slave ships.

The largest group of immigrants (voluntary newcomers) were the Scots-Irish. With encouragement from the English, their ancestors left Scotland for northern Ireland in the 1500s. Yet, roughly a quarter of a million of them left northern Ireland after 1680 because of discrimination by the English. Like other European immigrants, some Scots-Irish were misled about what to expect in America by immigrant recruiters. But reliable letters from friends or relatives in the colonies helped many more. Most paid their passage across the Atlantic by becoming indentured servants (contracting to labour without wages for four to seven years in the colonies). When their term of service was finished, they usually took their 'freedom dues' (a small sum of money and tools) and settled on the frontier where land was cheapest.

Constantly looking for better land, the Scots-Irish are the source of the stereotype of frontier folk, who feel it is time to move if they can see the smoke from a neighbour's chimney. This moving broke family ties and scattered their settlements from western New England to the hill country of Georgia. Although they built schools and churches wherever they settled, many abandoned Presbyterianism on the frontier.

The period's 200,000 German immigrants aroused more opposition than the Scots-Irish for a number of reasons. They were the largest non-English-speaking group in the colonies and believed their descendants had to learn German if their religion and culture were to survive in North America. To preserve their heritage and help each other economically, they concentrated their settlements in the Middle Colonies, mostly in Pennsylvania. Here, German families lived so closely together in some areas that others found it hard to settle among them. Like the Scots-Irish, Germans lived on the frontier, but they usually stayed behind when settlement moved farther west. Developing German-speaking towns, they kept to themselves and showed little interest in colonial politics.

As a result, German immigrants met considerable hostility. For some Anglo-Americans, the final straw was the Germans' prosperity. They were renowned for their hard work, caution, farming methods and concern for their property. They were too successful, according to their envious neighbours. Benjamin Franklin expressed what many feared when he said they might 'Germanize us instead of us Anglicizing them'. In a period so near the religious wars of the Reformation, the reception Germans met also varied according to whether they were nonconformists, reformed Lutherans, or Catholics.

Other smaller groups added to the first wave of immigration. They showed contrasting ways that ethnic groups can adjust to new and varied circumstances. England sent some 50,000 convicts and perhaps 30,000 poor people as indentured servants to ease problems at home while supplying the labour-starved American economy. Immigration from Ireland included thousands of single, male, Irish Catholic indentured servants. They assimilated even more rapidly than the Scots-Irish, because of religious discrimination and the difficulty of finding Catholic wives. The Scots, perhaps because of their hatred of English attempts to suppress their culture at home, followed a pattern more like that of the Germans, using compact settlement, religion, schooling and family networks to preserve their culture for generations in rural parts of New Jersey, Virginia and North Carolina. In similar fashion, a small French enclave persisted in South Carolina.

The French Huguenots and Jews, who settled in port towns and engaged in trade, illustrated a contrasting tendency. English colonists severely limited their civil rights and sometimes attacked their churches or synagogues, but accepted intercultural marriage with them as long as they converted to the religion of their spouses. Through intermarriage, the colonial Huguenot and Jewish communities virtually vanished.

This first wave of immigration transformed the demography of the colonies. By 1776 the English were no longer four-fifths of the population but a bare majority (52 per cent). Equally important, non-immigrant African-American slaves had become on average 20 per cent of the population and were a majority in large parts of the Southern colonies. Except in isolated pockets of wilderness, the East Coast Native-American cultures had been forced inland to or beyond the Appalachians. Non-English peoples were a majority in the coastal towns, Pennsylvania, the South, and parts of all the other colonies. However, the cultural, political and economic dominance of Anglo-Americans was clear.

The second wave: the old immigrants, 1820–90

Between 1776 and the late 1820s, immigration slowed to a trickle. The struggle for independence and the effort to establish a new nation welded the colonies' diverse peoples together and gave them a sense of being Americans. The pressure of the dominant Anglo-American culture and the passage of time also weakened the old ethnic communities. Although Dutch and German areas of influence remained locally strong, most ethnic groups found the Americanizing process irresistible and were assimilated.

Both Americans and immigrants in the 1820s, therefore, thought their situation was unprecedented. Few newcomers were aware of the colonial enclaves, and Americans reacted as if the new ethnic districts that formed were completely novel.

The momentous changes occurring in Europe and the US also made the situation seem different. A range of factors pushed Europeans from their homelands. Religious persecution drove many German Jews to emigrate, and political unrest forced out a few thousand European intellectuals and political activists. But economic push factors were decisive for most of the northern and western Europeans who are commonly called the 'old' immigrants. The first of these was the doubling of Europe's population between 1750 and 1850, due to an improved diet, better hygiene and medical advances. In Ireland and parts of Germany the diet of rural people depended entirely on the potato, which yielded more food per acre than grain. Another factor was the rapid growth of cities, which encouraged farmers to switch to more efficient large-scale production based on farm machinery, the elimination of small holdings, and enclosure of common lands. These changes meant a large rural population could no longer make a living in the countryside.

The industrial revolution and an international trade boom spread from Britain to the Continent and the US during this period, but reached different regions at different times. If nearby cities offered industrial work or jobs in shipping, emigration rates were lower. But the population surplus from the countryside was so large that huge numbers of people left anyway. Stage migration (moving first to the city and after some years from there to a foreign country) became common. Forced to follow changes in the international Atlantic labour market, people moved to where the jobs were.

As the steam engine improved land and sea travel, international migration became easier and cheaper. 'America letters' from family and friends in the US gave a remarkably accurate picture of changing economic conditions there. Of the 60 million people who left their homelands between 1820 and 1930, two-thirds settled in the US. During the 'old' immigration, 15.5 million people made America their home.

The largest immigrant groups, in order of size, were Germans, Irish, Britons and Scandinavians, but many other peoples, including French Canadians, Chinese, Swiss and Dutch also came in large numbers. The factor that attracted most of these people to the US was land, of which the country seemed to have an unlimited supply, especially since few respected the claims of Native Americans. But another pull factor was the work immigrants found in building transportation networks, exploiting mineral or forest resources, and supplying the engineering trades, skilled crafts and unskilled labour needed by America's expanding industries. American railroad companies, which had been granted enormous tracts of land by the federal government, and state and territorial governments sent immigration agents to Europe to recruit people with promises of cheap fertile farms or jobs with wages many times higher than they could earn at home. News of boom times in the US, land giveaways such as the Homestead Act of 1862, or gold in California brought peaks of immigration that rose ever higher.

While the newcomers settled everywhere, they were particularly numerous in the urban Northeast and the recently settled farmlands and frontier cities of the Midwest and Pacific coast. The 'old' immigrants found many economic niches, supplying much of the market for domestic servants, mill and factory workers, miners, loggers, sailors, fishermen and construction workers. Except for the 'famine Irish', most came with enough funds to travel to places where countrymen could help them adjust to American society. When a potato rot ruined the crop that supported Ireland's rural population, mass starvation and emigration followed. Huge numbers of Irish immigrants arrived in the 1850s and 1880s with so little money that they stayed in the cities where their ships landed.

British immigrants attracted so little attention that they seemed nearly invisible. Because they spoke English and had a culture much like Anglo-Americanism, their ethnicity was largely ignored. They also won the gratitude of important American businessmen as up to the 1850s, Britain's industry was the world's most advanced, and they brought the knowledge of recent machine designs and industrial organization in their heads. Protestant and White, Scandinavians had language problems but faced comparatively mild problems of adjustment.

But nativism (the dislike of people and things foreign) plagued many 'old' immigrants in spite of their apparent similarity to native-born Americans. Germans were welcomed for their technical knowledge and industry, and admired for a culture that was Europe's most respected at the time. But they were also stereotyped as Prussian marionettes or Bavarian louts, criticized for clannishness, and targets of temperance movements that attacked their habit of drinking in beerhalls after church on Sundays. German Jews experienced exclusion from education, the professions and many social circles.

The Irish suffered many forms of discrimination and were often stereotyped as dirty, lazy and drunken. The most serious opposition they faced, however, came from anti-Catholic bigots, who burned convents and churches as early as the 1830s. All the large immigrant groups found themselves involved in controversies over the control and content of the public schools. But none were so critical of the schools' attempts to Americanize immigrant children as the Irish (usually through the reactions of Irish-American priests).

Anti-foreign agitation reached its first peak in the 1850s, when the Know Nothing or American Party proposed tripling the length of time needed to gain US citizenship and restricting immigrants' voting rights. On that platform, Know-nothings won dozens of seats in Congress and numerous state and local offices, especially in the Northeast. Internal divisions and the coming of the Civil War defused this nativist movement. But another arose in the 1860s in the West and achieved its goal, the Chinese Exclusion Act, which effectively ended Chinese immigration in 1882. Racism and the fear of unemployment and depressed wages motivated the labour organizations that spearheaded the campaign.

The third wave: new immigrants and immigration restriction, 1890–1930

The 'new' immigration marked a change in the origin of most immigrants. Around 1890 immigration from northwest Europe began to decline sharply (but did not stop), while arrivals from southern and eastern Europe rose. By 1907, four of five newcomers were 'new' immigrants. Between 1890 and 1914, the volume of immigration also soared, topping a million annually several times and equalling the 15.5 million of the old immigration in just twenty-four years. In numerical order, the largest 'new' groups were Italians, Jews, Poles, and Hungarians, but many Mexicans, Russians, Czechs, Greeks, Portuguese, Syrians, Japanese, Filipinos and other nationalities also immigrated.

To most Americans, the change involved not so much numbers or national origins, as the feeling that the typical immigrant had become much less like them. The religions, languages, manners and costumes of the Slavic peoples seemed exotic or incomprehensible. Eastern Orthodox Jews, the Mediterranean nationalities and Asians also appeared to belong to other races. But this tidal wave of people was in several ways similar to its predecessors. The basic economic push and pull factors had not changed. The commercialization of farming, urbanization and industrialization had simply spread east and south. The new immigrants had the same dream of bettering their own and their children's future. And like the Puritans, Eastern European Jews emigrated because of religious persecution, chiefly the bloody Russian pogroms.

But transportation improvements also increased the flow of migrants. Peasant farmers now left home because they could not compete with cheaper grain imported from distant lands. Cheap train and steamship tickets (often pre-paid by relatives in America) made migration affordable even for the very poor and young. Cheap travel also permitted people to see immigration as a short-term strategy, instead of a life-long decision. Many new immigrants were sojourners, 'birds of passage', who stayed only long enough to save money to buy land or a small business in the old country. In general, the new immigrants were younger, more often unmarried, and more likely to travel as individuals rather than in family groups.

The opportunities in America had changed somewhat too. The closing of the frontier around 1890 meant the era of government land giveaways was over. Less than a quarter of the newcomers found employment in agriculture. The Japanese in California are the best example of those who succeeded by buying unwanted land and making it productive. Nearly four-fifths of the immigrants went where the jobs were: to the industries in the big cities of the Northeast and Great Lakes Midwest. America had an enormous need for workers in its factories, but as a result of mechanization, most of the jobs were unskilled and poorly paid.

The size of the new immigration and the altered job market resulted in larger urban immigrant quarters than Americans had ever seen. The crime, overcrowding, unsanitary conditions and epidemics in immigrant ghettoes had been a focus of alarm and reform since before the Civil War. But these urban problems seemed insurmountable, especially as many Americans doubted that the more 'exotic' foreigners were capable of assimilation or integration into American society. Reactions to the situation in the cities were various. Urban reformers established so-called settlement houses and inner-city charities to help immigrants adjust, worked to Americanize them, and fought for better housing and parks. For all their faults, the ghettoes were important as buffer zones, where immigrants could use their mother tongues and follow old-country traditions while gradually becoming accustomed to American conditions. But critics argued that the ghettoes proved restrictive immigration laws were needed.

In 1909, Israel Zangwill's play, *The Melting Pot*, popularized the idea that *all* population groups in the US would eventually fuse through intermarriage and become an entirely new people. To many a native-born reformer, the melting-pot view of American society meant that the immigrants should conform to Anglo-American culture, for their own good. Nativists of the time could not imagine a greater calamity than such a melting pot 'mongrelization' of the White race. The opposite view was the traditional one that the US should be pluralistic, a collection of cultures united by loyalty to the same political and civic ideals. But even pluralists split over the issue of race. Although they made the national motto '*e pluribus unum*' (out of many one), in the Naturalization Act of 1790, the founding fathers permitted all foreigners to become American citizens, as long as they were White.

Restriction, even regulation of immigration, was very slow to develop in the US. The federal government only asked local authorities to count immigrants and passed an act *encouraging* the importation of contract workers until 1875. Except for a brief period, aliens could become citizens in five years. In 1891, the national authorities finally took responsibility for regulating immigration and the next year opened Ellis Island, the country's most famous receiving and screening depot for immigrants.

In the 1920s, however, the pessimists who believed the US could no longer successfully integrate all immigrants won passage of severely restrictive, racist immigration laws that remained in force until 1965. The National Origins Quota Acts represented the climax of a campaign for restriction that achieved its first result in 1875, when the federal government began a piecemeal listing of banned groups. Between that year and 1917, convicts and prostitutes, the Chinese, lunatics, idiots, those likely to depend on public charity, contract labourers, polygamists, anarchists and other radicals, people with specific contagious diseases, the Japanese and illiterates were put on the list of undesirables. This is an official record of Americans' economic, racial, moral and ideological fears and prejudices. The influence of the pseudo-scientific racism of the early 1900s, which purported to prove experimentally the superiority of Anglo-Saxons over all other 'races', was evident in the list and later legislation. So was the combination of First World War superpatriotism that demanded 100 per cent Americanism and the ideological insecurity that grew after the Russian Revolution of 1917.

Finally in 1921, Congress passed the first general limitation on immigration, set the annual number of European newcomers at 358,000, and introduced the principle of national origins quotas. Each European nation's allotment of immigrant visas per year equalled 3 per cent of the foreign-born in the US from that country at the federal census of 1910. But the dissatisfaction of restrictionists with this law revealed the immigrant groups they feared most, Asians and the new immigrants from Europe. In 1924, a new National Origins Act met their demands. The new quotas equalled 2 per cent of the people of that national *background* in the US in 1890.

These changes aimed to make the quotas of southern and eastern Europeans minuscule. They calculated national quotas by choosing a census from *before* the arrival of most new immigrants and rewarded the accumulated weight of Northwestern

PLATE 2.4 A young Haitian ponders an uncertain future in the US *(Rex Features)*

European stock in the US population. In 1924, the Oriental Exclusion Act ended Asian immigration. In 1929, when the final national origins quotas went into effect, Britain's was 65,361, while Italy's, for example, was 5,802, and Syria received the minimum of 100 visas.

Wartime policies: displaced persons and refugees

Writing immigration law that functions as intended has proved difficult. The Quota Act, as its supporters hoped, ended the new immigration but it did not lead to increased immigration from northern and western Europe. Those nations left their quotas

PLATE 2.5 The 'good life' in the New World
(*Jacky Chapman/Format*)

unfilled. Nor did it occur to Congress that arrivals from 'non-quota' nations, such as Mexico, the West Indies, Canada and the American territories of Puerto Rico and the Philippines would soar into the millions by 1960.

Events during these years also defied governmental plans. The Depression of the 1930s put a stop to *voluntary* mass immigration. Local authorities and 'vigilantes' forcibly deported an estimated half million Mexican Americans, many of them US citizens, during the decade. The rise of the Nazi and Fascist regimes, on the other hand, caused an enormous flow of refugees, 250,000 of whom Congress admitted as non-quota immigrants under special laws. Many more, including 20,000 Jewish children, were turned away because the US was unwilling to put aside its national quota system when hard times at home had produced both high unemployment and rising anti-Semitism.

The Second World War and the Cold War caused several contrasting shifts in policy. The government agreed to import contract labour from Mexico under an intergovernmental agreement called the 'bracero program' (temporary worker plan) because of the wartime shortage of farm labour. It lifted the ban on Chinese immigration because of foreign policy considerations. Yet it also bowed to panicky racists on the West Coast, who feared foreign spies, and confined 110,000 Japanese Americans to 'internment camps', confiscating most of their property. After the war, federal law provided for the entry of the families formed by US service people while they were abroad. Several hundred thousand *displaced persons* (those so uprooted by the war that they had no homes to return to) were admitted by Acts of Congress. Between 1948 and 1959, Cold War refugees from communist countries, like Hungary and Cuba, also came. The total of non-quota immigrants for those years reached 750,000.

These events made a mockery of the idea that quotas based on the origins of the US population could be the basis on which most immigrants were admitted to the country. Moreover, during the Cold War, when the US competed with the USSR for the allegiance of non-aligned nations, the racist principles underlying the quotas were a foreign policy embarrassment. In 1952, the McCarran–Walter Act attempted to eliminate this racism by stating that race was no longer a reason for refusing someone an immigrant visa or American citizenship. Merit, defined as skills needed in the US, would determine who received the first 50 per cent of visas for each country. But because the law kept the national origins principle, gave many Third World countries tiny quotas, and made communist or socialist associations a bar to immigration, it was also suggested that an entirely new approach was needed.

The Immigration Act of 1965 provided this new approach, but also had unforeseen consequences. It abolished national origins quotas and replaced them with hemispheric limits to annual immigration: 170,000 for the Eastern Hemisphere and

U.S. IMMIGRATION & NATURALIZATION SERVICE

PLATE 2.6 US immigration *(Barnaby's Picture Library)*

120,000 for the Western. To emphasize equal treatment, all nations in the Eastern Hemisphere had the same limit of 20,000 immigrants annually. A system of preferences stressed the principles for selecting immigrants.

Unifying families was the goal of several preference categories, which together reserved about three-quarters of immigrant visas for relatives of American citizens or resident aliens. Spouses, minor children, and parents were admitted outside the limits, and grown children (married and unmarried) and brothers and sisters were given specific preferences. Like the 1952 law, the Act established a 'brain drain', reserving another 20 per cent of visas for people who possessed skills needed in the US. Humanitarian values were served by giving the remaining 6 per cent of places

73

to refugees. Having corrected the bias of its earlier laws for European and Asian immigration, Congress extended the 20,000 national limit and preference system to the Western Hemisphere in the 1970s.

Congress intended to make up for past injustices to southern and eastern Europeans through the large number of places reserved for family, especially for siblings and grown children, which it hoped, would lead to the reappearance of 'new' immigrants. For ten years larger numbers of Italians, Greeks and Portuguese came. By 1980 it became clear that the family preferences benefited people from other nations much more. In 1965 Europe and Canada provided the majority of immigrants to the US, but by 1980 less than a sixth came from those places and four-fifths were almost equally divided between Asia and Latin America. Expecting 'family' to be like western nuclear families, American politicans did not anticipate how useful Latinos and Asians would find the family unification clauses for bringing in large extended families.

The fourth wave: 1965 to the present

The 1965 law ushered in the fourth major wave of immigration, which gained strength through the early 1990s and may produce the highest immigration totals in American history by the end of the decade. In addition to the many immigrants allowed by the hemispheric limits (changed to a global total of 320,000 in 1980), the wave has included hundreds of thousands of immediate relatives and refugees outside those limits. It has also contained millions of illegal aliens, who cross borders without papers (or with false papers) or arrive at airports on student or tourist visas and then overstay.

Between 1961 and 1990 close to 20 million people settled in America. The order of the twenty largest nationality groups in the first column of Table 2.1 shows mostly Latino and Asian immigrants but a few prominent European groups. By 1996 some 7 million more newcomers had arrived. The second list, of groups

TABLE 2.1 The twenty largest immigrant groups, 1961–93

1961–90	1966–93
1 Mexicans	1 Mexicans
2 Filipinos	2 Filipinos
3 Chinese/Taiwanese	3 Chinese/Taiwanese/
4 Canadians	Hong Kong Chinese
5 Cubans	4 Vietnamese
6 Koreans	5 Koreans
7 British	6 Asian Indians
8 Dominicans	7 Dominicans
9 Vietnamese	8 Cubans
10 Asian Indians	9 Jamaicans
11 Jamaicans	10 British
12 Italians	11 Canadians
13 Germans	12 Salvadorans
14 Colombians	13 Haitians
15 Salvadorans	14 Italians
16 Haitians	15 Colombians
17 Portuguese	16 former Soviets
18 Greeks	17 Iranians
19 Poles	18 Poles
20 Iranians	19 Germans
	20 Portuguese

Source: US Immigration and Naturalization Service

after the passage of the 1965 Act, reveals its unexpected benefits for the Third World immigrants of the fourth wave.

Like the earlier waves of newcomers, the fourth includes a broad range of socio-economic groups. One result of saving visas for needed occupations is that a very noticeable minority are highly skilled workers, professionals (especially engineers, doctors and nurses), and entrepreneurs with capital. The large majority of both legal and illegal immigrants are similar to those who have arrived since the 1820s. They are above average educationally and economically in their homelands but below average in these areas

75

in the US. They have come because commercialization and industrialization (now revolutionizing the Third World) have disrupted their traditional economies.

At the socio-economic bottom of this wave are people who obtain visas because they are near relatives of recent, more skilled immigrants or take jobs Americans do not want. Among the latter are Latino women recruited by agencies as live-in domestic servants and nannies. Spreading the word about these jobs and moving into better paid work once they have acquired more English, they bring their families and forge the links in 'chain migration' based on a network of female contacts.

The nationalities and skin colours of most people in this wave are different, however, and they arrive in different ways and settle in different places. There are colonies of Hmong in Minneapolis, Vietnamese on the Mississippi Delta, East Indian hotel owners across the Sunbelt, Middle-Eastern Muslims in New Jersey, and very large concentrations of Latinos in the Southwest, Chicago, and New York. These colonies have given rise to contemporary forms of racism and nativism. Groping for ways to adjust to the changes in their country's population, Americans are again resorting to broad stereotypes. The Gallup Poll results in Table 2.2 come from Americans' answers when they were asked if ethnic groups had, on the whole, been good or bad for the US. In general, the longer the group has been in the country, the more favourable the public response to it is. Racial attitudes, however, appear to be decisive in creating long-term low opinions of non-White ethnic groups.

Large numbers of Asian immigrants in the fourth wave arrive with more capital and a higher level of education than most Latinos. Those facts and the popular view of some Asian cultures' emphasis on respect for parents, education, and hard work have led some media commentators to lump all Asian Americans together under the label of the 'model minority'. This ignores the large majority of Asian immigrants who come with little money and education; the special problems of Asian refugees who have experienced wartime traumas; and the rising job discrimination and violence against Asian Americans.

TABLE 2.2   Public opinions on immigrant groups

	Good (%)	Bad (%)
English	66	6
Irish	62	7
Jews	59	9
Germans	57	11
Italians	56	10
Poles	53	12
Japanese	47	18
Blacks	46	16
Chinese	44	19
Mexicans	25	34
Koreans	24	30
Vietnamese	20	38
Puerto Ricans	17	43
Haitians	10	39
Cubans	9	59

Source: Gallup Organization, 1982

For its own convenience, the federal government invented a word that gives the impression that the hugely diverse Spanish-speaking cultures in the US are a single monolithic group called 'Hispanics'. This is not only a handy label for official statistics but a word easily identified with illegal immigrants in the popular mind, even though 'illegals' come from countries as diverse as Ireland and Iran.

Illegal immigration caused much debate over government policy during the 1970s and 1980s. One segment of public opinion stressed that illegal immigration encouraged a disregard for the law in general, and was at variance with the 1965 law that gave all nationalites an equal chance to apply for immigrant visas. Other Americans emphasized that illegal immigrants were often paid less than the legal minimum wage; worked in substandard conditions; and while needing the benefits of social welfare programmes, dared not reveal the facts of their situation for fear of being deported.

PLATE 2.7 Puerto Rican couple, New York *(Barnaby's Picture Library)*

The federal government responded to the problems connected with illegal immigration by passing the Immigration Reform and Control Act of 1986 (IRCA). The law has two main provisions. The first establishes 'employer sanctions', rules that fine employers who hire illegal aliens and set penalties, including a jail sentence, for people who repeatedly violate this part of the law. IRCA also attempts to prevent discrimination in employment. Separate rules outlaw firing or refusing to hire people merely because they look foreign. The second major provision of IRCA offers 'amnesty' (legal immigrant status) for illegals who entered the United States before 1982 and remained, and for temporarily resident farmworkers (Special Agricultural Workers or SAW) employed in American agriculture for three months in 1985–6.

By 1992, most of the 3 million people who had applied for amnesty had been granted it. Their improved situation was the one great success of the legislation. A few employers were convicted for hiring illegal aliens, but it proved difficult to document that employers had broken the law. Illegal immigration, while it declined sharply at first, seemed to approach earlier levels by 1990.

In spite of rising reactions from some old-stock American organizations against increasing immigration, national policy became more liberal through the Immigration Act of 1990, which *raised* the annual number of immigrant visas by 200,000. The Act also increased the limit on entries from individual nations to 25,000 and doubled the annual number of asylum seekers who could become permanent residents. Business lobbies successfully won inclusion of provisions that made immigration easier for entrepreneurs, highly trained labour and migrant workers. Civil rights interest groups won the elimination of clauses that since the early 1950s had prevented the entry of homosexuals, socialists and communists.

Congress also bowed to pressure from a wide range of ethnic communities. European-American groups, led by Irish-Americans such as Senator Edward Kennedy, claimed that since 1965, American policy had unintentionally put some nationality groups (mostly European) at a disadvantage. The largest categories of immigrant visas allowed by the 1965 law went to close relatives of citizens and resident aliens, but Europeans' family connections in the US were too indirect to qualify. Asian-American and Latin-American groups replied that this call to permit the entry of more Europeans (to preserve ethnic 'diversity') would represent a return to the earlier discrimination against Asians and Latin Americans. In a compromise acceptable to both sides of the debate, Congress established 'diversity' visas for nations adversely affected by the 1965 law but also included a broadened category of visas for family members (still almost three-quarters of those granted annually) that now includes spouses and children of illegals given amnesty in the late 1980s and early 1990s.

The 1990 Act is all the more remarkable when one considers the mood of the general public when it was debated and passed. Opinion polls indicated that the public was less than enthusiastic about a new tide of immigrants as the country slid into an economic recession. When the economy improved, however, the public backlash against high levels of immigration continued to rise, especially in the seven states (California, New York, New Jersey, Florida, Texas, Illinois, and Arizona) where over three-quarters

79

of newcomers settle. Yet, after debating drastic proposals for restriction in 1996, Congress left much of US immigration untouched. It did, however, deny *legal* immigrants federal welfare benefits (illegal immigrants never received them) through the welfare act the President signed, and then promised to amend to include immigrants' children if re-elected. The 1996 immigration law provides for more border barriers, more immigration agents, stiffer penalties for 'people smuggling', easier deportation of illegals and terrorists, and less easily forged border crossing cards. But it does little to discourage record levels of legal newcomers. In an election year, it only responds to anger over illegal immigration, critics say, because of the growing power of immigrant voters (especially Latinos) and the need for workers in today's booming economy.

Internal migration: changing patterns in the American mosaic

The US has always had an unusually mobile population, not only because of the many millions who have immigrated, but also because of internal migration (population shifts within the country). The best-known of these shifts is the frontier movement to the west. It became a two-front war forcing native peoples into the Great Plains and Rocky Mountains after the discovery of gold in California resulted in a rush of the American-born and immigrants to the West Coast in the mid-1800s. The frontier movement resulted in areas with large minorities of conquered peoples, such as the remnants of Native-American cultures on reservations and the old Spanish-culture centres of the Southwest.

From the 1830s until the late 1940s, millions of people also left the countryside for the cities. Old-stock Americans and the descendants of immigrants abandoned farms as mechanization enabled fewer people to produce more food and industrialization created more urban jobs. Until the late 1920s, this process concentrated the nation's population in its urban, industrial core, from Boston to Milwaukee in the North and from New York to St Louis in the south. Then two other forms of internal migration

PLATE 2.8 Harlem, New York *(Barnaby's Picture Library)*

replaced immigration and urbanization as the main source of population shifts. The population of the 'core' began to decline. So many Whites moved to the South and West, both to cities and rural areas, that the large numbers of Blacks leaving the South for the North's industrial cities did not fully replace them. Jobs in defence industries during the two World Wars and the Cold Wars attracted even more Blacks to the North, but also brought industry to the West Coast and a few southern cities. The trend continued over the next decades, as air conditioning, the discovery of oil and gas, low property taxes and inexpensive labour encouraged firms to leave the core Rustbelt for the Sunbelt, from Atlanta, Georgia to Los Angeles, California.

The census of 1990 showed the nation's population approaching 260 million and demonstrated the importance of another population shift, the departure of city residents for the suburbs. Observers had long noticed the recurrent pattern of recently arrived immigrant groups replacing established ones in urban areas, as earlier arrivals moved into better paid jobs and left the cities for the suburbs. Through this migration (often half-accurately called 'White flight'), less successful Blacks, Latinos, and White ethnics from southern and eastern Europe inherited the political power and problems of many big cities by the 1970s. By the 1992 elections, a clear majority of middle-class voters lived in the suburbs for the first time. These areas, rather than the city centres with their Asian and Latino immigrants and Black 'under-class', now hold decisive socio-economic and political power.

The American population mosaic today shows many signs of internal migration. It also illustrates the effects of earlier waves of immigration through regional and local variations in the mixture of ethnic groups. Though they are Americanized and can be found all over the country, recognizable concentrations of German and Scandinavian Americans are still found in the Upper Midwest, as are southern and eastern European-Americans and Irish-Americans in the Northeast and Great Lakes region. In today's seven 'immigration' states, fourth-wave immigrants are particularly visible. Replacing the shift to the Sunbelt, movement to both coasts from inland states has become the main form of internal migration in the 1990s. Finally, in the mid-1990s the Mountain States, especially Utah and Nevada, reported the highest rates of in-migration in the nation. Some observers speculate that these patterns of internal migration represent American society's continuing search for opportunity on a new 'frontier'.

■ Examine and explain the following terms:

indigenous peoples	Middle Colonies
pluralism	pantheists
first wave	national origins quotas
Great Chain of Being	old immigrants
1965 Immigration Act	stage migration
immigrant (*contra* founder)	fourth wave
Virginia	nativism
IRCA	Northern colonies
new immigrants	push and pull factors
melting pot	internal migration
1990 and 1996	chain migration
Immigration Acts	

■ Write short essays on the following topics:

1 Explain why the encounters between Native Americans and Europeans were so disastrous.

2 Describe one or more of the four major waves of immigration and discuss causes for the kind of reception the newcomers received from the native-born population.

3 Debate which of the metaphors for understanding the nature of American society is most accurate and enlightening. Include a discussion of the vision of the US in 'The New Colossus'.

4 Critically discuss the evolution of American immigration law and the social forces that produced it.

Chapter 3

The people: women and minorities

The reason for American women's and minority history

Discrimination has given women and some minorities a special status in American society. For much of American history, men (or male-dominated society) have forced women, Native Americans, African Americans, Asian Americans and Latinos into inferior categories, legally and informally. As a result, these groups have their own histories, as subjects of changing fashions of opinion and government policy, even though their experiences are integral parts of the nation's history.

All these groups have powerfully moulded American history through their struggles for equality and resistance against unfair practices. Discrimination has affected all aspects of life. Inequality could and can be documented through the group differences it helps bring in attitudes, economic class, occupation, income, health, housing and crime. The gap between national ideals and the realities of institutionalized prejudice have agitated the nation's conscience and prompted a very uneven but persistent progress towards greater equality.

There has been constant debate over the proper means of creating a more just society. Neither policy-makers nor the subjects of that policy have agreed on the course to follow. Some women and minority group members have not wanted what reformers defined as 'progressive' legislation. Division and debate within all groups and compromise legislation have been the rule. Over a century of federal civil rights laws has proved that changes in the law often do not function as intended, or assure changes in attitudes.

Even defining what equality means has proved difficult. Most Americans have supported equality of opportunity (an equal chance to develop one's abilities and be rewarded for them) but not equality of results (an evening out of economic, social and political power). Thus most attempts to redistribute wealth have failed or

PLATE 3.1 Cowgirl *(Range/Hanley)*

been short-lived. Affirmative action programmes that call for preferential treatment of women and minorities to correct the effects of past discrimination are still in effect but have aroused strong opposition. Political representation of minorities has improved because of legislation requiring the creation of minority election districts, but many of the new districts have been found unlawful by the courts. Although Americans favour equality, they are at odds about what it is and the degree to which government can or should provide it.

Women in America

Numerically a majority, women in America today experience unequal treatment in significant ways. They are assigned prescribed roles, and do not as often work in the most prestigious occupations, earn as much money, or enjoy positions of equal social status as men. Popular attitudes continue to keep women in their traditional place. Mostly working in poorly paid service jobs, they are grossly under-represented in politics and the highest levels of business management. But great changes in their position have occurred.

Historically, women's legal status in America was determined by English common law. From 1608, when the first female colonist arrived, until the mid-1800s, the law regarding women was that upon marriage, a woman experienced a 'civil death', which meant she ceased to exist legally except through her spouse. She had no right to own property, control her wages, or sign contracts. Divorce, seldom granted except in extreme cases, was easier for men to obtain than for women. Single women could inherit and own property until they married. A single woman was, however, expected to submit to her father's or brother's will until she entered matrimony.

Claiming they were by nature physically frail and mentally limited, men kept women economically dependent. Physical work could endanger their ability to bear children, and rigorous intellectual pursuits would overstrain their brains. Women ought, therefore, to have little education and no political influence. Church leaders said women's weaknesses and subordinate position were God's punishment for Eve's original sin. Clerics cited St Paul's injunction that women should not speak in public meetings. The appropriate place for women, in the accepted view, was at home where their limited strength and learning could serve their male relatives.

But there were historical circumstances and attitudes that worked against or contradicted this conventional view of women. On the frontier of settlement that moved west for over 250 years, women's skills were as essential as men's. The westward movement resulted in a scarcity of women on the frontier, where they were consequently highly valued but could not be pampered. It also meant a shortage of men in the East, where widows and single women were often needed to fill the occupational roles of men.

From the earliest colonial days, most American women have worked. The churches proclaimed idleness a sin for both sexes. Before the industrial revolution most necessities of life were made at home, and women were expected to be as proficient at handicrafts as men. Women were in a majority among the first factory workers when the industrial revolution began in the New England textile mills. Before the Civil War they worked in over 100 industrial occupations, but they were concentrated mostly in the less skilled jobs and earned on average about one-quarter of men's wages. Women were among the first workers involved in strikes and demonstrations for higher pay and better working conditions. From its beginning they joined the labour movement, and formed their own unions when men showed little interest in organizing them.

In fact, a very small elite of women in North America did only housework or were leisured before 1900. All Native-American cultures assumed women were needed for crucial tasks. African-American women were almost all slaves or poor, and thus had to work to survive. The large majority of White women, many of them immigrants, had to work in addition to performing the duties of a homemaker. They often did piecework in the 'cottage industries' (factory work done at home for which people were paid for the number of items they completed).

The nineteenth century

Some middle- and upper-class White women were leisured or had no paid work at home. Among these were the founders of academies and seminaries for girls between 1800 and 1850 and of famous women's colleges, such as Vassar, Smith and Mount Holyoke, in the late 1800s. These social classes also produced most of the century's female reformers. Such women were prominent in the crusade against alcohol abuse and led movements to improve conditions in US prisons, insane asylums, hospitals, schools and immigrant ghettoes.

The first movement for women's rights was closely related to female reformers' experiences in abolitionist (anti-slavery) campaigns. Women abolitionists publicized parallels between discrimination against Blacks and women after they were attacked as 'unwomanly' for speaking to mixed audiences of men and women. In 1848 two abolitionists, Lucretia Mott and Elizabeth Cady Stanton, led the first women's rights convention in Seneca Falls, New York. In language taken from the Declaration of Independence, the convention's 'Declaration of Sentiments' called for property and divorce rights, educational and employment opportunities and the vote.

Thereafter, the women's movement held regular conventions and with mixed results, worked to realize their stated goals. Before the Civil War Susan B. Anthony led successful efforts to improve women's marriage and divorce status as well as their economic rights under New York state law. A few years later, however, these liberal provisions were repealed. Women were increasingly accepted as teachers, and moved into nursing and government office work during the Civil War. Feminists joined the successful campaign for the constitutional abolition of slavery through the Thirteenth Amendment. But their movement split in two when it became clear that only Black men were offered the vote in the Fourteenth and Fifteenth Amendments.

One group of women thought the linkage between the oppression of women and Blacks was so natural that they opposed all proposals for broadening the franchise that excluded women. They insisted that the movement had to champion a wide range of women's rights and pursue the vote through a federal women's suffrage amendment. Other female activists believed that women should not risk causing the defeat of suffrage for Black men by creating more opposition through demands of their own. They thought the best plan was to present women's voting rights as a separate issue, avoid involvement in other causes that would alienate influential groups, and concentrate on winning the vote on a state-by-state basis.

The latter group first tasted victory when Wyoming Territory granted female suffrage in 1869. But of the seventeen states that considered women's suffrage between 1870 and 1910, only Colorado, Idaho and Utah approved it. Several other states gave women voting rights limited to municipal or school issues and elections. Although men continued to deny women membership in unions for skilled workers, the more ambitious female activists assisted unskilled women's unionization and mounted successful campaigns against child labour. On the other hand, their fight for abortion rights, birth control and membership on juries met with failure until after the Second World War.

The twentieth century

The movement united behind efforts for ratification of the Nineteenth Amendment, which granted women the right to vote in all elections in 1920. Women had strongly supported efforts to deal with political corruption and urban social problems at the turn of the century. Therefore, many male politicians thought they would vote for a broad range of social reforms or form a women's party to defeat conservative male candidates.

In practice these fears proved to be unfounded, as women voters divided over issues in much the same way as men. Nor did having the vote bring significant change in employment for women. Many women's rights organizations disbanded soon after suffrage was won. Women's economic position improved slowly in part because of disagreement within the movement about whether there should be any legal differences between the sexes. Female social welfare reformers demanded protective measures that treated women as a special category. Some groups, for example, successfully lobbied for laws limiting women's working hours and occupational choices to protect their safety and health. Until the 1970s civil rights legislation for women and court decisions affecting their rights were generally based on such a *protectionist* approach.

Other feminists insisted that this approach kept women in poorly paid jobs that offered little overtime. Protective legislation, they said, prevented equality with men because it was founded on the assumption that women are the weaker sex. These activists proposed another constitutional change as early as 1923, the Equal Rights Amendment (ERA), to eliminate the remaining legal inequalities between men and women. Some early opponents of the ERA feared it would lead to the overturn of protective legislation for women. Such dissension and the generally conservative mood of the country contributed to the relative dormancy of the women's movement between the late 1920s and the beginning of the 1960s.

The turning point in women's employment came after the Second World War. Many married women who went to work during the war continued to work in peacetime and many more joined them in the following decades. While 15 per cent of married women were employed in 1940, by 1970 almost 50 per cent had jobs. Not only were many more married women working, but the majority in 1970 were middle-aged and middle class. Husbands accepted the change with little protest for several reasons. Though wives' wages were usually low, they were essential for joining or staying in the middle class. Working in the traditional role of helping their families, moreover, most women did not take jobs until the children entered school. Meanwhile, larger numbers of poor and single women were also working.

Thus, when a new women's movement appeared in the 1960s, challenging the view that women's place was keeping house, many middle-class Americans agreed. The reality they lived no longer squared with conventions of the past. The women's movement was also stimulated by Blacks' demands for civil rights. Again women discovered more keenly their own oppression as they fought racial discrimination. The 1964 Civil Rights Act was the first such legislation to explicitly ban discrimination based on sex as well as on race. By the mid-1970s laws were passed that promised women equal treatment in the job market and admission to higher education, equal pay for equal work, and equal availability of loans and credit.

In 1973 the Supreme Court legalized abortion through the *Roe v. Wade* decision and since then has limited abortion rights only marginally. In a series of rulings during the 1970s and 1980s, it also supported laws mandating *affirmative action programmes* in employment and education. Essentially, these require that businesses and institutions take steps to make up for the effects of past discrimination. The aim is to increase the number of women and minorities among employees or students until it is about equal to the number of such people in the local population or work force. In the 1978 *Regents v. Bakke* case the Court struck down a policy of using numerical quotas for affirmative action. But it currently supports programmes requiring companies and institutions to actively recruit women and minorities by setting up affirmative action plans that include specific goals and timetables, and by advertising opportunities where these groups are likely to notice them.

The contemporary situation

Today court action has reduced the legal hindrances to equality between the sexes. 'Protective' laws based on sexual stereotypes have been repeatedly overturned. Employment ads may not ask for applicants of only one sex. Most large private organizations that prohibit female members are banned. Federal Courts support strict laws against *sexual harassment* (unwanted sexual advances). Polls indicate that since law professor Anita Hill accused Supreme Court nominee Clarence Thomas of sexual harassment during televised Senate hearings in 1991, more women are prepared to take men to court over sexual offences and more men expect them to do so. Judicial approval of state laws granting unpaid maternity leave in the late 1980s led more employers and public authorities to institute maternity leave programmes. Through the Family and Medical Leave Act of 1993 Congress mandated unpaid leave after the birth of a child for the estimated 42 million workers covered by the law. As the percentage of married women working outside the home approached 60, employers increasingly offered day-care centres for working mothers.

The only major recent initiative for women's rights that has failed is the ERA. Its text stated that neither the states nor the federal government could deny or limit a person's rights on the basis of sex. In 1972 Congress passed the ERA with little opposition. To become a part of the Constitution, the Amendment then had to be approved by three-quarters of the state legislatures within seven years (within ten when Congress extended the deadline). After passing in many states in the early part of the decade, support lagged (three states even reversed their approval), and the ERA fell three states short of ratification in 1982.

Differing explanations for the failure of the ERA have been offered. Some critics believe the conservative swing in public opinion that elected Ronald Reagan also worked against ratification. Opposition among women who felt their accepted role would be undermined convinced some state legislators that the risks of voting against the ERA were small. Some critics note that national opinion polls throughout the period showed clear majorities for ratification among voters. They emphasize that the three-quarters majority of states required to amend the Constitution allows a determined minority to frustrate the wishes of the majority. Other observers comment that the ERA was not necessary by the 1980s because civil rights laws and court decisions had accomplished the same goal.

The National Organization of Women (NOW, founded by a group of older, moderate women in 1966) and other supporters of the ERA claimed that the struggle for ratification was well worth the effort. Raising women's awareness of their social position, it involved them in the political process on their own behalf, and helped pass equal rights provisions to many state constitutions. 'Radical feminists' expressed scepticism about male society's sincerity in offering women equality.

By the 1990s, however, women's groups and others who reviewed the progress made since 1970 often remarked that legal equality clearly had only limited effects on the achievement of social and economic parity between the sexes. The incidence of rape and other forms of sexual harassment appeared to be rising at an unprecedented rate, according to some measures, which some attributed to women's increased willingness to complain and others thought was part of a 'backlash' against the women's movement. Women's groups focused on the easy availability of pornography and media violence as causes of child and wife abuse but this won few policy changes.

For the first time, over half of all bachelor's degrees were awarded to women in 1990. They were also earning higher degrees, but mostly in fields traditional for women that offer lower earnings (the fine arts, foreign languages, nursing, teaching and library science). Men still comprised the large majority of the country's professors, doctors, lawyers, architects and engineers. Women ran for and were elected to public office in record numbers in the 1990s but were still far outnumbered by men in government and business management.

Perhaps most worrying, women's economic position seemed to illustrate in exaggerated form the increasing distance between the rich and the poor in the 1980s. The 'feminization of poverty' continued to increase. Women's earnings were still only two-thirds of men's in the mid-1990s as they remained largely segregated in the semi-skilled service sector. The income of women bringing up children alone increased less than that of other families. Women were six times as likely to be living in poverty than men, and female-headed families made up nearly half of all poor families.

Native Americans

Viewing Native Americans as a minority amounts to discussing their relationships to the European Americans that became the dominant population group in the US. The story is one of invasion and prolonged military conflict followed by pressure on native peoples to adjust to the demands of White hegemony. The history involved is complex but has two primary aspects: the popular behaviour and governmental policy of Whites towards 'first Americans' and the responses these actions provoked.

The conflict was always an uneven one. In early days, Native Americans were outnumbered at the point of contact. Diseases reduced their population drastically while the influx of Europeans became enormous. Europeans' metal goods from kettles to firearms, their textiles, and their written languages and books gave them a decisive technological advantage. European cultures were also more aggressively expansive and acquisitive.

Patterns formed in the colonial period

British settlers came in much greater numbers than colonists from other European nations and primarily sought land of their own, rather than trading partners or mineral riches. The British presented Native Americans with a threatening front of compact settlement rather than scattered trading posts like the French. And, unlike the Spanish, the British brought their own women to the

New World and segregated themselves from the natives. Thus, no mixed race of *mestizos* appeared in British America.

Relations with the natives in English colonies were marked by distrust, resentment and disastrous wars. A predictable sequence of events set the pattern for almost three hundred years of contact. First was a period of relative peace when the settlers exchanged technology for land, furs and knowledge of the Indians' survival techniques. In a few years, conflicts caused by trade disagreements, expanded White settlement and cultural misunderstanding escalated to the second phase: full-scale war. In the 1620s and 1630s the natives tried forcibly to expel the intruders and threatened the existence of the Virginia and New England colonies.

During the third phase, massive retaliation by Whites, the natives were defeated militarily. Often the colonists received help from tribes that were traditional enemies of those that had attacked the settlements. Then followed the last phase, Anglo-American policies aimed at easing the expansion of settlement while minimizing the 'Indian threat'.

For the most part, colonists were left to devise their own solutions to this threat until the 1750s. In the heat of victory they usually tried to exterminate native opponents, drive them farther inland, or enslave and deport them. Often, the settlers negotiated treaties based on a policy of *forced separation*. To free more territory for White settlement and end violence, the natives were moved to distant lands that (Whites promised) would be theirs permanently. In short, the 'Indian reservation system' dates back to the 1630s and 1640s.

Colonial authorities promised to protect the rights of reservation natives. Some Whites also encouraged them to adopt European ways and Christianity. In New England, villages of Christianized natives were known as 'praying towns', for example. But assimilation on distant reservations failed. Native peoples further west attacked the reservations because they objected to intrusions into their territory. Colonists squatted on reservation land when it was no longer distant from White settlement, and colonial authorities rarely acted to limit settlement. Native Americans resented and resisted attempts to assimilate them.

Thus one cycle of violent conflict followed another, and Native Americans were continually pushed further west.

In the eighteenth century, Britain and France competed for power in North America. Both vied for native allies, which led Indian groups to offer their allegiance to the highest bidder. The Iroquois Confederacy in western New York and Pennsylvania, for instance, was especially successful in playing one European power against the other and for a long time was able to channel White settlement to the south of its territory. The French generally won support from more tribes because their trading activities seemed far less threatening than the advance of British settlement.

To change this, the British government established a new policy during the French and Indian War (1754–63). It gave gifts to native leaders, by-passed the colonists through direct negotiations with the Indians, and most important, set a western limit to White settlement. The Proclamation of 1763 made a line west of the Appalachian Mountains the official boundary of British America. To the west of the line was 'Indian Country', which settlers had to leave.

Parliament's action was the colonists' policy of separation applied to both settlers and natives and the creation of a huge reservation. But it brought enough tribes to Britain's side to bring victory over the French, who gave up much of their land claims in North America. It infuriated the colonists, who ignored the Proclamation but cited the limit on western settlement as a reason for rebelling against the mother country. When the American Revolution came, most tribes remained loyal to Britain despite American efforts to dissuade them. The US therefore treated several tribes as conquered nations after the war and demanded that they give up their lands without payment, which, for example, led to the rapid decline of the Iroquois Confederacy.

1783 to 1860: conquest and removal

Through the treaty of 1783, Britain ceded to the US all the land between Canada and Florida to the Mississippi River and asked no protection for Native-American rights. With the coming of peace, tens of thousands of settlers moved into the area. But well over 100,000 Native Americans blocked their way. In the Great Lakes region a powerful native confederacy formed to protect tribes there from the fate of the Iroquois, and would not permit settlers north of the Ohio River. On the southern frontier, several tribes refused to give up lands, despite pressure from southern states.

First, the US sent military forces against the northern confederacy to take their lands by conquest. When American armies suffered repeated defeats, however, they were willing to negotiate a treaty after their first major victory. The confederacy ceded huge amounts of land but won annual payments of goods and cash in return. Thus the US government set an important precedent that recognized Native-American land claims and the need to pay for lands taken by Whites.

Abandoning the hope of relying on military conquest, many American leaders promoted a new version of the assimilation policy. Congress funded an educational programme that sent teachers and missionaries to the natives with the goal of transforming them into independent small farmers who could live within the framework of American society. The Indians were not asked if they wanted to be 'civilized', and those who favoured harsher policies said their resistance was proof that assimilation was impossible.

Meanwhile, observing the rapid growth of the White population west of the Appalachians between 1800 and 1810, the Shawnee leaders Tecumseh and The Prophet worked to form a grand alliance of tribes east of the Mississippi to limit US expansion. Tecumseh also applied to British authorities in Canada for help when he heard that the two White nations might be on the verge of war. But the difficulty of unifying tribes that had warred for centuries proved fatal to Native Americans' last attempt to control the land east of the Mississippi River.

While Tecumseh was lobbying for support among southern tribes, his forces in the north were defeated by American armies who had heard of his plan, and British weapons were discovered at his headquarters. A year later Tecumseh and his allies joined the British against the US in the War of 1812, and Tecumseh was killed. Loss of leadership and British support led many tribes to move further west after 1814.

Most tribes who remained found themselves forced to accept a revival of the old separation policy, which Americans now called *removal*. By this they meant moving Native Americans west of the Mississippi. Thomas Jefferson supported the idea as early as 1803, when he used it to argue for buying the area from the Mississippi to the Rocky Mountains (the Louisiana Purchase) from France. Removal gained popularity even with so-called friends of the Indian who said it was the only way to save them from squatters, disease, alcohol and poverty. Removal would give the natives a chance to acquire social and political skills. In sum, these 'friends' argued assimilation could be best achieved away from the evils of White society.

In 1830 President Andrew Jackson, famous as an Indian fighter in the War of 1812, signed the Indian Removal Act. Many tribes north of the Ohio River had signed individual removal treaties before that time and moved to parts of present-day Kansas. Now, federal policy required the removal of all remaining tribes to a permanent 'Indian Territory' in undesirable areas of today's Oklahoma. State authorities so terrorized southern tribes that all but two (the Seminoles and the Cherokees) accepted removal as the only alternative to extermination.

The Seminoles held out for seven years through guerrilla warfare in the Florida Everglades. The Cherokees had adopted many White institutions including industries, schools, a newspaper, and an American-style government and constitution during the earlier period of federal assimilation programmes. Influenced by the society around them, some Cherokees (mostly those intermarried with Whites) were slaveholders. As a sovereign nation, the Cherokee appealed to the US federal courts to fight the state of Georgia's annulment of their constitution and seizure of their lands, as well as the federal plan for removal.

The Supreme Court handed down rulings in this case that in some ways still define Native Americans' rights and status. The court said an Indian tribe (or reservation) was neither an independent nation nor a state but a 'domestic dependent nation'. Within US borders, tribal lands were still outside American political structures. By right of first residence, Indians had sovereignty over their lands and could lose them only voluntarily and with just compensation. The federal government alone could negotiate with a tribe. State laws did not apply on Indian lands or reservations, where native laws took priority. American citizens could not enter Indian lands except by permission or treaty right. By implication, the Removal Act and Georgia's actions were declared illegal.

President Jackson and Georgia ignored the Court's rulings. Federal troops and state militia in the winter of 1838 'escorted' the Cherokee to Indian Territory. Because of the weather, harassment by Whites, and poor government planning for food and shelter, a quarter of the Cherokees died during the march along the path called 'The Trail of Tears'.

By 1840 nearly 100,000 Native Americans had been forcibly removed to Indian Territory. Here, the great differences in the terrain and climate required painful adjustments for eastern woodlands peoples. Put on much smaller parcels of land than they were used to, groups with long traditions of mutual hostility were forced to live side by side. Western Indians, such as the Comanches, resented the newcomers' intrusion into their lands and raided the Territory for food and livestock. Unable to cope with the situation and often not given the protection and material aid promised by the federal government, between 1840 and 1860 many Native Americans in the Territory sank into dependence, alcoholism and poverty.

1860–1934: war, concentration and forced assimilation

During the Civil War, several southern tribes in Indian Territory supported the South, earning money by supplying Confederate armies with food. Consequently, they were asked to give up even more land at the war's end. Removal was replaced with a policy of *concentration* as Americans occupied the prairies and plains that had been considered the 'Great American Desert' and rushed in to profit from gold and silver strikes in the West. US government support for trans-continental railroads increased the influx of settlers and quickened the slaughter of the buffalo on which the Plains cultures depended. Native Americans were to be concentrated on reservations to free as much land as possible for development.

Between 1850 and 1890 the Indians in the West struggled unsuccessfully to keep their lands. The familiar pattern of White settlement, conflict escalating to war, treaty-making and treaty violation leading to new wars repeated itself again and again. At the famous battle of the Little Big Horn, Lieutenant Colonel Custer and his men were killed by Dakota warriors under the leadership of Sitting Bull and Crazy Horse. The battle resulted from US cavalry attempts to punish Dakota warriors for attacking gold prospectors who broke the treaty with the Dakotas by entering their sacred Black Hills.

The era of open warfare ended with the so-called battle of Wounded Knee. This bloodbath resulted from clumsy attempts by American authorities to suppress the Ghost Dance religion that promised believers a return to the happy conditions before the appearance of Whites. Accused of promoting the religion, Sitting Bull was arrested and killed by Native-American police while in custody. When US soldiers tried to disarm a nearby group of Dakotas at Wounded Knee Creek, they fought back in anger over reservation conditions and the death of Sitting Bull. The panicked troops sprayed the men, women, and children with machine-gun fire until all 300 were dead.

From the 1870s to the 1930s the US made energetic attempts to assimilate the Indians quickly. The motives of assimilationists ranged from an unselfish wish to free natives from the dependence and poverty of the reservations to a barely disguised desire to acquire reservation lands cheaply. Assimilation programmes also caused dissension within native groups. Native Americans who had White relatives, were the children of mixed marriages, or who were already rather Americanized tended to favour adoption of White institutions. Racially unmixed natives were more likely to be cultural traditionalists who resisted all forms of assimilation.

US efforts at assimilation took three main forms during the period. The first was the deliberate eroding of the tribes' legal authority. Being on reservations weakened the importance of native leaders because everyone knew agents from the US Bureau of Indian Affairs (BIA) made the final decisions. In 1871 Congress removed any appearance of local control by declaring the end of tribal sovereignty and treaty-making. Henceforth, the federal government made its own laws for Native Americans, often without seeking their advice. In the 1880s, Congress granted private companies rights to use Indian land without their consent and substituted federal for tribal law in criminal cases involving Indians.

Granting US citizenship was also seen as a way to weaken tribal authority, because it gave Native Americans individual rights they could defend in court and made them responsible as individuals to state and federal law. By 1905 over half of all Native Americans had US citizenship, and in 1924 Congress extended citizenship to the rest.

Americans who believed assimilation could be achieved in a single generation put their faith in the second major plan for assimilation: educating Native-American children at boarding schools far away from their own reservations. To break all ties with tribal culture, the pupils were forbidden to wear native clothing, practise native customs or religions, or speak their native languages. Both academic and vocational, the curriculum stressed American history and government. In the 1880s and 1890s the BIA founded some two dozen of these schools, as well as day and boarding schools on reservations, where the discipline and curriculum were similar.

Allotment programmes (dissolving reservations into small farms owned by Native-American families) was the keystone of the third key method of assimilation. Tried out with tribes before the Civil War, allotment became US policy for all but a few tribes under the Dawes Act of 1887. Typically, allotment plans granted each Native-American family 160 acres and single adult members of a tribe half as much. This nearly always left a huge amount of 'surplus' reservation land available for sale to non-Indians.

Native Americans who accepted allotment and left their tribes were rewarded with US citizenship. When a reservation had undergone the allotment process, the BIA took control of tribal schools and introduced the usual programme of Americanization. Thus, the Dawes Act combined all three major means of forcing Native Americans to assimilate.

Supporters of the Dawes Act believed that Indians would experience the American dream of becoming economically self-reliant and politically independent farmers through allotment. The process would as effectively Americanize them as it had millions of European immigrants, in the opinion of many. But critics pointed out that Native-American farming was communal, not a collection of individual holdings. Without safeguards, therefore, allotment was likely to produce starvation and huge numbers of landless Indians. To prevent this, the Dawes Act forbade the sale or leasing of allotted land for twenty-five years.

As long as that provision remained in force, allotment proceeded slowly. However, when Congress removed these restrictions in 1891, it took place rapidly. By 1934, some 4 million acres of reservation land had been declared surplus and sold to Whites or sold by failed Indian farmers. Allotment did not successfully assimilate Native Americans, and instead provided a bonanza for speculators and land-hungry settlers.

1934–1970: tribal restoration and termination

By the 1930s public and private studies had repeatedly blamed allotment for the extreme poor health, poverty and low educational levels of Native Americans. Franklin Roosevelt's 'Indian New Deal' attempted to correct the mistakes of the past. The full range of relief and employment programmes available for other Americans suffering from the Depression were now extended to Native Americans. New better-staffed hospitals for Indians were built. Most boarding schools were replaced with local schools offering religious freedom, bilingual education and programmes to nurture Indian culture.

The Indian Reorganization Act of 1934 was the centrepiece of the tribal restoration plan. It repealed allotment, restored considerable 'surplus' land to tribes, allowed the return of allotment farms to communal ownership, and provided federal funds for adding to tribal lands. The BIA was now required to help develop self-government on reservations. Money was made available for founding these governments, which were offered federal credit for the conservation and economic development of local resources. Each tribe could accept or reject the Act through a referendum. All in all, the Indian New Deal made effective progress towards providing social services, an economic base and self-government to Native Americans, until funding for the programme dried up with the beginning of the Second World War.

By 1953 advocates of rapid assimilation again constituted a congressional majority, however, and pushed through three new programmes. The first was a concerted effort to settle all Native-American claims against the US by offering financial compensation for lost lands and treaty violations. Once such claims were resolved, the BIA proposed *termination* (dissolving the tribe/reservation as a legal entity and making Indians ordinary citizens of local and state governments). Then the BIA could complete the process of assimilation, the argument went, by helping as many former members of the tribe as possible to find work in urban areas. Instead of making Indians 'regular' Americans by transforming them into farmers, this new policy (called *relocation*) aimed to accomplish the same end by turning them into industrial workers.

By the 1960s most of the progress of the New Deal years had been reversed, and the policy of assimilation again seemed bankrupt. Termination and relocation had increased welfare dependency and social alienation rather than producing self-sufficiency and social integration. Native-American interest groups formed to seek justice through lobbying and court actions. Protest organizations, such as the American Indian Movement (AIM) employed direct action to capture mass media attention. Activists occupied Alcatraz Island in San Francisco Bay as Indian territory, marched on Washington along 'The Trail of Broken Treaties', and barricaded themselves against federal authorities for weeks at Wounded Knee to publicize the need to review the history of US treaty violations.

1970 to the 1990s

In this period Native-American law firms have won important victories through lawsuits in defence of Indian claims. Traditional religious practices, tribal independence, mineral and water rights, improved health and education services, and the return of ancient artefacts and skeletons have all been successfully pursued through the federal courts. Vast tracts of land have been returned or paid for to honour old treaties. The courts have returned to the early nineteenth-century definition of tribes' status as dependent domestic nations.

In 1975 Congress confirmed this status in the Indian Self-Determination Act, which gave tribal councils most of the powers exercised by state governments. Not least, the councils have been encouraged to use their authority to develop an economy and social institutions tailored to their own natural resources and values. The BIA is to offer assistance at the tribes' request, but the agency's role is to be phased out as they achieve autonomy. In recent years councils have founded industries, irrigation systems and tourist resorts. Today the US has over a hundred tribal gambling casinos that earn Native Americans around a billion dollars a year. A few tribes have grown rich on mineral deposits, for example, about 20 per cent of US oil and two-thirds of the country's uranium are on reservation land. As life on the reservation has improved, the flight of Indians to US cities has been reversed.

At the 1990 census, only one out of four Native Americans was a 'reservation Indian'. The other three lived in urban areas where jobs were more plentiful and varied. The adjustment to the city has not been very successful for Native Americans. About 20 per cent live below the poverty line, unemployment is high, and those with jobs frequently earn low wages. A small well-educated elite enjoys a much higher standard of living and frequently is well integrated in American society.

Most 'reservation Indians', however, still live in appalling conditions. Of all American ethnic groups, they have the highest unemployment, alcoholism, school dropout and suicide rates. Many cases of malnutrition and mental illness as well as an exceptionally short life expectancy indicate that much remains to be done to improve the situation.

African Americans

The more than 30 million African Americans today are mostly old-stock Americans but also include immigrants from the Caribbean and African countries. Although their living standards on average have improved, and more Blacks achieve higher education now, their average per capita income is 65 per cent less than Whites'. Most Blacks today live in urban areas.

When Africans were brought to the American South in the early 1600s, they were at first indentured servants rather than permanently enslaved from generation to generation. By the late 1600s, however, hereditary slavery had become the rule and Blacks were degraded to the status of property. Some owners treated their slaves better than others, but all had ultimate power over what was theirs. For Blacks, slavery meant extremely hard work, poor living conditions and humiliation.

Keeping slaves became very important to the Southern economy, at first on large tobacco and rice plantations in Virginia and Maryland, and later in the more important cotton business in the expanding Deep South. When the US became independent about 20 per cent of its population were slaves.

But dependence on slave labour diminished as tobacco and rice grew less profitable in the early 1800s. At the same time, moral indignation over the slave trade grew so strong that in 1808 the importation of slaves was banned. But then new technology in the cotton industry made slave labour more important than ever before. Eli Whitney's cotton gin (the machine that cleaned cotton many times faster than was possible manually) meant that plantation owners could greatly increase their profits if they had more slave cotton pickers to keep their cotton gins in full operation. By 1860 the slave population had grown to just under 4 million.

As importing slaves was illegal, this increase came mainly from the large size of slave families and labelling children of mixed parents Blacks and hence slaves. With a booming cotton economy (and cheap land available from 'removing' the Indians), the cotton South expanded westward. This often meant that slave children had to move away from their parents to serve their masters, who were often the younger sons of slaveowners, on newly developed plantations.

Between 1820 and the outbreak of the Civil War, several political compromises were reached in Congress to keep the number of slave states and free states equal. Anti-slavery supporters felt this policy amounted to condoning slavery, while slaveowners thought each state should be able to decide whether it wished to be 'slave' or 'free'. Compromise finally failed, and the Civil War began in 1861.

Lincoln freed the slaves in the undefeated parts of the secessionist South in early 1863 through the Emancipation Proclamation, and after Union victory, Amendments to the Constitution ended slavery in the US, granted the former slaves citizenship, and gave Black men the right to vote. Congress repealed the *black codes* the southern states passed to limit the rights of former slaves. However, without land and education, most Blacks had to work as sharecroppers or lease land and equipment from their former masters. Rents were so high that they had to give most of their crop in payment and so had little to sell to get them out of debt.

The new constitutional amendments were enforced in the South by the presence of the Union Army during the period of Reconstruction. But in 1876 the troops were withdrawn and racial segregation became public policy in the South by 1900. Most Southerners could not accept Blacks as equals, and passed laws which denied them social, economic and political rights and segregated almost everything. These 'Jim Crow laws' remained in effect in most southern states until the 1960s. In 1877, northern leaders abandoned the cause of the former slaves, and for eighty years the federal government let the South alone. On the Supreme Court a Southern majority interpreted the Fourteenth Amendment to mean no *government* should deny equal protection, but private persons could. The *Plessy v. Ferguson* case in 1896 established the *separate-but-equal doctrine* which gave segregation the Court's approval.

In 1909 a group of Blacks and Whites founded the National Association for the Advancement of Colored People (NAACP) to fight for African Americans' civil rights in general and get the Supreme Court to repeal the separate-but-equal doctrine in particular. At the time, most Jim Crow laws affected most African Americans because about 90 per cent of Blacks lived in the South. In 1915 the NAACP persuaded the Court to annul the grandfather clause (which denied the vote to persons whose grandfathers had not voted in the 1860s).

In 1935 the NAACP also won the invalidation of some residential segregation laws, but with little effect. By then many African Americans had migrated to northern cities, and during the Second World War even more went North (and West) to take jobs in the war industries. By the 1950s almost half the nation's African Americans lived outside the South. *De jure* segregation (separation of the races by law) was the rule in the South, while in the North, *de facto* segregation (racial separation through informal means) was almost universal.

The young African-American lawyer, Thurgood Marshall, who later was to become the first Black justice to serve on the Supreme Court, led the legal defence group of the NAACP from 1938, and more liberals gained seats on the Supreme Court during the next twenty years. These developments helped the NAACP achieve more success in the courts, where it concentrated on attacking the separate-but-equal doctrine by showing the inequalities forced on Black students by school segregation. Although the Supreme Court did not invalidate the doctrine, during the next decades its decisions made segregation almost impossible to implement in graduate and high schools. Not until 1954, however, in the *Brown v. Board of Education* case, was the separate-but-equal doctrine reversed. The NAACP at last proved to the Court, and Chief Justice Earl Warren in particular, how unjust the *Plessy* doctrine was, and the Court followed up this historic ruling with the annulment of *de jure* segregation in public places. These rulings sent a message to Blacks that the time was right for fighting their cause.

Implementing these changes, however, was difficult. The South offered massive resistance, and the Court did not get help from other branches of government. President Eisenhower had publicly supported segregation, and a conservative coalition of Southern Democrats and Republicans dominated Congress. Not until violence broke out in Little Rock, Arkansas, when nine Black students tried to attend a White school in 1957, did the President send the national guard to repress the riot and enforce the Court's ruling. The next president, John F. Kennedy, several times used the guard or federal marshals in other southern districts to desegregate the schools. Defiant Southerners therefore avoided desegregation in other ways. Whites who were able to send their children to private schools that were not bound by federal law. By 1964 only 2 per cent of Black children in the South attended desegregated schools.

In 1969 the Supreme Court ordered the desegregation of all public schools, and later approved measures to force integration, such as racial quotas, the grouping of non-contiguous school districts and busing in order to achieve racial balance in the schools. But since segregation still determined residential patterns (most Blacks lived in the inner cities, while Whites lived in the suburbs), there was strong opposition to busing. After the Court ruled against busing plans between cities and suburbs unless discriminatory districting could be proved in 1974, few new attempts to bus pupils were made. Some thirty years after the *Brown* decision around 70 per cent of America's schools were racially mixed, but those in inner cities were still mostly Black, and/or Latino.

Separate schools was only one form of the *de jure* racial discrimination in the South in the 1950s. Blacks then were prevented from voting, as well as kept out of jobs and White facilities. In 1955 Rosa Parks, a Black woman from Montgomery, Alabama, was arrested and fined for taking a seat in the White section at the front of a bus. This incident sparked a Black boycott against the city's bus system, led by the young Baptist minister Martin Luther King, Jr. One year later the federal courts ruled that segregated transportation was in violation of the Fourteenth Amendment. The African-American civil rights movement of the 1950s and 1960s was under way.

Martin Luther King, Jr was one of the organizers of the Southern Christian Leadership Conference (SCLC) which coordinated civil rights activities. His 'I Have a Dream' speech, to more than 250,000 people at the Lincoln Memorial in 1963, is regarded by many as one of the most inspiring calls for racial equality in American history. White officials' brutal suppression of civil rights protests in the South (shown now on nationwide TV) made Americans elsewhere more conscious of racial injustice. President Kennedy addressed the problem for the first time from the White House, calling fighting racism a moral issue. The Civil Rights Act of 1964 outlawed discrimination in jobs and public accommodation, and the following year the Voting Rights Act opened the voting rolls and transformed politics in the South.

This has been called the non-violent revolution. However, while Martin Luther King, Jr was advocating non-violence, there were other Blacks who felt changes were too slow in coming. Radical Blacks wanted to establish an alternative Afro-American culture inside the US. Some of these formed the Black Power and Black Panther movements. Malcolm X became one of the most famous of the Black Muslims, who created their own variant of Islam and rejected White America's lifestyle and politics. These movements became involved in violent conflicts with the police. For many Blacks, non-violence seemed defunct as a means of winning civil rights when Malcolm X was killed in 1965, and Dr King was assassinated in 1968.

In retrospect, it is clear that passing laws was the easy part. The nation has still not found a way to enforce civil rights laws.

PLATE 3.2   Most black people have a traditional loyalty to the Democratic Party   *(T.L. Litt/Format/Impact Visuals)*

Malcolm X had hoped that violent revolution would not be necessary, that warning of the violence that would result from not listening to Dr King would be enough. But it was not. And how can one-third of Blacks be brought out of poverty? The issues of violent protest and how to deal with poverty were among the questions that fractured the movement.

To make use of equal opportunity, Blacks in general need the higher education and skills to obtain the better paid jobs that in turn will enable them to afford better housing and improved living standards. Despite the Fair Housing Act of 1968, the large majority of Blacks who try to buy or rent housing are still faced with discrimination. As a result, desegregation of housing has been minimal and equal standards in the schools have therefore not been achieved. Attempts are being made to rectify this, however, and some states have had more success with their programmes than others.

More Blacks complete high school today. In 1990 11 per cent of Blacks had earned at least a bachelor's degree, compared to 22 per cent of Whites. By 1994 there were nearly 7,000 Black officials in the South, while there were less than 100 in 1964, and in the latter year Congress had forty Black members. But persistent socio-economic inequality and the unkept promises of public policy and ideals in the 1990s lie behind the appeal of racist figures like Louis Farrakhan and incite Blacks' participation in ghetto riots from LA to New York.

Asian Americans

'Asian American' is a convenient term that lumps together a diverse collection of immigrant and American-born population groups. It includes, for example, both Hmong tribespeople who came as refugees after the Vietnam War and the descendants of Chinese who settled before the Civil War. The principle of continental origins is used to justify putting in one category people with different religions, skin colours, socio-economic backgrounds and historical experiences. In 1990 Asian Americans numbered over 7 million people (about 3 per cent of the US population) and were the nation's fastest-growing minority. In the latter part of the decade their prominence in the current wave of immigrants and their diversity was greater. It is the old-stock American perception that all these people *look* Asian (and the different treatment that perception has caused) which have given them related experiences in the US.

Early Asian immigration

The first large group of Chinese, some 370,000 of them, came with the second-wave 'old' immigrants between the late 1840s and 1882. One-fifth of them settled in Hawaii and the rest on the West Coast, mostly in California. About 400,000 Japanese immigrated between the 1880s and 1908 and settled in roughly equal numbers on the West Coast and in Hawaii (where they composed the largest Asian immigrant group). Small groups of Koreans and East Indians (about 7,000 each) came to the islands and west coast states from 1900 to 1930. During the same period, approximately 180,000 Filipinos immigrated, about three out of every five of them first arriving in Hawaii.

The situation of Asian immigrants varied greatly between Hawaii and the mainland. In the islands, most were recruited as contract workers on sugar plantations, where they performed back-breaking labour under military-style discipline and the supervision of abusive overseers. Nationality groups were segregated in different camps and pitted against each other to keep wages low and prevent the formation of a unified labour movement. But plantation owners were dependent on these workers, and so provided food, housing and medical care. To get workers to stay when their contracts ended, they helped women immigrate, encouraged family life, supported religious and ethnic customs and built schools and community centres.

The discrimination Asian Americans suffered in Hawaii was much milder than that on the mainland because they made up a large majority of the islands' workforce. In 1920, when they were working in every part of Hawaii's economic life, Asian Americans comprised over half of the islands' population, and about two of every five people there were Japanese Americans. Thus, the vast majority of Japanese Americans on the mainland but less than 1 per cent of those on the islands were put in concentration camps during the Second World War. In the 1930s, Asian Americans began to assume prominent positions in Hawaiian politics. Since 1959, Hawaii has been the only state in the US in which they have regularly played major roles in state politics and also represented the state in Congress.

On the mainland the situation of Asian Americans was fundamentally different until the mid-1940s. Always a tiny minority compared to European Americans, they could much more easily be made victims of systematic discrimination. Anti-Asian campaigns in the Pacific West were designed to segregate Asians from Whites, prevent them from competing economically and end their immigration entirely.

Anti-miscegenation laws (laws to prevent racial mixing) forbade marriages between Asians and Whites. Many private businesses refused them products and services. The only place they could find housing was often in Asian-American ghettoes. A series of Supreme Court decisions determined that they were non-Caucasians and therefore ineligible for citizenship. Most western states passed alien land laws, which prohibited those banned from citizenship from leasing or owning land. In 1882 the Chinese were excluded from immigrating. The 1908 Gentlemen's Agreement, prohibiting the entry of Japanese labourers, was followed in 1921 by the 'Ladies' Agreement' that banned Japanese women's immigration. Three years later all Asians were barred from immigrating.

With assistance from sympathetic Whites, Asian Americans fought these forms of oppression. They found loopholes in the land laws, circumvented immigration exclusion laws, created their own job opportunities by starting businesses, formed union and protest organizations, and through these, stood up for their rights through strikes and lawsuits. For all Asian-American groups but Japanese Americans, the Second World War brought decisive social and economic improvements.

Public attitudes became positive to the Chinese, Koreans, Filipinos, and East Indians, whose homelands were American allies. Members of these groups joined the US armed forces or intelligence networks. (Some tens of thousands of Japanese-American youths even left the concentration camps to serve in the American military and prove their loyalty.) War industries gave Asian Americans professional and skilled work that previously had been denied them. By the war's end, all four groups could immigrate, and all but Koreans had won citizenship rights. Between 1945 and 1965, discriminatory laws against Asian Americans were repealed or struck down by the courts.

Recent newcomers from Asia

Refugee laws permitted the entry of Asians who had married American military personnel during the period, and in 1965 a new immigration law opened the way for the huge wave of Asian immigration that is still continuing. As a result of the Vietnam War, hundreds of thousands of Vietnamese, Laotian and Cambodian refugees have settled in the US. The recent newcomers are quite different from the earlier immigrants in some ways. A quite significant minority consists of well-educated professionals, and many more come from urban areas, where they worked in modern industries. More of the recent immigrants also arrive as families rather than as single men and plan to settle permanently. On the other hand, many refugees are destitute, poorly educated and ill prepared for city life. Now the number of Japanese newcomers is small while the totals from other Asian nations have set new records.

Since the mid-1960s the popular media have often depicted Asian Americans as the country's most successful ethnic groups, its 'model minority'. Their high median family incomes, unusual level of academic achievement, and low rates of unemployment, crime, mental illness and dependence on welfare have been held up as examples to other minority groups. A closer look at the situation, however, shows that significant numbers of Asian Americans have serious socio-economic problems and face considerable discrimination.

Studies reveal that Asian-American family incomes are higher than most White groups, but only because more family members work for longer hours than is common for Whites. In personal incomes Asian Americans have not caught up with Whites. One important reason for this is that they are more concentrated in semi-skilled service trades and low-level professional and management positions. Asian Americans' educational attainments, on average, often surpass Whites' but a so-called 'glass ceiling' of prejudice keeps them out of the higher levels of industrial management and professional firms. The slums of major American cities often overlap with parts of Asian-American communities that have a high incidence of poverty, health problems, drug abuse and teenage gangs.

The media image of Asian Americans' success, moreover, has caused resentment that feeds a rising wave of anti-Asian activity. In 1986, the US Civil Rights Commission reported dozens of cases of racial slurs, violent assaults, vandalism and harassment against Asian Americans. Across the nation, conflicts have occurred between Korean storeowners and residents of the Latino or Black communities where many of these shops are located. In the 1992 Los Angeles riots, their shops became the special target of looters and nearly 2,000 Korean businesses were destroyed.

Latinos

A Spanish language and cultural background is the inexact basis for calling people with ethnic origins in the Caribbean, Central and South America Latinos (or Hispanics, according to the US Census Bureau). Thus the term does not apply to people from countries in the Americas that have been influenced by other European cultures, such as Brazil, Haiti or the Bahamas.

Those commonly called Latinos include the descendants of Native-American peoples, African slaves, immigrants from other European nations and Asia, and mixtures of these peoples. Although the majority of Latinos are Catholic, significant numbers are Protestant or members of other religions. Most are relatively recent immigrants, but Mexican Americans have been coming in large numbers since the late 1800s and include the descendants of the early Spanish settlers from the 1500s.

Over 22 million people (or about 9 per cent of the population) were counted as Hispanics in the 1990 federal census. Today Latinos are the second-largest minority group in the US. About 60 per cent of Latinos are Mexican Americans and live in the Southwestern states or in large Midwestern cities such as Chicago. All of the other groups are small by comparison. Puerto Ricans make up 12 per cent of Latinos and have concentrated their settlement in New York City and other Northern urban areas. The third largest group, Cuban Americans, comprise about 5 per cent of the Latin-American population and have founded their largest communities in Florida. The remaining 23 per cent represent about thirty nationalities, the largest of which are Salvadoran, Nicaraguan, Guatamalan, Columbian, Ecuadoran and Peruvian.

Like Native Americans, Blacks and Asian Americans, Latinos have faced race prejudice and economic discrimination in jobs, housing, education and politics. The current high number of Latino newcomers, especially illegal immigrants, has led to rising hostility against Latinos. In the Southwest, border patrols and local police often stop and harass Latinos on the assumption that they might be illegal aliens. Over twenty states have declared English their official language mainly in reaction against the use of Spanish by Latinos. Opinion polls in 1993–4 showed that President Clinton and the governor of Florida had widespread public support for intercepting Cuban boat people at sea and preventing their entry as refugees.

For decades, Latino children were sent to segregated 'Mexican' schools in the Southwest. When federal courts declared them Whites in the 1940s, the situation improved somewhat, but a decade later racist local officials frequently used these rulings to 'integrate' the schools by creating districts where nearly all the pupils were Latino or Black, while non-Latino Whites were placed in other schools. Today the great majority of Latinos still go to school in segregated districts. In the past they were often punished for speaking Spanish and met many pressures to anglicize their culture at school. In the late 1960s and 1970s court cases established their right to instruction in Spanish but most bilingual education programmes (education offered in both the pupils' mother tongue and English) are designed to ease the transition to English rather than maintain the pupils' Spanish heritage.

In part because of the poorer quality of schools in minority districts, in 1990 Latinos were less likely to complete high school or college than non-Hispanic groups. Almost one out of every five Latinos was then illiterate. In 1982, Latinos won an important victory when the Supreme Court decided that the children of illegal immigrants were entitled to public education. That ruling was challenged by Proposition 187, passed in California in 1994, that would deny the state's illegal immigrants all social services except emergency medical attention but was blocked by court actions brought by civil rights groups. In 1996 a clear majority of California voters approved Proposition 209, ending all state affirmative action programmes, including ones that have helped many Latinos secure better education and jobs. It remains to be seen whether that policy change will be implemented.

In the Southwest, Florida and the New York City area Latinos have achieved political influence by being elected to office at all levels of government. In the 1960s and 1970s, they organized 'brown power' protest movements that fought for civil rights on the streets and in the courts, enhancing Latinos' pride and stimulating a variety of cultural institutions. Latinos have long been actively involved in union movements of many kinds despite the prejudice of some White labour leaders. The largest occupational group of Latinos was for many years migratory farm workers. César Chávez became the first nationally well-known Latino leader in the 1960s through his successful strike negotiations as head of the United Farm Workers Union of California.

■ Examine and explain the following terms:

equality of opportunity

abolitionists

women's suffrage

ERA

affirmative action

   programmes

'domestic dependent nation'

Indian New Deal

Asian contract workers

alien land laws

hereditary slavery

'Jim Crow laws'

NAACP

non-violent revolution

minority school district

César Chávez

English common law

  (regarding women)

Seneca Falls Convention

protectionist legislation

Roe v. Wade

forced separation

forced assimilation

Self-Determination Act

anti-miscegenation laws

'model minority

black codes

Plessy v. Ferguson

de jure segregation

illegal immigrants

bilingual education

■ Write short essays on the following topics:

1   Discuss the factors that have contributed to the improved status of American women since the colonial period.

2   Evaluate the motives and effects of US policy towards Native Americans.

3   Give a critical review of the aspects of African Americans' struggle for equality that you find distinctive from that of other minority groups.

4   Compare and contrast early and recent Asian
     American immigrants and the treatment they have
     received in the US.

5   Describe the make-up of America's Latino popula-
     tion and discuss the kinds of discrimination it has
     faced.

Political institutions

STABLE POLITICAL INSTITUTIONS have been particularly important in a nation of immigrants. Many commentators feel that loyalty to the basic structures and principles of government has acted as the cement that has held together so large and diverse a nation. Today, the US holds several records for political stability and longevity. Arguably the oldest functioning democracy, the country also has the world's oldest written constitution and political party (the Democratic Party).

But much has changed in American government and politics since the nation declared its independence in 1776. The constitutional framework from 1787 has endured not least because it has proven amenable to changing interpretations, and open enough to assimilate important extra-constitutional elements. Even so, political institutions in the US have been, and continue to be, the subject of heated debate. Serious doubts may be raised as to whether they (particularly the federal institutions) still have widespread support.

Historical origins

The English authorities initially allowed the American colonists to evolve political institutions (governors, assemblies and courts) with little outside interference. Partially based on local control and the consent of the inhabitants, these traditions of self-government later inspired the independence movement, formed the foundation for the constitutions of the independent states after 1776 and served as the model on which the federal government was erected through the Constitution of 1787.

In the first glow of independence, most Americans opposed strong central government, which they identified with British oppression. The country's first constitution, the Articles of

PLATE 4.1   The US Capitol, Washington, DC   *(Barnaby's Picture Library)*

Confederation (1781–8), established a loose league of independent states under a very weak central government. With no executive or judicial branch, the national government consisted only of a one-house legislature that lacked financial, diplomatic and military power. Much like the United Nations, the Confederation had to ask the member states for everything, from military forces to money for operating expenses. Each state kept the right to refuse any request and often did, even after promising support.

By the late 1780s the chaotic condition of the nation's economy and international relations made members of the merchant classes support efforts to set up a stronger central government. These leaders (the Federalists) argued for the adoption of the new constitution drafted in Philadelphia in 1787. They were opposed by the Antifederalists, who pictured the country's future as largely agricultural. They thought the new constitution should be rejected because it endangered the sovereignty of the states and lacked a bill of rights to protect individuals.

The thirteen original states ratified the Constitution on the understanding that ten amendments, including many of the Antifederalists' demands, were added. The first session of Congress (the federal legislature) formally proposed these ten, later known as the Bill of Rights, and the states ratified them in 1791. Thus, the new framework of national government reflected ideas from both sides of the debate.

This Constitution returned to the colonial tradition of a government with three branches (the legislative, executive and judicial). But unlike revolutionary era state governments, it did not make the legislature paramount. Instead, it provided for branches that had to cooperate to perform the functions of government. It also changed the nature of the union. The loose confederacy became a federation whose national government had powers that remedied the weaknesses of the Articles. Federal law became supreme in the areas covered by those powers. But the states' territorial integrity and their sovereignty in all other areas were guaranteed.

Three compromises were necessary to gain the states' approval for this new government. The first balanced the representation of small and large states in Congress. In the House of Representatives the number of seats per state was made proportional to population to please the states with large populations. In the Senate every state was given two seats, regardless of population, to please the small states.

The second compromise was needed to patch over conflicts between the North and South over slavery. Once representation in one chamber of Congress was made dependent on population, the issue was how to count the large number of slaves in the South, who were not citizens and legally property rather than people. In the North, the states had abolished slavery or contained very few slaves. The compromise stated that three-fifths of the slaves would count for representation in the House, but that importing of slaves could be outlawed by 1808.

The drafters also compromised on economic disagreements by permitting Congress to tax imports but not exports, which simultaneously kept the prices of Southern agricultural exports low and opened the door for tariffs to protect Northern manufactures from cheap imported goods. Critics, then and since, have pointed out that two of these compromises tacitly approved slavery by incorporating advantages for it into the fundamental framework of the federal government. (See the Appendix on pp. 400–26 for the annotated text of the Constitution, including Article I with the three famous compromises.)

The constitutional framework

Some four-fifths of the original text of the Constitution remains formally unchanged, and only seventeen amendments have been added after the Bill of Rights. Yet its thought and language have remained flexible enough to be interpreted differently by succeeding generations. The changes in US constitutionalism have been significant but few. They have come largely through formal amendments, judicial review, and gradual, evolutionary processes rather than revolutionary upheavals. Before looking at these changes, it is important to understand the enduring elements of the Constitution.

Federalism

The US has a hierarchy of law. The federal Constitution is the supreme legal authority to which all other law must conform. States' laws must conform to the state constitutions, and the states' legal structures (as well as Acts of Congress) must not contravene the US Constitution. This legal hierarchy led the federal Supreme Court to assume the role of final interpreter of the US Constitution. Connecting the state and national institutions, it became the body that hands down decisions on what government activity is permissible, under the limits imposed by the Constitution, on any level.

The essential purpose of that document is to restrain the power of government. Its Preamble stresses popular sovereignty (the idea that 'we the people' are the ultimate power behind the government). Representatives of the people created this charter of government and can also alter or totally replace it. The rights guaranteed the people in the Bill of Rights (1791) restrict the actions of the authorities. In addition, the Constitution limits government by specifying the powers delegated to the federal government by the states. Through the *Tenth Amendment*, it further reserves to the states or people those powers not so specified or reasonably inferred from the language of the Constitution.

The Constitution establishes the principle of federalism as fundamental to American government through the concepts of 'reserved' and 'delegated' powers in the Tenth Amendment. These concepts indicate a political union in which the ultimate governing power (sovereignty) is shared between the national government and the states. The powers of each are limited by the reservation or delegation of some powers to the other level of government. The powers of both are limited by the rights preserved for the people.

The provisions for amending the federal Constitution also stress the federal principle. Amendments can be proposed by two-thirds majorities in Congress or by a constitutional convention called by two-thirds of the states. Any changes must be ratified by the legislatures of or conventions in three-quarters of the states.

But the Constitution's broad language has allowed the Supreme Court to expand federal power into areas that originally were the province of the states. Congress, for example, has extended its activities through clauses giving it power to regulate commerce; provide for the general welfare; and create all laws that are 'necessary and proper' to carry out the other powers granted to the federal government in the Constitution. In practice, therefore, government activity in the US today falls into three categories: that allowed the states alone; that permitted only to the national government; and that shared by both levels of government.

The separation of powers

Articles I to III of the Constitution create a federal government with three branches: the legislative (Congress and support agencies); the executive (the President and executive bureaucracy); and the judiciary (the US Supreme Court and other federal courts). In this non-parliamentary system, no person may serve in more than one of the branches at the same time. Thus the President and the heads of the executive departments, as well as federal judges, are constitutionally prohibited from sitting in Congress. The separation of powers is institutionalized in other ways as well. Representatives, Senators, and the President are selected through independent elections that do not all occur at the same time. The areas from which they are elected (congressional district, state, the whole nation) are different and so are the lengths of their terms of office. Thus they each feel responsible to different voting constituencies and develop quite dissimilar political loyalties and priorities. As a result, one or both of the houses of Congress are often controlled by one major party while the presidency is held by the other.

Constitutional provisions further distinguish the branches by listing the powers of each one. They thus outline the limits of legislative, executive and judicial action. As intended by the drafters of the Constitution, separating the branches prevents the concentration of power in any one and creates both cooperation and tension between the branches.

Checks and balances

The branches must also share power through a system of checks and balances. The President nominates federal judges, including justices of the Supreme Court, but the Senate must confirm their appointment. Senatorial approval is also needed for treaties negotiated by the executive branch and the President's candidates for other high federal offices. The President can veto legislation passed by Congress, but a veto can be overridden by two-thirds majorities of both houses.

One house of Congress balances and checks the other in that bills must pass both. Congress can remove members of the other branches from office through impeachment procedures. On the other hand, the President has the power to pardon people accused of federal crimes, and Supreme Court justices are appointed for life terms, dependent on their 'good behaviour'.

The Congress has the power to raise money through taxes and to allocate that money to government programmes. But when implementing laws, the President and executive departments control the way these funds are used by setting administrative rules that interpret the language of federal law. By tradition, as well as constitutional provision and interpretation, Congress has exercised the power to create, regulate, or eliminate elements of the executive branch below the Vice-President and of the judicial branch below the Supreme Court. It can thus respond to the other branches' attempts to frustrate its intentions. Finally, if a citizen challenges an Act of Congress or an executive order or procedure, the Supreme Court can declare the Act or executive action unconstitutional. It can thus force the other branches to revise their actions to find a means of reaching political goals that it can approve. In all these ways the Constitution checks the unrestricted exercise of power by each branch and balances the powers of the branches against each other.

Constitutional change

Important changes in the constitutional framework have come through both formal and informal means, that is, through the amendment process as well as through evolving customs and changing historical circumstances. Amendments have generally enhanced federal power, while reducing states' prerogatives, and have democratized participation in government. The three Civil War Amendments written by the victorious Union Congress contributed to both these general trends. They abolished slavery (the Thirteenth), gave all the former slaves citizenship (the Fourteenth), and allowed former male slaves the right to vote (the Fifteenth).

In the twentieth century, the Fourteenth Amendment, which requires states to respect the rights of US citizens by extending to them 'due process of law' and the 'equal protection of the laws', has proven particularly important in restricting state government actions that limit the civil rights of individuals. Other amendments contributing to the democratizing of American politics are the Seventeenth (1913) which provided for the selection of US senators by a popular vote rather than by the choice of the state legislature; the Nineteenth (1920) which granted women the vote; and the Twenty-sixth (1971) which lowered the voting age to 18. The Sixteenth Amendment (1913) gave the federal government much greater financial power than the states have by granting Congress the right to tax incomes, whatever their source.

The informally achieved changes in the Constitution (those that occur without resort to the amendment process) have been even more important. Among these are political parties, primary elections, the congressional committee system, the Executive Office of the President, and the Supreme Court's power of judicial review. Since 1945 the federal government, supported by the constitutional interpretations of the Supreme Court, has steadily increased its power at the expense of the states. But the US has remained a country characterized by decentralized political power in a federal union. Citizens still find that state governments are those which most touch their daily lives.

The political parties

The Founding Fathers viewed political parties as *factions* (interest groups that are dangerous because they pursue narrow private interests rather than the common good). They therefore designed a constitutional system that, together with the size and diversity of the country, was meant to keep factions so divided that no one of them could gain significant power. Yet, parties emerged almost immediately, and it can be argued that the Constitution was one cause of their appearance.

The separate and staggered elections required for Senators, Representatives and the President (and the republican form of government guaranteed the states) create many fragmented electoral interests. But they also ensure many and frequent elections. Parties arose in part because organizations were needed to recruit, screen and nominate candidates for these elections. The constitutional separation of powers helped create parties because a tool was needed to coordinate the policy initiatives of the separated branches.

The Founders set up a system that encourages two parties, rather than no parties. Only one person is elected from each electoral district, and that person needs only a *plurality* (more votes than any other candidate) to win the election. Thus coalitions tend to form *before* elections. Political parties become few in number, and usually, are coalitions of interests with middle-of-the-road programmes whose vagueness results from the compromises made to unify several dissimilar elements. Since 1856 there have been only two successful national parties: the Democrats and the Republicans.

Two other factors have also been important for the development of a two-party system in the US. First, the presidency is such an important office that winning it has inspired two broadly based national coalitions, one consisting of supporters of the party in the White House and the other of everybody else. Several of these 'presidential coalitions' have defined the major parties and the agenda for national politics for decades. Second, since the early days of the republic there has usually been a polarization of the country into two camps on the most important issues, such as those for or against slavery or government regulation of the economy.

Differences between the parties

Despite their broad diversity and the diffuseness of their ideologies, the two major parties represent distinct political orientations. One measure of their differences can be seen in the view the voters and activists for each have of themselves. Traditionally more conservative than Democrats, Republicans twice as often identified themselves as conservatives in a *Washington Post* poll in 1992.

Until recently, the major American parties could be distinguished by their strength in different regions of the nation. In the decades after the Civil War, both parties were competitive in only a few states. The South blamed the party of Lincoln for the war and so voted almost exclusively for the Democrats. The rest of the nation tended to be heavily Republican. Between the 1890s and 1930s this regional division deepened as Southerners disenfranchised African Americans through discriminatory state election laws and the Republican Party became more clearly associated with big business.

Franklin D. Roosevelt's New Deal Coalition complicated the picture, because he forged a national majority by appealing to both the White supremacist South and the urban multi-ethnic, multiracial Northeast and Midwest. From 1932, when FDR was first elected President, until 1968, Democrats were conservative in the South but often liberal in other regions of the nation. Republicans were conservative in the rural Midwest and the West as a whole, but frequently moderate or liberal in the Northeast.

During the last twenty-five years, regional differences have gradually become less important. In 1968, Southern Democrats left the party to support Alabaman segregationist governor George Wallace as an independent candidate in the presidential election because of the party's support for the African-American Civil Rights movement. Since then conservative White Southerners have increasingly voted Republican, at first mostly in presidential elections, but since the late 1980s also in congressional and state contests.

Meanwhile, large increases in African-American voters, the influx of people from other regions, and the economic modernization and urbanization of the South have made it a genuinely two-party region. Across the nation today the Democratic Party label tends to represent a moderate to liberal political orientation. During the same period, the Republican Party has become more uniformly conservative as its moderate to liberal wing in the Northeast has shrunk and lost influence to conservative activists.

The ideological centre of the Republican Party supports small government, minimal regulation of business, low taxes and private solutions to poverty and social problems. Since the 'Reagan revolution' in the 1980s, party allegiance to these policies has become more pronounced as its centre shifts progressively to the right. In 1996, presidential candidate Bob Dole, known for his talent for legislative compromise, seemed quite moderate compared to most delegates at his party's national convention.

Democrats are more in favour of government management of the economy, a public social safety net and the union movement. Bill Clinton, who has been tugging the party to the political centre ever since he first ran for president in 1992, had a party majority behind his New Moderate Democrat label but nearly alienated his party's liberal wing in 1996. From the 1960s, opinion in the parties has also tended to divide over a number of social issues. More Democrats have favoured civil rights and affirmative action programmes for minorities, gun control and unrestricted abortion rights. Republicans have more often favoured reducing government spending and balancing the federal budget, but President Clinton has adopted both of these positions and milder forms of typically Republican stances on welfare reform, taxes and small government. In the late 1990s the parties still seem distinct, but both have moved to the right.

A range of economic and social indicators continue to show differences in the groups that identify with each party. Democrats have on average lower incomes, less education and

PLATE 4.2 Clinton supporters at the Democratic National Convention in Madison Square Garden
(T.L. Litt/Format/Impact Visuals)

less prestigious occupations. They are also more often female, Jewish, urban and members of racial minority groups. Until the 1980s, most White Catholic ethnics were also Democrats, but now they more evenly split their allegiance.

Party organization

The federal system results in parties that organize and function on three distinct levels. State and local party organizations vary a great deal in size, strength and the make-up of their shifting coalitions. They are affiliated with but not controlled by the national parties, which usually do not interfere in their activities

133

except to offer funds or services. The formal structure of the parties is based on organizing committees at every level with the Republican and Democratic National Committees and their chairmen at the top.

Some critics say the cooperation between the party levels is growing stronger. Others note an advantage in the current separated levels. The party which loses presidential elections (as the Democrats did most of the time between 1969 and 1992) can sustain its strength in Congress and state governments. The obverse seems relevant now, as the Democrats control the presidency for a second term, while the Republicans gain strength in the states and majorities in Congress.

The state and local parties are active on a continuous basis, while the national organization lies mostly dormant between presidential elections. Both parties seem weak in some ways, compared with their European counterparts. Nearly all candidates label themselves as Democrat or Republican, but the party does not control their election campaigns or the governmental policies they advocate. Party loyalty is rather uncertain, except when political incentives support it.

Independent candidates and 'third' parties

Independent candidates and minor or splinter parties (so-called 'third' parties) have a long history in American politics. They seldom win federal elections because of the nation's election rules and the public's traditional loyalty to one of the major parties, which about half the voters inherit from their parents. Independents' victories nearly always occur in state or local contests in which exceptional circumstances play a larger role.

There are several types of third parties. In national elections, independents like H. Ross Perot (in 1992) and some third parties attract votes from people who are dissatisfied with the major parties and the government in general. Other third parties, such as the Socialist and Libertarian Parties, represent ideologies that have only small followings in the US. Others are single-issue organizations, such as the Prohibition, Women's and Right to Life Parties.

The most important third parties have been those that result from splits in the major parties. One of these was the 'Bull Moose' Progressive Party formed from the liberal wing of the Republican Party by Theodore Roosevelt. It won over 27 per cent of the vote in the presidential election of 1912, which helped put Democrat Woodrow Wilson in office by dividing the Republican electorate. The greatest impact of all third parties is perhaps seen in the adoption of their policy suggestions, such as primary elections, the direct election of senators, women's suffrage and the graduated income tax.

The legislative branch

In addition to the staffs of individual members and congressional committees, Congress draws expertise from its own library, research service, and accounting, budget and technology assessment offices.

During the crisis decades of the Cold War, some claimed the President was more important than Congress because of the executive's capacity for quick and decisive action. But since the 1970s, Congress has attempted to reassert its authority over the nation's military involvements and international commerce. It remains a very powerful institution, even though some argue that it is no longer the dominant branch of the federal government, as the Founders intended. Its main functions are law-making, forming administrative structures and programmes to implement policy, overseeing the resulting bureaucracy, raising and allocating government funds and advising the President on foreign affairs and appointments.

Differences between the chambers

While the chambers of Congress are in theory equally powerful, there are several significant differences in their membership, organization and practices. As originally intended, the House of Representatives continues to respond more quickly than the Senate to the electorate's mood. Elections every two years in smaller geographical units allow Representatives to more closely reflect the current views of local voters than do Senators, who serve six-year terms and represent whole states. The large majority of both chambers has always consisted of middle-aged White men, many of whom are usually lawyers. The House contains the more diverse membership. As a result of the 1996 elections, when record numbers of women and minority groups members ran for seats, it had 51 women, 37 African Americans, 18 Latino and 3 Asian Americans, while the Senate had 9 women (including the chamber's 1 Black member), 2 Asian Americans, one Native American, and no Latinos. Since 1992, when the number of female and minority members rose significantly, there have been only slight changes in this respect.

There are constitutional differences between the chambers as well. To qualify for a seat in the Senate, a person must be 30 years old, have been a citizen for nine years, and a resident of the state where elected. Representatives must be 25, seven years a citizen, and (by custom) a resident of their district. Financial bills must begin in the House, although the Senate can amend them. Treaties and presidential appointments must be approved by the Senate. Size, however, is the constitutional difference that has the most important effect on the chambers.

Because of its much greater size, the House must regulate its business carefully. The Speaker of the House and the Rules Committee are given considerable power to schedule the work of the chamber, limit debate, and restrict amendments to a bill from the floor. The Speaker also influences the assignment of members and bills to committees, decides which bills are brought up for a vote, and has total power over who speaks during debate. The Speaker is chosen by the majority party and in turn chooses his party's members on the Rules Committee. The majority party also elects a majority leader as the Speaker's next-in-command and a whip to help round up votes. The other party selects a minority leader and whip.

The smaller Senate has much more relaxed procedures and no officer with power comparable to the Speaker's. Bills can be considered in any order and at any time a majority of the chamber wishes. There are majority and minority leaders, and both parties use the whip system to get out the vote. The Constitution appoints the Vice-President as presiding officer of the Senate and requires the Senators to elect a president *pro tempore* to chair the chamber in the Vice-President's absence. Most members usually find the position so powerless that it is turned over to a junior Senator.

The real leader of the chamber is the Majority Leader, but even he has no formal power to limit debate or amendments. Members can therefore engage in a filibuster (an attempt to defeat a bill by talking until its supporters withdraw it so that other business can be finished). Only if sixty members of the chamber vote for cloture, which limits speeches to one hour, can a filibuster be stopped. In practice filibusters seldom occur. When they do, it signals an issue so important that Senators are unable to compromise, and therefore filibusters receive considerable notice. Amendments to a bill during Senate debates can be irrelevant to its subject or purpose. Some 'riders' are attached in an attempt to ensure the bill's defeat. Others are added to secure the passage of proposals that would have great difficulty in winning a majority if forwarded separately. During its last session, the Senate agreed to limit the use of riders, and Congress approved a line-item veto (the right to reject some parts of a bill while accepting others) for the President on financial bills, which is also likely to reduce the number of riders.

Congressional organization

Members of Congress organize themselves in several ways. The most important of these is by party, even though party discipline is much weaker than in a parliamentary system and is continuing to decrease as members become less dependent on party for re-election. Members divide along party lines on between a third and a half of the votes that take place in Congress. Special party groups pick the officers of each chamber and decide which committees the members will work on. Each party receives the number of places on committees that equals the percentage of seats it won in the last elections, and about two-thirds of committee staff workers are in the majority party's service. In 1994, when the Republican Party won majorities in both houses for the first time in forty years, there was therefore a major shift in the leadership, committee composition and staffing of Congress.

Members also cluster and act on the basis of other loyalties. In the House state delegations are important, especially since the members from states with large populations represent big, potentially unified voting blocks on some issues. Congress has well over a hundred caucuses (interest groups formed to lobby other members) that allow members to gather in groups that are increasingly important rivals to the parties as the source of policy proposals. There are conservative, moderate and liberal caucuses for each party, as well as caucuses formed to promote regional, economic, ethnic, racial and women's issues that cross both party and chamber divisions. Yet three decades ago Congress had only four caucuses. Today some commentators believe they cause the fragmentation of planning in the national legislature.

Powers and Functions of Congress

Article I, Section 1 of the Constitution grants Congress 'all legislative powers' in the federal government. Only Congress can make laws, and it has the power to write all the laws that are needed to put the rest of the Constitution into operation. The President, interest groups, and private citizens may want laws passed by Congress. But only if they can convince a member of *each* chamber to introduce their proposals, is there a chance that these will become Acts of Congress.

However, law-making is only the best known of the legislative branch's duties. Members are truly representatives of their constituents and much of their work involves 'casework' (handling pressure groups' and voters' complaints and requests). The national legislature has the 'power of the purse', which means it alone can make the federal budget. No federal funds can be raised, allocated, or spent without its approval and directions. Congress also has the constitutional authority to regulate foreign and interstate commerce. Congress alone has the power to raise, finance, and regulate military forces and to declare war. The legislative branch has great power over the other arms of the national government. Congress created all the federal courts below the Supreme Court, can (and has) changed the number of justices on the Supreme Court, and determines which cases the federal courts can hear by setting limits on their jurisdictions. Congress, not the President, established the departments, agencies and bureaux that compose the bulk of the executive branch.

The committee system

Congress does most of its work in committees, in which members gain the expertise and power to make their mark on public policy. The volume and complexity of legislation introduced each year are so huge that committees are an indispensable tool for the division of labour. The committee system assigns members to specific legislative work; the supervision of executive departments and agencies; hearings on public issues; and on some Senate committees, to the questioning of the President's nominees for high office.

Naturally, members strive for assignments to committees whose work is of the greatest concern to their states or congressional districts. As government has become involved in ever wider areas of life, the two dozen or so standing (or permanent) committees in each chamber have spawned numbers of subcommittees. Thus, it is not surprising to see a House member from Mississippi as the chairman of the agricultural subcommittee dealing with cotton, for example. The most senior member has traditionally been given the chairmanship of a committee and through this position has exercised considerable control over its power to 'kill' or promote a proposal. Since the early 1970s, however, subcommittees have won greater independence, and chairmen have been chosen by secret ballot, which has not always resulted in election by seniority.

How a bill becomes an Act of Congress

Bills can be introduced in one chamber first or in both simultaneously. The steps in the law-making process are similar in both chambers. After its introduction, the bill is referred to a committee, which usually refers it to a subcommittee. There members not only air their own views but commission written reports from experts and lobbyists and frequently hold hearings to collect a variety of opinion on the proposal. The next step is a 'mark-up session' during which the subcommittee agrees on changes in the text of the bill. It is then returned to the committee, which holds its own mark-up session before sending it to the whole chamber for debate and a vote on passage.

Most bills 'die' in committee or subcommittee because they were introduced only to publicize a member's willingness to 'do something' about an issue, or because they are too flawed or controversial for passage. If bills pass both chambers, in a minority of cases amendments added in one or the other result in different texts. In that case, a conference committee composed of members from both chambers produces a compromise text of the bill for final votes in the House and Senate. If the compromise bill passes, it is sent to the President, who may sign or veto it.

Congressional elections

Elections for Congress take place in two different subdivisions of the nation: congressional districts, each of which chooses one member of the House of Representatives, and states, each of which selects two members of the Senate. Congressional elections take place every two years, when all members of the House of Representatives and one-third of the Senate face re-election contests.

The House expanded as new states entered the Union and their populations grew. But in 1929 the size of the House was fixed at 435 (with three additional non-voting delegates from the District of Columbia). Since then, the seats are divided among the states according to their population by a process called reapportionment after every ten-year federal census. The Constitution guarantees each state a minimum of one Representative. The number any state has above this minimum depends on how large its population is compared to that of the other states. Since the size of the House is constant, states with declining or slowly growing populations lose seats, and those with more rapidly growing populations gain seats.

Since the mid-twentieth century, the political power of the Northeastern states' delegations in the House has declined while those of the Sunbelt states of the South and Southwest has risen. The 1962 Supreme Court ruling in *Baker v. Carr* required that reapportionment follow the one-man-one-vote principle by creating congressional districts with equal populations. Each district now contains about 530,000 people. The 1982 Amendments to the federal Voting Rights Act have added the requirement that a state's plan for redrawn district lines must make it likely that minority group members will be elected to the House in numbers equivalent to the group's portion of the population of the state. In the 1990s, successful court challenges to the constitutionality of these 'minority majority' districts have close to eliminated them, but so far there are few protests, since record numbers of minorities are getting elected to Congress.

The fifty two-member constituencies for the US Senate are the major exception to the basic principle of single-member election districts in American politics. Even these function as one-member districts because only one of a state's two Senators is elected in any election year, unless both of a state's seats in the Senate are vacant because of unusual circumstances, such as death or sudden retirement.

One key to understanding the nature of Congress lies in remembering that the US does not have a parliamentary form of government. In a parliament, the prime minister is usually the leader of the majority party in the legislature after a general election. Members of a parliament are kept in line with their party's policies because voting independently can result in defeat of the sitting government. In that kind of system, members owe their seats to political parties, and voters choose between parties rather than personalities. Voting independently in office can well lead to deselection by the party at the next general election.

In the US, Congress does not choose the chief executive. Its members can vote without fear that the government will fall if they do not support their party on important issues. This means that they can give their first allegiance to their state or congressional district, rather than to their party or to the chief executive. Members of Congress owe their seats to elections in which their personalities and individual positions on issues are more important than their party labels. The parties cannot control who enters congressional elections or directs these campaigns. And most candidates organize their own campaign staff and cover the cost of running for office through their own fund-raising activities. The party is but one of several possible sources of support.

To run for a seat in Congress, a person must usually win a *primary election* first. Thus, two or more candidates from the same party compete in a primary for the right to represent the party in the general election campaign that follows. They may put themselves forward or be recruited by the party. But state law ordinarily requires people to document the seriousness of their bid for the party label by collecting a certain number of signatures supporting their candidacy before their names are put on the primary ballot. Victory in a primary is often achieved with a plurality rather than a majority of the votes because the field of candidates is frequently between three and five. In some states, a *run-off primary* is held between the two front runners when no candidate wins a majority. In the general election there are usually only two candidates, a Democrat and a Republican, although independent or third-party candidates sometimes run.

Being a member of Congress has become a career. Between 1946 and 1996 more than 90 per cent of House members and about 75 per cent of senators won their re-election contests. Most observers agree that incumbents (sitting members) have advantages over challengers. They have greater opportunities to use their office for media attention, their names and faces are consequently better known, and they can take credit for helping to pass government programmes that benefit the state or district. Although voter dissatisfaction with Congress has reached new heights since 1990 according to opinion polls, incumbents were re-elected at only slightly lower rates in 1994 and 1996. On the other hand, larger numbers of incumbents chose to retire in those years to avoid possible defeat.

The Democrats had majorities in both houses of Congress for almost the entire time from 1954 to 1994, losing control only of the Senate between 1980 and 1986. The advantages of incumbency helped the party to stay in power so long, but since 1990 have backfired as voters made Democrats the target of their discontent with government. The mid-term elections (those between presidential election years) usually result in losses for the majority party, and in 1994 cost the Democrats the control of both chambers. Two years later, the Republicans increased their majority in the Senate by two, and despite polls showing 60 per cent disapproval rates for Republican Speaker Newt Gingrich, he and a majority of Republicans (though nine fewer) won re-election to the House.

The executive branch

Some 3 million people work in this largest branch of the federal government. The degree of control that the President has over the departments, independent agencies and government corporations that make up the federal bureaucracy depends on the arrangements set up by Congress. Over 99 per cent of executive branch employees, for example, are hired through competitive examinations required by the Civil Service Act, rather than by presidential appointment.

The President nominates the highest officials in the executive branch, such as the Secretaries and Assistant Secretaries who lead the fourteen departments; the chief administrators of agencies and commissions; and the ranking officers of American embassies around the world. His appointments to these offices must be approved by the Senate. Only the roughly 2,000 positions in the Executive Office of the President are filled without congressional approval.

The Executive Office of the President

The main components of the Executive Office of the President that operate outside the White House are the Council of Economic Advisers, the National Security Council, the Office of Management and Budget and the Central Intelligence Agency (CIA). Inside the White House are the First Lady's staff and the President's own staff, which includes his personal advisers (some of whom are often carried over from his election staff), his press secretary, congressional liaison officer and chief of staff. The actual structure and operation of the Executive Office and the upper levels of the executive branch vary greatly, depending on the style and character of the President. For instance, the President's cabinet, even though it is composed of department secretaries and other key officials, has played a relatively small role in the policy development of recent administrations.

Qualifications for and powers of the presidency

The President's powers and limitations reflect the clauses in the Constitution intended to prevent the development of presidential government while providing for strong national leadership. The President must be a natural-born citizen, at least 35 years old, and have been a resident of the US for at least fourteen years. He is more independent of the legislature than the chief executive officers of most democratic governments because he is elected separately from the Congress and cannot be removed from office by a vote of no-confidence like a prime minister.

The price of his independence is having no guarantee of majorities in the houses of Congress; the difficulties of lobbying for support in an institution of which he is not a member; and the limits put on his powers by the system of checks and balances. However, the chief executive is the only official elected by a vote of citizens in all the states, and on that basis, sitting Presidents routinely claim to be the sole politicians who rise above the self-seeking goals of party politics to serve the interests of the whole nation.

Presidential duties are either stipulated in the Constitution, delegated to him by Congress, or are the result of circumstances. His most important extra-constitutional responsibilities are acting as chief of state and party leader. The President became the nation's ceremonial representative on state occasions by default, because the Constitution provides no other office for that purpose. He evolved into the national leader of his party as parties developed into the main organizers of the nation's political life and the presidency became increasingly powerful. The President's degree of popularity with the voters can often affect the success of his party's candidates for other offices. After the 1994 mid-term congressional elections, for example, polls showed that a large majority of voters questioned claime that their votes expressed displeasure with the President's policies.

The office's constitutional powers are the result of interpreting rather vague phrases in the document that describe his functions. He is the administrative head of the nation because the Constitution states that 'the executive power shall be vested in the

PLATE 4.3 President Clinton at the White House *(Dennis Cook/AP)*

President'. What that and other constitutional phrases mean in practice has evolved from the claims that successive holders of the office have made without provoking Congress or the courts to effectively oppose them. As chief administrator, the President is required to see that the laws are carried out. This is understood to mean managing the bureaucracy and enforcing existing policies, but interpreted broadly it has enabled Presidents to break a strike or send troops to integrate a public school.

The Constitution names the President as commander-in-chief, making him the highest-ranking officer in the armed services, but gives Congress the power to declare war. The Founders' attempt to give the legislature control over the executive's military power proved so limited that Congress in 1973 passed the War Powers Act to restrain him by requiring congressional approval for deployment of American troops abroad within specified time limits. Presidents have unanimously called the Act unconstitutional and have followed its notification procedure only when it suited them.

The President's military power is one of several factors that strengthen his position as foreign policy leader. This is the arena where the executive branch has most clearly developed a dominant position. Presidents have learned to circumvent the constitutional clauses that require approval by two-thirds of the Senate for ratification of a treaty and a simple majority for confirmation of diplomatic appointments. The National Security Advisor, who owes his position solely to the President's choice, has become most Presidents' main advisor in formulating foreign policy. And decisions are most often carried out through executive agreements, which do not have to be approved by the Senate. In addition, the President has at his disposal four major organizations to support his conduct of foreign affairs: the Department of State, the Defense Department, the CIA and the National Security Council. Faced with these facts, Congress continues to assert its role in foreign policy but recognizes the executive's ability to act with greater expertise, speed and clarity.

The President's role as legislative leader developed in part from constitutional clauses requiring him to inform Congress about the 'state of the nation' and to suggest the 'measures' he considers 'necessary or expedient'. Another clause allows him to convene a special session of Congress if he deems it necessary. However, the President did not usually set the legislative agenda until the twentieth century.

In 1921 Congress weakened its monopoly on the 'power of the purse' by the Budget and Accounting Act, which delegated to the President the power to screen the budget proposals of executive branch departments and agencies. As a result, the White House routinely sets policy priorities in the process of proposing how much money shall be allotted to government programmes. But not until the Great Depression of the 1930s did the chief executive become heavily involved in drafting a coordinated 'package' of bills for congressional action. The New Deal proposals of Franklin D. Roosevelt marked a new era in presidential legislative activity, when the President sent his bills to Congress and let its members decide what to do with them. Today he is expected to follow their progress through the legislature closely and use a staff of legislative aides to ensure their passage.

If he is effective as a combined legislative initiator and lobbyist, the President has less need of his veto power. He can refuse to approve bills passed by the houses of Congress in two ways: by sending a veto message that explains his objections or simply by not signing a bill that comes to him within ten days of the adjournment of Congress (the so-called pocket veto). The President's veto power is limited. Congress may override it, and only since 1995 has he had a line-item veto on financial bills. This situation permits some members of Congress to press unwanted proposals on the President as 'riders' to non-financial bills.

Presidential elections

Electing the President is a long, complicated and costly affair. After conferring with political advisers for some time, individuals hold press conferences between eighteen months and a year before the election to announce that they are running for the office.

Several serious candidates from different factions or wings of each party commonly propose themselves. Over the following months these candidates 'test the water' to see how warm party and public support is for their candidacy in different parts of the nation.

From February to June of the presidential election year the states conduct the process of narrowing the field of candidates to one from each party. Most states use presidential primaries for this purpose, but a few hold party meetings called presidential caucuses. Both procedures are *indirect*. Party voters choose delegates to the party's national convention and give these delegates the authority to make the party's official nomination of a candidate.

Because they result in the choice of roughly 80 per cent of convention delegates, presidential primaries attract much more attention than the caucuses. Some are *closed*, that is, they are elections in which only registered party members can vote. Others are *open* primaries, voters from either party can participate. During the 'primary season' the media keep a running count of the delegates pledged to each candidate and track the front runners' progress towards a majority of delegate votes at the party conventions in July and August.

As a result, in recent years each party's choice has been clear before the convention. The situation becomes more interesting, however, if no candidate has accumulated a delegate majority by the end of the primaries. The proportional representation from primaries that the Democrats and a number of states now require sends more divided blocks of delegates to the conventions. Caucuses and primaries bind delegates only on the first roll-call ballot of the states. If no candidate wins a majority, delegates are free to switch loyalties on succeeding ballots, and the final choice of the convention could be unexpected.

But, if present trends continue, the interest in the convention will lie elsewhere. Because the convention is televised, both parties present a 'packaged media show' of unity to demonstrate that the internal disagreements of the primary season are forgotten. But sometimes, as at the Republican conventions in 1992 and 1996, elements in the party can gain delegate majorities and

PLATE 4.4   The Republicans celebrate, 1994
(Jacky Chapman/Format)

promote their views to the disadvantage of the candidate. The convention agrees on a policy programme called the platform. In the 1990s, Bush and Dole were at pains to distance themselves from the more extreme statements of their party's platform.

The Democrats' meetings in the 1990s have been the well-orchestrated media event that is typical of most of today's party conventions, with factions such as Jesse Jackson's Rainbow Coalition accepting a subordinate role. In 1992 Clinton even announced the choice of Al Gore as his vice-presidential running-mate in advance (denying TV viewers the only convention suspense in recent years), and Bob Dole followed suit four years later when he chose Jack Kemp.

The parties and their candidates eventually face each other in the post-convention campaign that runs from late August until the voters go to the polls at the beginning of November. Candidates still criss-cross the country to make their stands on

149

the issues, but increasingly rely on the media to take them into the public's living rooms. Short TV 'spots' are used by all candidates, but most depend on getting free coverage by making the evening news with their regular campaign activities. Only a multi-millionaire candidate like H. Ross Perot can afford to buy half-hour 'infomercials' on TV to present his views. In the closing months of the campaign, nationally televised debates between the candidates offer them the best chance to exploit the media for a campaign boost.

On election day the television networks display huge maps of the country to track two different tallies of the results. One is the 'popular vote' (a count of how many voters across the country have supported each of the candidates). At first these figures are estimates compiled by polling organizations who ask people how they voted as they exit the polling stations. In the evening after the polls have closed in the eastern states, the count for those areas may be official. But because of the difference in time zones, the popular vote in the Pacific west will not be known until some hours later.

The popular vote, however, does not determine who wins the election. Not only are the candidates chosen in an indirect fashion through the primaries, but the final election is also decided indirectly. In accordance with rules in the Constitution, the popular vote is not counted nationally, but by state. The second tally on election-day television screens is the electoral college vote. Each state receives a number of votes in the college equal to the sum of its members in Congress (two Senators plus its number of Representatives in the House). The District of Columbia has three votes, making a total of 538 'electors' in the college. After each ten-year census, the number of electors per state is adjusted to reflect the changing size of their congressional delegations.

The members of the electoral college travel to their respective state capitals in mid-December and cast the ballots which officially decide the election when they are counted in the Senate in January. However, the media make the electoral result clear long before then because, except for the electors from Maine and Nebraska, members of the college are pledged to vote together

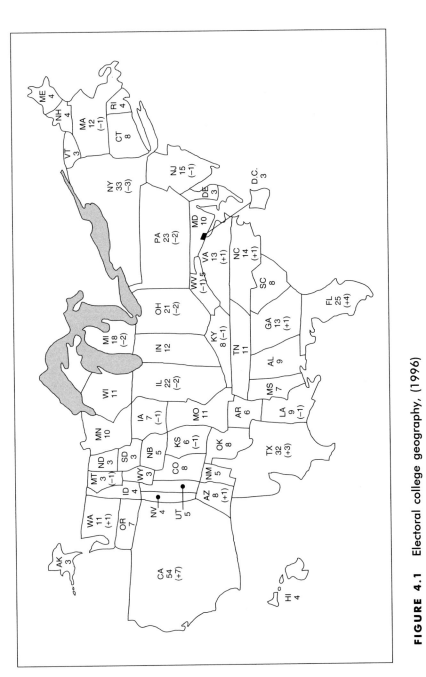

FIGURE 4.1 Electoral college geography, (1996)

Note: Changes in states' electoral votes because of the 1990 Census are shown in parentheses

for the winning candidate in each state. The Supreme Court has determined that states cannot *require* electors to vote for that candidate, but since 1820 only four electors have not.

The plurality system has its most dramatic effect in the electoral college vote. The candidate who carries a state (even with a minority of its popular vote) receives *all* the state's votes in the college. Most voters are unwilling to 'waste' their votes, and so presidential elections in practice become two-party contests. For example, independent Ross Perot won 19 per cent of the popular vote in 1992 but no votes in the electoral college.

There has been debate about whether indirect election of the President through the electoral college should be continued, but no concerted effort for change has emerged. Critics point out that it is currently possible for a candidate to win the popular vote but lose in the college, as in fact occurred three times in the nineteenth century. Supporters of the *status quo* note that usually the effect of the electoral college vote is to produce a clearer result by exaggerating the margin of victory in the popular vote.

In 1996, for example, Bill Clinton won only 8 per cent more of the popular vote than Bob Dole, but captured 379 electors to Dole's 159. Those in favour of the college emphasize that the electoral count correctly emphasizes the importance states should have in a federal system and the importance that the most populous states (most of which Clinton carried) should have in a democracy.

The judicial branch

The only court specifically mentioned by the Constitution is the *US Supreme Court*. However, the constitutional power given to Congress to establish lesser federal courts has resulted in a three-tier system as well as special courts for specific areas such as tax, customs, patent and military law. *District courts* have original jurisdiction in most federal cases. Only about one-sixth of the decisions of these courts are appealed further to the next tier, the *US courts of appeals*.

TABLE 4.1 US presidential elections, 1932–96

Year	Candidates[a]	Parties	Percentage of popular vote	Electoral vote[b]
1932	*Franklin D. Roosevelt*	*Democratic*	57.4	472
	Herbert C. Hoover	Republican	39.7	59
	Norman Thomas	Socialist	2.2	
1936	*Franklin D. Roosevelt*	*Democratic*	60.8	523
	Alfred M. Landon	Republican	36.5	8
	William Lemke	Union	1.9	
1940	*Franklin D. Roosevelt*	*Democratic*	54.8	449
	Wendell L. Wilkie	Republican	44.8	82
1944	*Franklin D. Roosevelt*	*Democratic*	53.5	432
	Thomas E. Dewey	Republican	46.0	99
1948	*Harry S. Truman*	*Democratic*	49.6	303
	Thomas E. Dewey	Republican	45.1	189
	J. Strom Thurmond	States' Rights	2.4	
	Henry A. Wallace	Progressive	2.4	
1952	*Dwight D. Eisenhower*	*Republican*	55.1	442
	Adlai E. Stevenson	Democratic	44.4	89
1956	*Dwight D. Eisenhower*	*Republican*	57.6	457
	Adlai E. Stevenson	Democratic	42.1	73
1960	*John F. Kennedy*	*Democratic*	49.7	303
	Richard M. Nixon	Republican	49.5	219
1964	*Lyndon B. Johnson*	*Democratic*	61.1	486
	Barry M. Goldwater	Republican	38.5	52
1968	*Richard M. Nixon*	*Republican*	43.3	301
	Hubert H. Humphrey	Democratic	42.7	191
	George C. Wallace	American Independent	13.5	46
1972	*Richard M. Nixon*	*Republican*	60.7	520
	George S. McGovern	Democratic	37.5	17
	John G. Schmitz	American	1.4	
1976	*Jimmy Carter*	*Democratic*	50.1	297
	Gerald R. Ford	Republican	48.0	240
1980	*Ronald Reagan*	*Republican*	50.8	489
	Jimmy Carter	Democratic	41.0	49
	John B. Anderson	Independent	6.6	
	Ed Clark	Libertarian	1.1	
1984	*Ronald Reagan*	*Republican*	58.8	525
	Walter Mondale	Democratic	40.6	13
1988	*George Bush*	*Republican*	53.4	426
	Michael Dukakis	Democratic	45.6	111
1992	*Bill Clinton*	*Democratic*	43.0	370
	George Bush	Republican	38.0	168
	H. Ross Perot	Independent	19.0	
1996	*Bill Clinton*	*Democratic*	49.4	379
	Bob Dole	Republican	41.0	159
	H. Ross Perot	Reform Party	9.6	

Notes: [a] Victor in italics. [b] In some elections a few electoral votes went to candidates whose percentage of the popular vote was insignificant.

153

PLATE 4.5 The US Supreme Court *(Priscilla Coleman)*

Most of the US Supreme Court's work consists of hearing cases from US courts of appeals or state supreme courts. All of these cases raise federal questions (controversies arising under the Constitution, federal law, or treaties). In addition, it has original jurisdiction in cases which involve a state or officials of the federal government. In 1990 it heard ten cases under its original jurisdiction and handed down decisions on 130 cases that it selected from 4,500 appeals for review. The decisions of lower federal courts become final in cases it refuses to hear, which means those judges may also exercise judicial review, though usually that means following earlier decisions set by the US Supreme Court.

The Constitution creates a separate judicial branch with a single supreme court that has an unspecified number of justices with terms of office dependent only on their 'good behavior'. In practice, the number of justices has varied between five and ten, according to the will of Congress, but in recent history has been eight, plus a chief justice. Terms of office have by tradition been

PLATE 4.6   Outside a polling station, Detroit   *(Format)*

for life or until voluntary retirement. As no justice has ever been impeached, life terms have given justices an impressive degree of independence. Of the 144 men and 2 women nominated to the Court, about 4 in 5 have confirmed by the Senate. In 1987 Richard Bork became the last presidential nominee to be rejected.

Judicial review

Today the fame and influence of the Supreme Court result from its power of *judicial review* (the right to evaluate whether congressional and presidential acts are in accordance with the Constitution and to declare them void if it deems them unconstitutional). This power, which is not explicitly granted in the Constitution, gives the Court an important role in the system of checks and balances.

The Court claimed the right of judicial review by stages and won gradual acceptance for its practice between 1796 and 1865. In the first year the Court asserted its right to invalidate state laws that it considered unconstitutional. In *Marbury v. Madison* [1803], it claimed the power to invalidate an unconstitutional federal law. Later decisions extended judicial review to cover executive acts and emphasized that the Court's exercise of its review power was necessary to maintain the supremacy of federal law and a uniform interpretation of the Constitution from state to state.

President Andrew Jackson ignored the Court's decision in 1832 when it upheld the sovereignty of the Cherokee nation against encroaching settlers. Emphasizing the Court's lack of financial or military power to carry out its rulings, he remarked, '[Chief Justice] John Marshall has made his decision – now let him enforce it!' States' righters from Thomas Jefferson to those who urged Southern secession insisted that the states rather than the Court had the power to nullify federal law. As a practical fact, only the Union victory in the Civil War established the supremacy of federal law and the Constitution and the Court as their interpreter.

Once that pattern of authority was accepted, Supreme Court decisions became a powerful force shaping public policy because they became precedents that all other state and federal courts followed in similar cases. But there remain two views on how the Court should exercise the power of judicial review. One, called *judicial restraint*, holds that the justices should limit their review to applying the rules explicitly stated or clearly implied in the Constitution or Acts of Congress. If cases raise questions not clearly answered by existing law, the Court should leave those questions for the elected politicians to decide. The other view, termed *judicial activism*, maintains that justices ought to let the general intent or principles underlying the text of the Constitution and federal statutes be their guide in applying often vague legal language to a changing society. In the activist view, the Court should not hesitate to intervene in political questions to protect the Constitution and prevent infringements on individual rights.

In the course of US history, there have been cycles of judicial activism and restraint. The activist period before the Civil War was followed by a cycle of restraint that lasted until 1937. During these years the Court generally held that the government's right to regulate the economy was not clearly implied in the Constitution. Instead it asserted that private business and property were protected from federal regulation by the Fourteenth Amendment, even though the Amendment was originally intended to guarantee the rights of former slaves.

In the 1890s the Court handed down a series of decisions that legalized racial segregation and the disenfranchisement of Blacks in the South by ruling that the regulation of public facilities and elections exceeded the constitutional powers of the national government. In the 1930s the Court invalidated so many of the economic programmes in Franklin Roosevelt's New Deal that he proposed 'packing' the Court with more amenable justices until one member of the court provided a majority for the President by adopting new views in 1937.

A new period of judicial activism began in that year, extending to the end of the 1980s, during which the Court rarely invalidated economic legislation but overturned dozens of laws that it believed infringed individuals' rights. It reversed its earlier stand on segregation in the *Brown* decision [1954] and since then has protected minority voting rights, affirmative action programmes to increase educational opportunities for racial minorities, abortion rights and the right to unrestricted political expression, even if that means burning the American flag.

Republicans Reagan and Bush appointed five justices whom they hoped would move the Court into another period of judicial restraint. But once on the bench, justices have frequently surprised and disappointed their sponsors. Moreover, in his first term moderately liberal President Clinton has appointed a second woman, Ruth Bader Ginsburg, whose views may not coincide with those of the supposed conservatives. Clinton will likely have the chance to appoint more justices in his second term of office. Thus, the recent trend in rulings suggesting a more restrained Court may not last long. For the present, however, the Court is allowing more government discretion in limiting abortion rights and affirmative action programmes and is showing a willingness to reconsider earlier decisions in voting rights and segregation cases.

Some commentators criticize a system in which an appointed judicial body can overrule the democratically elected branches of government. Others point out that in over 200 years the Court has invalidated only around 120 sections of federal law but nearly ten times as many provisions of state law. These rulings, it must be remembered, were all in response to disagreements between specific parties and limited to the particular points of law raised by those parties. Nevertheless, the Court's judicial review can be overridden, since Congress and the President (and state governments) can revise their Acts and constitutional amendments can be passed.

The Court's decisions also relieve the other branches of taking positions on politically sensitive questions. The Court has reversed itself when older decisions no longer seem valid and, according to a study covering its rulings from the mid-1930s to the mid-1980s, was in line with public opinion at least as often as the other branches. Thus the question of whether judicial review by the Supreme Court is a democratic process turns out to be more complicated than it at first appears.

■ Examine and explain the following terms:

Articles of Confederation	'third' parties
incumbents	popular sovereignty
Speaker of the House	presidential appointments
'reserved' powers	Majority Leader
line-item veto	filibuster
presidential caucuses	separation of powers
congressional caucuses	electoral college
winner-take-all system	reapportionment
original jurisdiction	a two-party region
primary elections	judicial review
'necessary and	
proper' clause	

■ Write short essays on the following topics:

1   How are the principles of federalism and limited government protected by the Constitution of 1787 and its amendments?

2   Compare and contrast the chambers of Congress, giving particular attention to the effects of their different size, membership and terms of office.

3   Discuss the powers of the President and contrast his position with that of a prime minister in a parliamentary government.

4   Describe American parties and elections and discuss the causes and effects of their most distinctive elements.

5   What are some of the arguments for and against the Supreme Court's power of judicial review?

State and local government

BOTH ADVOCATES AND CRITICS of the European Union have compared it to a 'United States of Europe'. Certainly Europeans are presently grappling with dilemmas of government structure similar to those weighed by the drafters of the Constitution of 1787. The vastly different historical situation of European nations today makes comparison dubious. Still, leaders in both times and places have considered the similar issues of how much power should be centralized and which functions should be left to national (state in the US) or local government.

The answers the Founding Fathers gave to these and related questions defined the particular brand of federalism originally established in the US. But, as we shall see in the following pages, such issues are not decided once and for all. They are part of an on-going debate about the nature and purposes of government. The answers given at different times provide a map of the evolving character of American federalism and state and local government.

The place of state government in American federalism

A whole article of the Constitution is devoted to the states. Article 4 recognizes states' limited sovereignty by denying the federal authorities the power to alter the boundaries of existing states without their permission. The federal capital, Washington, could be founded only after Maryland and Virginia agreed to give up some territory to create the District of Columbia. Constitutional rules for the admission of new states on an equal footing with the original thirteen and a clause guaranteeing them a republican form of government also recognize states as the main building blocks of the US system.

The importance of the states is woven into other provisions of the Constitution as well, such as the rule that membership in both chambers of Congress and the election of the President are determined by state. In addition, amendments to the Constitution can only be made with the approval of three-quarters of the states. These protections and privileges go a long way towards explaining the current movements for statehood in Puerto Rico and the District of Columbia.

The drafters of the Constitution were representatives of states, who did not want to create a tyrannical federal government. They also intended to design a division of powers between the national authorities, the states, and the people that was appropriate to each. As one Founding Father, James Madison, explained it, 'the great and aggregate interests' were 'referred to the national, and the local and particular to state governments'. Some powers are denied the states. They cannot coin money, conduct foreign policy, keep military services, make war or set customs duties.

All these are recognized as *delegated powers*, aggregate interests given to the national government to prevent conflicts among the states and between them and the federal government. In addition, the Constitution specifically assigns the national government the duty of protecting the states from invasion and rebellion. To protect the people from both levels of government, rights such as a jury trial are included in the main document and many more are granted to citizens through the ten amendments in the Bill of Rights.

The states kept for themselves a long list of *reserved powers* (state and local powers denied to the federal government). Only states can establish local governments. State functions also include protecting public safety and morals, which today means providing police, fire and sanitation departments, as well as deciding 'moral' questions such as the legality or availability of drugs (including alcohol) and sexual practices. They also provide educational and health facilities, as well as raise taxes and borrow money to fund all these activities.

States write their own codes of civil and criminal law. They maintain transportation networks, issue licences for intrastate activities, and incorporate businesses as part of their regulation of state commerce. State legislatures also determine voting qualifications and conduct elections for all levels of government. The Tenth Amendment, which reserves to the states or people those powers not granted the federal government, remains an important constitutional guarantee of the states' sovereignty.

Some government activities are commonly understood to be *concurrent powers*, ones shared by the states and national authorities, because the Constitution does not designate one level of government as primarily responsible. These functions include lawmaking, establishing courts, levying taxes, borrowing and providing for the general welfare. A basic principle of federalism is that two levels of government exercise authority and powers over the same territory. Such overlapping has not usually been problematic because the national government applies these powers to relations between the states, while each state exercises them only within its borders.

Over time, however, the existence of concurrent powers and disputes concerning them have worked to the advantage of the federal authorities. Despite the kind of federalism the Constitution defines, power has shifted dramatically from the states to the federal government for that and several other reasons. Briefly put, historical circumstances and practical politics have determined the balance of power between the states and the nation more than has constitutional theory.

Not only the defeat of states' rights advocates in the Civil War but a series of historical crises (the two World Wars, the Depression, urbanization and industrialization and the Cold War) were beyond the capacities of the states and so strengthened the national government. During these crises, accepted limits of national power were judged too confining for the solution of problems. The federal government therefore interpreted its constitutional powers quite broadly, and the states (and usually the courts) accepted a transfer of power that usually became permanent after the crisis.

A number of changes that increased national power resulted from constitutional amendments. For example, until after the Civil War, the Bill of Rights was assumed to apply only to relations between citizens and the national government. But two general phrases in the Fourteenth Amendment (1868) require *states* to offer citizens 'due process of law' and 'equal protection of the laws'. The US Supreme Court has interpreted these phrases to mean that states also must meet the standards set in the Bill of Rights. The Court has therefore upheld federal civil rights legislation as well as the demands of individuals for protection from state actions. Other amendments and civil rights rulings limit state power over tax revenues, voting rights and elections.

Most of the growth in federal power, however, has come through lawmaking. Congress has used the so-called *elastic clause* of the Constitution to set precedents for federal legislation in almost every area of life. That clause gives Congress the right to make any laws that are 'necessary and proper' to carry out its other powers. Often the President has lobbied Congress to invoke this and other broad constitutional phrases because the public expects the chief executive to lead the nation out of troubled times. Both federal branches have cited their concurrent power of promoting the 'general welfare' as a reason for encroaching on state authority.

Federal laws often include *grants-in-aid* (funding for specific purposes) as a means of persuading states to give the national government a say in their internal affairs. Grants-in-aid hold out the possibility of gaining resources to solve pressing problems, but require states to accept regulations determining how the money is used. Many grants are offered as *matching funds*, which means a state receives no more support from Washington for a project than it contributes itself.

The promise of funding operates as a powerful incentive. The threat to deny funds is as powerful a pressure for getting states to give up their own standards for federal standards. And simply by choosing to fund some kinds of activities and not others, the federal government has often been able to set states' policy agenda. The combined effects of concurrent powers, national crises, constitutional amendments, Supreme Court decisions, congressional legislation and grants-in-aid have been a strong trend towards centralized government.

The evolution of state government and federalism

The Supreme Court laid the foundation for the expansion of federal powers between 1803 and 1865, when it established its power of judicial review and tradition of broadly interpreting the federal government's constitutional powers. Yet, both the national and the state governments exercised their powers in a small way for most of the nineteenth century. Until the 1930s the main way the federal government affected most citizens was through its help to promote the economy by developing the frontier. Its armies fought Native Americans and forced them farther west. It gave new states federal land for schools and joined states and private entrepreneurs to build roads and canals. From the 1860s onwards, Congress wrote legislation providing free or cheap land on the frontier for settlers homesteading in the wilderness and companies engaged in building transcontinental railroads.

When the federal government attempted to legislate in the areas of public health, safety and order in the 1800s, the Supreme Court ruled that these were *solely* the concern of the states. Likewise it decided that the regulation of business was purely a matter for the states. On the whole, the Court acted in accordance with the theory known as *dual federalism* (the theory that state and federal governments have clearly separate spheres in which each is sovereign). The Court also interpreted the Constitution narrowly, limiting government activity on any level to explicitly granted powers. Thus, it commonly approved neither federal nor state laws regulating industry and labour. Strongly influenced by *laissez-faire* economic theory, from the 1880s through to the 1920s it refused to accept laws to regulate child labour, minimum wages and working hours, safety or working conditions.

At the start of the Great Depression, the states still provided most services understood as reserved to them by the drafters of the Constitution. Washington did not regulate citizens' behaviour and provided few services beyond the Post Office. The combination of the economic crisis, FDR's New Deal legislation, and the Court's advocacy of a new theory of federalism had transformed the governmental landscape by 1939.

By then the national authorities' regulation of the economy and creation of a social security safety net had ushered in the era of *cooperative federalism*. The Court interpreted the Tenth Amendment and elastic clause broadly. It viewed the division of powers between state and federal governments as less distinct and important than the ways they might work together. Many of the most vital activities of the authorities were now assumed to be concurrent powers of government. Sweeping expansions of both state and federal powers resulted from the change in the Court's philosophy, but Washington's share of all money spent on domestic needs nearly tripled while the states' spending on these problems stayed the same.

Grants-in-aid programmes began with the New Deal laws and grew rapidly in number for almost forty years. In the 1950s such grants resulted in heavy federal involvement in secondary and higher education as part of the effort to compete with the Soviet Union's technological progress. They also supplied states with funds for the massive interstate highway system built at the time. In the 1960s grants helped pay for efforts to enforce civil and voting rights laws as well as the goals of Lyndon B. Johnson's ambitious Great Society and War on Poverty programmes, which aimed at the realization of equal opportunity and a better quality of life for all Americans.

Grants-in-aid mushroomed in kind, number and expense. Washington became active in local law enforcement, low-rent housing projects, urban mass transit, health services and job training. It shared responsibility for virtually all the services that had been functions of the states. For the first time, moreover, it encouraged applications for aid from local governments and private community groups, frequently bypassing the state authorities in its decisions on financing.

By the early 1970s, a counter-reaction had set in. State and local governments complained of over-regulation, wasteful bureaucratic red tape, and the tendency of the national government to place new duties on them without supplying sufficient funding. Conservatives in both parties called for a return to dual federalism, and President Nixon's proposals in 1972 amounted to just that, although he called them the *New Federalism*. His revenue-sharing cut most strings attached to federal grants so that the lower levels of government could gain more power in setting priorities and standards. Combining many grant programmes into 'block grants' for health, welfare, or education aimed to accomplish the same purposes.

The New Federalism had little success in stopping the shift of power from the states to the national government. Members of Congress were unwilling to give up taking credit for and exercising control over the distribution of federal money to their districts or states. Revenue-sharing ended in 1986, and grant programmes returned to their former pattern.

President Reagan promised to revive New Federalism, but the main effect of his administration was to reverse the trend of increasing federal aid to state and local government. Such aid dropped by 25 per cent in the early 1980s, and to date has grown only slightly, in part because federal budget deficits leave little leeway for increased spending. Since then, federal grant programmes continue to grow in number, but states and local governments have had to bear more of the cost of new programmes themselves. In exchange, congressional leaders and all Presidents since Nixon have agreed to set fewer binding federal regulations on grant programmes.

In fact, during the last decade or so the federal government has left the solution of growing numbers of national problems to the states. That inevitably means that inequalities among the states have grown, because cuts in federal grants hurt poor states most. By the 1990s, the wealthier states had more than made up for the loss of federal funds and were financing new activities in economic development and social services. The poorer states, by contrast, hovered near bankruptcy, cut services, and found that payments for the poor made up a growing part of the federal money they received.

Most political commentators and politicians interpreted the results of the 1994 mid-term elections as a sign that the national mood still favoured the devolution of power and responsibility to the states. The Democrats, traditionally viewed as the party that supports central government programmes to solve social problems, suffered their greatest losses in decades. House Speaker Newt Gingrich led his chamber's new Republican majority in an attempt to enact a 'Contract with America', which many say embodies a *new* New Federalism. Events in 1996 continued this trend. The voters returned Gingrich and Republican majorities to power, and President Clinton not only signed a welfare reform act that returned the responsibility for welfare to the states but won re-election as a 'moderate Democrat' (one supporting a smaller, less intrusive federal government).

The structure of state government

As the fundamental principles of all American governments were first developed by states, it is hardly surprising that the structure of state government parallels that of the federal government. Each of the fifty states has a written constitution. Each also has a separation of powers among three branches, which share power through a system of checks and balances.

All of the *state legislatures*, except Nebraska's, have the same format as Congress with two houses, usually called the state senate and state assembly. State legislatures also work through committees and pass laws through a process very like that used in Congress. Like the President, the chief executive of a state, *the governor*, enjoys the powers of administration, appointment and veto. The structure of a *state judiciary* is also broadly parallel to the federal court system. In most states there is a state supreme court and under it appeals courts and (parallel to the US district courts) county or municipal courts.

There are, however, some important differences in the structure of state governments. State constitutions are typically several times longer than the US Constitution because they contain many more detailed provisions and much more specific language. Instead of reserving whatever powers are left undefined to a lower level of government or the people, the drafters of state constitutions attempt to be as explicit as possible. Such detailed documents less easily adapt themselves to broad interpretation and so are much more frequently amended. New York State's constitution has been amended over 200 times in the last century, for example, while only twenty-seven amendments have been added to the US Constitution since 1787. Most states have written new constitutions or extensively rewritten their old ones several times.

The branches of government also have distinctive elements at the state level. Most state legislators are part-time law makers. They often divide their time between the legislature and a law practice or business in their home districts. State legislators have fixed terms of office like members of Congress, but they do not run for re-election as often. Instead, they go back to full-time work in their private jobs or use their government experience to enter a new line of work. Thus, over a third of state legislators are newcomers at any time and as many are rather inexperienced.

State legislators' interest in careers in government is low for several reasons. Compared to what they can earn in the private sector, the annual salary is low. And travelling between the capital and the member's district, as well as keeping an office in both places, require time and expense. Yet, sitting in the state legislature brings little prestige, even though it disrupts family life and leads to the forced neglect of members' other part-time profession or business.

Some experts on American government argue that the states should change to full-time, professional, legislators with higher pay. But tradition and the enormous cost of converting to full-time lawmakers make the present situation likely to persist. The traditional view is that having part-time legislators is an advantage. Their jobs in local districts keep them concerned about the well-being of the community they represent. As one political scientist explained, they 'really have something at home, unlike Congressmen who don't have anything to come home for except trying to get votes'. In practice, the debate may be moot, because the federal government's increasing withdrawal from grants-in-aid programmes has forced state governments to assume more responsibility. The increased workload of state lawmakers has already produced a movement towards full-time legislatures in the more populous states.

There are also important differences between a governor's situation and the President's. Most governors have two powers the President lacks: they usually have more complete control over the state budget and most also have a broad line-item veto, which allows them to accept some parts of a bill while vetoing other parts. The President's line-item veto (not approved by Congress until 1995) is much more limited.

On the other hand, in many states the governor's power is weaker than the President's in four important ways. First, many are not free to make as many appointments as the President does. More state officials are elected. Second, many states have a tradition of electing several of a governor's department heads, for example, the state treasurer, attorney general and commissioner of education are often elected. These other state executives are popularly considered part of the governor's 'team' at election time. But each must get elected separately, and that makes them more independent of the governor. Many times, these department heads do not even belong to the governor's party. State parties often seem less important to voters than selecting a team of state executives that represents a range of different races, ethnic groups and economic interests.

Third, governors have less control over suggestions for new laws. Starting early in this century, many states developed two procedures for taking suggestions for new laws (or changes in old laws) directly to the voters, bypassing the governor and usually the legislature. The *initiative* allows citizens to call for a vote on a state law or constitutional amendment, in the legislature or by the public at an election. Those proposing the initiative must petition the state for this vote by collecting signatures from somewhere between 5 to 10 per cent of the state's registered voters. About half of the states currently permit some form of voter initiative.

The *referendum*, a direct vote of the public on an issue, may be the result of a successful initiative, a requirement for amending the state constitution, or an item put on the ballot by the state legislature. Known as *propositions*, referenda are allowed in half the states. Referenda on constitutional changes are required in all but one state.

It is politically dangerous for governors to oppose procedures that make state government more democratic by giving ordinary voters a say in state lawmaking, even though some propositions may have harmful effects. Thus state executives have found it difficult to speak out against proposals similar to Proposition 13, passed in California in 1978, which so reduce taxes that state and local governments must cut back on basic services. The use of referenda has grown rapidly, which numbered nearly 250 in every election year during the 1980s and reached a new record in 1996. Many critics now doubt whether the public is informed enough to vote intelligently on so many issues. Politicians, however, make little protest, even though the most common and successful proposal these days is term limits (putting limits on the number of terms people can run for office).

The fourth way governors have lost power is through *special district governments*, authorities designed to deal with a specific problem that crosses governmental boundaries. Some special districts have become so powerful that they are popularly called regional governments. Most special districts have been established since the First World War. Some have been suggested by federal authorities, but like all forms of local government, special districts are created by the states.

State legislatures do not aim to weaken the governor's position by founding special districts; rather, legislatures simply recognize that growing problems, such as air pollution, land and water shortages, refuse disposal and regional traffic jams, cannot be efficiently handled within one legal jurisdiction. Several states and often many local governments share the responsibility for dealing with these problems.

Coordination between so many separate authorities becomes difficult if not impossible. Many of America's big cities are merely the centres of much larger metropolitan areas that include many suburbs, several satellite cities and even 'pockets' of rural territory. Most special districts have been established in just these areas, where the need for coordinated public services is greatest.

Special districts are governed by official delegates from the various local and state governments in the area where regional problems exist. But special districts also have their own staffs and budgets. Usually both are funded mostly by grants from the federal government and are therefore outside the governor's control. Presidents Reagan and Bush said they intended to reduce the role and importance of special districts. Though the number of special districts reached nearly 30,000 by the beginning of the 1990s, however, neither President took any significant action in the matter, because the problems the districts are set up to solve have only become more serious. Since then, they have gradually taken more planning initiative from state governors and state governments generally.

The judiciary branch in state governments is different from the federal judiciary in two important ways. First, many state and local judges are elected, rather than appointed, to terms of office that vary from between four and fifteen years. In many states, even the state supreme court justices are elected. The election of judges is meant to make them more responsive to changes in public opinion. It is also meant to make the removal of unpopular or incompetent judges easier. Of course, as a result of their election, state and local judges are more frequently accused of being swayed by political pressures. Once on the bench, judges are required by law to be impartial. Therefore, it is not considered unusual that both major parties will endorse the same person for judge, if that candidate is known as a fair and competent jurist.

Second, the state supreme court cannot be sure of handing down the final decision in the most important cases that come to it. The federal constitution takes precedence over all other law, and so the US Supreme Court has the power to review the constitutionality of both federal and state laws.

Local government

The fifty states are divided into some 83,000 units of local government. In addition to the special districts, there are counties, towns, cities, boroughs and school districts. The states create these (and other) kinds of local governments and determine their powers.

No local government in the US has sovereignty, power in its own right. Units of local government are not mentioned in the federal constitution. They exist because they have been created by the states as instruments, tools to help the state carry out its responsibilities. Some local governments have been established by state constitutions while others came into being through acts of state legislatures. Special districts often result from agreements among two or more states.

Local governments vary tremendously across the country, because each state has developed its own system of local authorities. Most states are divided into *counties*, but, in Louisiana, the parallel unit of government is called a parish and in Alaska a borough. Counties also vary greatly in population, size and functions. Still, most counties share several general responsibilities. They are usually the main units of government in rural areas. They rarely have lawmaking power, but instead act as agents of the state. They serve as administrative units that carry out some state-wide programmes in local areas, such as keeping records and issuing licences.

All the powers of local governments are really powers of the states. The state just delegates the work of providing local facilities and services to smaller units of government. Thus, the states set general standards and guidelines, but ask counties to carry out the functions that are delegated. These include providing local transportation, schools, fire and police protection, water and sanitation systems and medical programmes and buildings. Counties also collect the local property taxes to pay for these services.

County government usually consists of a board of between three and twelve members, a county court, and the chief officers of county departments. Board members, or commissioners (as they are often called in more populous counties) are elected and serve on a part-time basis. Their powers usually include deciding how local taxes should be raised and spent for county programmes, as well as the authority to establish zoning codes that regulate the purpose for which land may be used.

The boards have no influence over the county court, but their power of the purse and zoning gives them significant control over local department heads. The county superintendent of schools, for example, must have the board's support to raise more money for local schools or to have a site for a new school approved. Other administrative officers commonly found in a county include the county sheriff, medical examiner or coroner, commissioner of health, recorder or registrar of property deeds and clerk (who issues licences and keeps population records). Because they carry out state law on a daily basis, all these officers of county government usually determine what the law means in practice for most residents.

In built-up, heavily populated areas, the states have usually created substitutes for county government. In urban areas, most tasks once performed by counties have been taken over by *municipal governments*: cities, towns, villages, boroughs, or special districts. The meaning of these common terms varies widely, according to the state's definitions. 'City' usually indicates an urban unit of local government with a population of at least several tens of thousands.

Most states define smaller built-up areas as villages, towns, or boroughs, but there are many exceptions to this rule of thumb. In Kansas, a 'city' may have a population of no more than 200 people. In Illinois, the 'village' of Oak Park has a population of about 60,000. The term 'town' also has various meanings in different parts of the country. In New England, much of the land had been divided into towns *before* state governments were established. Counties were mapped out later and never became as important as towns in providing the main services of local government in the New England states.

The confusion of terms is not made easier by the US Census Bureau, which has developed its own vocabulary for analysing units of population. Documents from the federal government often discuss 'metropolitan statistical areas' (MSAs) and 'consolidated metropolitan statistical areas' (CMSAs). These terms are very useful for showing the population concentrations that cross the boundaries of state and local governments. They have often helped demonstrate the need for special districts, but they have no legal status.

Most states have granted urban units of government some form of *home rule*, a legal status amounting to limited local autonomy. This gives them a degree of legislative power to establish local law and usually a municipal charter that functions as a kind of local constitution. Ordinarily this *charter of incorporation* cannot be altered without the approval of local residents. However, if there is disagreement with the state over the limits of the powers granted in the charter, state and federal courts almost always interpret the municipal government's powers narrowly.

The structure of municipal governments varies widely. In most a *mayor* is the chief executive, and the mayor decides policy together with a *city council*. But the amount of power allowed the mayor under the city charter may make him merely a figurehead or the primary decision-maker in local affairs. Since the early 1900s, a large number of cities have experimented with or adopted 'city manager government', in which the city council is the chief political organ of government and a professional administrator, the city manager, carries out its decisions.

The council writes local laws, called *ordinances*, in the policy areas granted it by the state charter. The mayor may or may not have the veto power over such council legislation. As in counties, a range of officials carry out local policy in specific sectors of local government activity. The mayor or city manager usually prepares an annual budget proposal based on these officials' requests for money and available sources of income, and submits it to the council for approval.

Until recently the financing of both county and municipal government came primarily from real estate taxes, but today property taxes supply only about a third of funding. Another third comes from state governments and a tenth from the federal government. Both state and federal financing is generally tied to grants-in-aid programmes that give these other authorities an important role in local decision-making and often aim to alleviate the effects of local poverty or socio-economic inequality. The rest of local funding generally comes from a variety of fees and charges. To make ends meet and launch new programmes, large

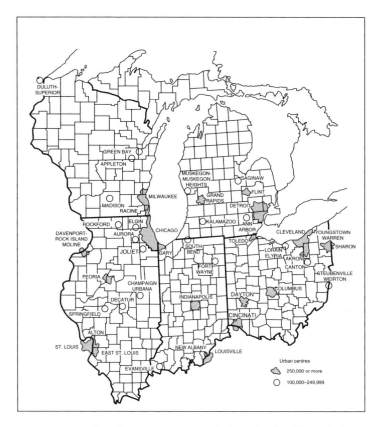

FIGURE 5.1 Local governments and cities in the Great Lakes region

cities have increasingly raised additional revenue through sales and income taxes.

The meanings and powers of local governments vary so much for three main reasons. First, local authorities developed in several different historical periods. Second, these governments reflect the effects of local conditions, such as climate, natural resources and the various population groups that have settled there over time, bringing with them a variety of traditions for handling local affairs. Third and most important, each state is free to give local governments whatever powers and functions it chooses.

177

To citizens, the state's definitions of local governments are very significant. In practice, local governments are delegated the job of providing most of the vital services citizens expect today. And the territory of local governments often overlaps. Towns, villages and cities often have authority inside parts of a county. Therefore, citizens must learn which local government is responsible for each service. Otherwise, it becomes impossible to apply for the local services that state law gives people a right to expect. A citizen cannot even complain effectively about problems with the water supply, garbage removal, school system, and so on without knowing what unit of local government to contact.

There are arguments for and against the great number, variety, and overlapping authority of governments in the US. Some observers maintain that the situation is quite democratic in that it gives many citizens opportunities to participate in government and affect the making of policy. Critics, however, note that voter participation is highest in national elections and lowest in local elections. Some suggest that US voters participate less in *all* elections than people in other developed countries because there are more opportunities for participation than the public has the capacity to focus on.

Another disadvantage often cited is that the complex sharing of powers and functions by all levels of government has become too difficult to disentangle for many people, so that they have great difficulties securing the very services government is instituted to offer. The same complexity makes individuals turn to organized lobbies that have the time and resources to influence policy. Thus, instead of bringing government to the people, some observers complain, the current situation encourages the growth and power of special interest groups.

Benefits of multiple governments are emphasized by other commentators. Some believe state and local governments with significant powers allow the nation to experiment with alternative solutions to problems on a small scale. That is why the states have long been termed '50 laboratories for democracy'. In recent years both states and cities have pioneered new plans for health service management, pollution control and welfare reform. Many, if not most, governmental reforms since late in the last century have been tested out at lower levels of government before being adopted nationally.

Other observers insist that only such varied and overlapping governments can respond to the sharply contrasting conditions that exist in a country as diverse as the US. Smaller units of government can respond more quickly and appropriately to such differences. But local solutions are bound to generate inequality as well, and that is why the federal government must step in to protect minority rights and to even out economic disparities.

EXERCISES

■ **Examine and explain the following terms:**

delegated powers	dual federalism
propositions	concurrent powers
cooperative federalism	special districts
elastic clause	New Federalism
counties	grants-in-aid
state constitutions	municipal governments

■ **Write short essays on the following topics:**

1 Discuss the causes of the transfer of power from the states to the federal government since 1787.

2 Compare and contrast the structure of the state and federal governments.

3 Give a critical evaluation of the use of the initiative and referendum in state government.

4 What are some arguments for and against the election of judges?

5 In your opinion, does the variety of overlapping governments in the US represent a factor for increased democracy?

Chapter 6

Foreign policy

A nation apart: American perceptions of the world

The foreign policy of the US, like that of all nations, has always resulted from a mixture of self-interested concerns and the attempt to act according to commonly held ideals. As in other lands, self-interested concerns have frequently been clothed with the rhetoric of high ideals. Yet a number of factors particular to the US have led many Americans to view their foreign policy as unique. The nation's geographical position is the first of these.

If one looks at the globe as Americans do with the US in the centre, two 'facts' that have coloured much of US foreign policy history seem clear. First, broad oceans separate the Americas from the other continents. Second, most of the world's population and farmland, and *all* of the other great powers, are located in Europe and Asia.

For nearly 300 years the relative physical isolation created by the oceans encouraged those migrating to North America to believe they were leaving behind whatever they disliked in their home societies. Here was the basis for US *isolationism*, the belief that Americans could withdraw from involvement with the rest of the world and focus on domestic (internal) affairs. As the country expanded across the continent, its great size offered another excuse for believing the US 'was world enough' for its inhabitants. Successive transportation, communication and weaponry revolutions, as well as the internationalization of the economy, eventually made isolationism founded on geographical separation an indefensible foreign policy position. But traditional attitudes continue to influence the views of many Americans.

Paradoxically, geographical separation has also contributed to a tradition of national insecurity. Looking outward and seeing the great powers of Europe and Asia on all sides, Americans have periodically felt surrounded. That anxiety resulted in a determination to create national security in the North American quarter of the globe. The US has sought to be the only great power on the continent, worked to drive European powers out, and has striven to control the land, sea, air and finally the space approaches to North America.

The felt need for continental security has been regularly advanced as a justification for territorial expansion through war, purchase, or negotiation. The peoples who first bore the brunt of this preoccupation with security were Native Americans. Success in driving them westward fuelled Americans' ambitions and sense that they had a destiny to 'civilize' the continent. Security was also the rationale for a ring of far-flung military bases and later, of radar stations beyond the country's borders. The US, it should be remembered, entered both World Wars primarily because of threats to its control of the continental sea approaches. President Reagan's strategic defence initiative (or 'star wars' plan) sought to extend this 200-year-old principle of quartersphere security to the space approaches to the US.

A second factor that makes a nation's foreign policy distinct is its size and strength relative to other nations at critical times in its history. For the US, this factor has been most important in relation to the European nations most involved in the settlement of North America. Only in the twentieth century have other nations significantly challenged the Euro-centred character of American foreign relations. This situation, of course, also results from Europe's leadership in world affairs generally during much of American history and the predominance of Europeans among immigrants to the US until recently.

Its history of settlement and immigration is a third major influence on the character of US foreign policy. European colonists and later immigrants have usually had mixed feelings towards their homelands. They emigrated to escape aspects of their home societies but simultaneously harboured deep attachments to the old country. Consequently, immigration has produced both isolationism and internationalism in American foreign policy, as Americans expressed their wish to avoid or cultivate contacts with former homelands. Immigrants brought with them their homelands' history of international relations and often lobbied the American government to fight the old country's enemies and help its friends. Longer-settled Americans have periodically doubted the loyalty of recent immigrants. The US has a history of perceiving threats to internal security from foreign agitators which has caused repression at home and strained its relations abroad.

Before Europeans founded lasting settlements on the East Coast, 'promotional literature' written by European explorers established the idea that 'America' would evolve a new and better phase of civilization. Uncorrupted by the past, America would offer people a chance to start over and do better. From the earliest colonists, migrants to America have wanted to prove advertisements of this 'promise of America' true to justify their decision to emigrate. Thus grew up the rhetoric of *American exceptionalism*. This is the belief (rhetorical or sincere) that America's foreign affairs, unlike those of other nations, are not self-interested but based on a mission to offer the world a better form of society.

The Puritan leader, John Winthrop, had in mind a religiously reformed community that would be a model for change in England when he spoke of a 'City on a Hill that the eyes of all people are upon'. But later American leaders from George Washington to Ronald Reagan who echoed Winthrop's words were confirming Americans' sense that they had a unique mission to set an example for the rest of the world, to export American freedom and democracy and so conduct a foreign policy unlike that of any other nation. Whether real or imagined, American exceptionalism has had palpable effects on the history of US foreign relations.

In reality, the basic concerns that greatly influence the foreign relations of other nations have also played major roles in the formulation of American policy. Of necessity, the US too has protected what it saw as its vital interests: economic success at home and abroad, access to important natural resources, support for its ideological views, respect for its military power, and assistance in times of crisis. In practice, the US has often seemed as concerned with *realpolitik* as other nations.

Major periods and trends in US foreign policy

The first period in the history of American foreign affairs covers the years from 1776 until around 1830. During this time, it can be argued, US policy towards other countries (especially the European powers) resembled that of the newly established Third World nations in the twentieth century. Like those nations, the US tried to steer clear of alliances with great powers and instead strove to keep its neutrality in foreign affairs and to act unilaterally. Fear of becoming a pawn of British or French schemes for expanded international power was the mainspring of American policy in this period.

Around 1800, the US was a political and economic midget. It was hemmed in by British colonies to the North, French Louisiana in the west, and in the south by the rich and powerful Spanish Empire that included Florida and today's Southwest. During the colonial period, every war between the European powers had its American phase, and the new nation could not afford to have that pattern continue if it was to stabilize its political institutions and economy. Thus the US for many years stayed aloof from the Napoleonic Wars and refused to become involved in the French Revolution, even though the French had been an indispensable ally in the War for Independence from Britain.

After serving as the nation's first President, George Washington stated the existing policy in general terms in his so-called *Farewell Address* (1796). Its main principle consisted of avoiding political and military alliances while cultivating trading relations with other countries. President Washington also advised the nation to remember its uniqueness and resulting need for unilateral action. When the US strayed from these principles by entering the Napoleonic Wars on the side of France in 1812, the results were disastrous. British forces burned Washington, DC; the US won not a single important victory; and the cost was enormous. After that object lesson, the core ideas of the Address remained a pillar of American foreign policy until after the Second World War.

185

The *Alien and Sedition Acts* (1798) were more evidence of the American fear of becoming a pawn of European powers. These laws, however, were directed against foreign subversives who might undermine the nation from within. Fear of French sympathizers inspired the Acts, but they allowed the President and courts to fine, imprison, or deport any foreigner who seemed a danger to national security. The Acts were an early sign of deep insecurities about the loyalties of newcomers in a nation of immigrants.

The foreign policy statement from the early period that contributed most to the development of later policy was the *Monroe Doctrine*. Between 1800 and the 1820s, many Spanish colonies in Central and South America rebelled and declared their independence. The US wanted to recognize these new nations but feared conflict with Spain and the possibility that Britain or France would intervene and return them to Spanish control. America was too weak to prevent European interference in Latin America, but it formally expressed its opposition to outside meddling in their affairs through the Monroe Doctrine.

The Doctrine can be reduced to three basic principles. The first (called non-colonization) is that the US opposed any new colonies in the Americas. The second (non-intervention) demanded that the European powers remain uninvolved in the affairs of New World nations. In return for Europe's compliance with these rules, the US would observe a third principle (non-interference) that amounted to accepting the presence of the remaining European colonies in the Americas and keeping aloof from European affairs. The US could not enforce any of these principles until around 1900, when it had constructed a powerful navy. Until then, the British navy prevented other European nations from violating the Doctrine, and opened Latin America for British economic influence.

The Monroe Doctrine transformed American neutrality into isolationism and combined it with the country's sense of having a special mission in the world. The Americas were declared the US's exclusive sphere of interest. European-style kingdoms and Old World politics were to have no place in the hemisphere, so that only the US's brand of republican government would influence Latin America. In short, the Doctrine expressed the mixture of idealism and ideological domination that was to become typical of US relations with Latin America.

Expansionism

The second period of American foreign policy overlaps with the first but extends into the early years of the twentieth century. During this time, the US was preoccupied with developments that Americans often viewed as internal affairs: the settlement of a frontier that constantly moved further west; the struggle over whether slavery should be extended into new states or abolished; the effort to construct transportation systems to bind the continent together and ease the exploitation of its resources. Because all these processes consisted of or were related to territorial expansion, they were also central to the conduct of foreign affairs.

Early in the nineteenth century, the US roughly tripled its territory through treaty and purchase. Agreements with Britain added the land between the Appalachians and the Mississippi River, the northern section of Maine, and parts of Minnesota and the Dakotas. America bought Florida from Spain, and France offered the US the land from the Mississippi to the Rocky Mountains in the Louisiana Purchase. Most Americans viewed these as legal and unaggressive ways to consolidate US territory and minimize the dangers of European interference. It was assumed that the European powers could legally transfer hegemony over the Native Americans with the right to their homelands. In reality, much of American foreign policy up to about 1900 consisted of war and treaty negotiations with these native peoples.

Such enormous increases in the country's size inspired the growth of an intense national pride. The feats of frontier settlers evolved into myth and a set of idealized character traits. The farther west people and institutions were, the more truly American they appeared in the popular mind. Some advocates of expansion emphasized that only a nation spanning the continent could effectively isolate itself from external threats. Others told themselves that they were extending the benefits of democracy to less advanced peoples. Forthrightly racist expansionists said the red and brown peoples were inferior and therefore had to be confined, conquered, or at least dominated.

By the 1840s, the idea of America's expansion to the Pacific was being popularized as the nation's *manifest destiny* (its apparently inevitable, divinely determined fate). Since it was obviously meant to be, that expansion was also right, argued the expansionists. 'Oregon fever' sent thousands trekking across the plains and mountains. Facing threats of armed conflict, Britain gave up its claims to the present-day Pacific Northwest and parts of the Mountain States in border negotiations.

Americans were more militantly aggressive towards Mexico. American settlers seized power in Texas and asked that the area be annexed to the US. When the Texas border with Mexico was disputed in 1846, the US offered to buy the territory in question but took the first excuse to take it by war after Mexico refused to sell. But expansion in the Southwest aroused strong opposition, expecially in New England, where many argued against acquiring a slave-owning republic and endangering the lives of US troops to make more territory available for slavery. So Texans waited ten years for annexation and the Mexican War was the source of violent congressional debate. In 1848, however, the treaty at its end added the Southwest, California, and most of the southern Mountain States to US territory.

In the decades after the Civil War, expansionists gained support from several sources. Businessmen and farmers demanded the opening of new markets abroad to prevent overproduction from causing economic depression at home. Military strategists pointed out that a strong navy and overseas bases were necessary to keep these markets open and protect US shipping. Religious leaders fused the ideas of manifest destiny and the 'White man's burden' to support overseas missions and the 'civilizing' of foreign peoples. Nationalists, now using the language of Social Darwinism, claimed Americans were surely the fittest to survive in the international competition for territory and influence. When the federal government declared the western frontier closed in 1890, some people feared that Americans would lose their strength and endurance if they did not find frontiers abroad.

Buoyed up on this wave of public opinion, US foreign policy became territorially and economically imperialist around the turn of the century. That is to say, America imposed its control on overseas peoples both formally (through colonization, annexation and military occupation) and informally (through military threats, economic domination and political subversion). In 1898 the US declared war on Spain as an imperialist power that was stifling Cuban freedom. Yet, having won that 'splendid little war' (as the American Secretary of State called it), the US acquired economic control over Cuba and the right to intervene in its affairs. It also acquired (as colonies) Puerto Rico, Guam Island and the Philippine Islands, where Filipino nationalists fought a bloody campaign for independence from the US.

American trade expanded rapidly, especially in Asia and Latin America. Hawaii, Samoa and Wake Island were annexed and served as suitable bases for further economic expansion eastward. In an effort to protect its growing trade in China, the US contributed troops to an alliance of European powers that put down a Chinese rebellion. It also announced the *Open Door policy* (which demanded equal access to Chinese markets) to counter the Europeans' claim to exclusive trade rights in China. In Latin America, President Theodore Roosevelt instigated and ensured the success of a Panamanian revolt against Columbia in 1903 in order to secure the right to build and control the Panama Canal. A year later he announced the revision of the Monroe Doctrine known as the *Roosevelt Corollary*. According to the Corollary, the US was justified in intervening in the internal affairs of Latin-American nations if their politics or economies became unstable. The European powers, however, were again warned that America would not passively permit their intervention in the Western Hemisphere. Between 1900 and 1917, the US intervened in six different Latin-American countries.

Critics known as the 'anti-imperialists' actively opposed overseas expansion. As a result of their efforts, for example, Cuba was not annexed and the Philippines were promised their freedom as early as 1916 (although the promise was not kept until 1934). Some anti-imperialists claimed that sending US military forces abroad for intervention or colonization upset the balance of power in foreign policy between the President and Congress by increasing his importance as commander-in-chief.

Other opponents of imperialism stressed that America could gain access to foreign markets without oppressing other peoples. Prominent leaders of the Progressive Movement protested that America ought to clean up its political corruption and inequalities at home instead of exhausting its energies abroad. Both traditionalists and the Progressives also asked Americans to remember their historic commitment to self-determination in the Declaration of Independence.

1914–45: isolationism and internationalism

For nearly three years the US maintained the fiction that the First World War was a European conflict that did not concern America. That was the neutral pose that President Woodrow Wilson held because it reflected the traditional isolationist views of the US electorate. But neutrality was impossible to preserve for three reasons. Wilson, along with many other US politicians, felt strong sympathies for the Allies. The majority of Americans shared his belief in loyalty to Anglo-American traditions, while vocal German-American and Irish-American minorities opposed an alliance with Britain. Finally, the US economy depended on trade with the warring nations, who each tried to prevent goods from reaching its enemy.

Most Americans had taken sides but were still reluctant to commit their fortunes and lives to intervention. Both Wilson and the public needed to believe they were entering the war for high moral reasons rather than the country's selfish economic interests. Some two months before the US declared war, Wilson provided that rationale in his famous *Fourteen Points*, which appealed to the tradition of the American mission to create a new world order.

The essential elements of the Fourteen Points can be reduced to three major categories. The first was all nations' right to self-determination. National boundaries were to be redrawn after the war so that every 'people' could freely determine whether it wished to be an independent country. The principle of self-determination amounted to a vague plan for popular referenda on ethnic nationhood (in Europe, of course) with no formula for determining how this would be implemented. The second category was a general set of principles for governing international conduct after the war. Among the main principles included were free trade, freedom of the seas, global disarmament and the outlawing of secret alliances. The remaining points described Wilson's proposal for a League of Nations that would put self-determination and the other principles into effect. Except for the League, most of the points were cornerstones of America's traditional rhetoric if not of its practical policy.

The Fourteen Points constituted Wilson's public justification for participating in the war, and were but one set of conditions meant to limit US involvement. American troops remained separate from the Allied armies and fought under American commanders. Wilson called the US an 'associate' rather than an ally to emphasize that it was in an emergency coalition, not a lasting alliance (and therefore remained true to the injunction against such alliances in Washington's Farewell Address).

When it finally came, American participation in the war was decisive but very limited. Significant numbers of American troops fought in Europe only during the last eight months of the war. About 110,000 US soldiers died in that time, compared to the 900,000 British, 1.4 million French, and almost 2 million German troops who died in four years.

The conditions on American aid to the Allied war effort, combined with the Allies' very different experience with a long and destructive conflict, made the US position seem morally arrogant. Although America claimed to be materially disinterested, its call for freedom of the seas and free trade would benefit the US most since its industrial plant was booming and its fleet was the least damaged. The Allies wanted revenge and to make Germany pay for war damages. They rejected all the Fourteen Points but the League.

The US Senate failed to ratify the treaty Wilson brought home from the Paris peace conference. Many Senators rejected the idea of the League because they were unwilling to bind the US to membership in a permanent international alliance. The foreign policy-makers who took over after Wilson were not isolationists. Rather, they wanted to design safeguards for peace that would not limit America's traditional freedom to act unilaterally in world affairs. In 1921, the US negotiated separate treaties with the defeated Central Powers. The League was formed but, without US participation, it never became an effective international force.

During the rest of the 1920s, US foreign policy centred on eliminating obstacles to American trade. International peace and stability were essential largely so that, once established, US trade would remain free of interference. Many Americans also believed free trade fostered peace by making nations more open and familiar with each other. Moreover, the US called for arms reductions and the destruction of some 2 million tons of navy ships. It reaffirmed and extended the Open Door policy. Finally, it initiated the Kellogg-Briand Pact in 1928 under which sixty-two nations signed a pledge not to use war as an instrument of national policy. Critics called this pact and others the US entered at the time, a 'paper peace' since it depended on voluntary compliance alone.

In the 1930s, however, this limited internationalism was replaced by isolationism. As the German war machine marched into country after country and the rest of Europe rearmed, American voters made it clear that their last wish was to be dragged into another 'Old World' war. Over four-fifths of the people surveyed in a Gallup poll in March of 1941 were opposed to US intervention. About that time, President Franklin Roosevelt had won congressional approval for the *Lend-Lease Act*, a disguised give-away plan he invented because domestic opposition to open aid to the Allies was massive. Under Lend-Lease, the President could sell, but also let the Allies borrow or lease, war material on the promise that it would be returned after the war.

The Japanese surprise attack on Pearl Harbor on 7 December 1941 accomplished overnight what Roosevelt could not in years of effort: it united the American people in a fervent commitment to war. In a few days Congress had declared war on all the Axis powers and announced its support of the Allies. Almost as quickly, Roosevelt constructed a vision of a new world order for the post-war period. Determined to succeed where Wilson had failed, Roosevelt called the Allies the 'United Nations' almost from the start. He also ensured that American troops were integrated with those of Britain and France. Joint command and cooperation, he had decided, would prevent complaints about American arrogance.

Roosevelt's vision for world order after the war was expressed in his so-called Four Freedoms and proposal for the United Nations (UN). The Four Freedoms were cleansed of advantages to US business because they were rights contained in the American Bill of Rights (freedom of religion, speech and expression) or broad extensions of those, such as freedom from want and fear, that amount to a version of the American dream. The UN was to help make the Four Freedoms realities. A number of the UN's features were intended to make it a more effective organization than the League had been. Unlike its predecessor, the UN can take preventive action, ask members to contribute troops to an international 'peace-keeping' force, and act against aggressors (whether or not they are members) without approval from all its members.

At the Yalta Conference in February 1945 Roosevelt won Stalin's and Churchill's support for the UN. On other important issues, the results of the Conference were much less clear. Roosevelt could not convince the other leaders to give up the concept of spheres of influence in Europe. However, he thought they had agreed to the establishment of democratic governments, under no other nation's direct control, in Eastern Europe. All three leaders agreed that post-war Germany should not again quickly become a military power, but they could not resolve their differences on how to prevent that from happening. They therefore had to put off specific plans for dealing with post-war Germany.

The Cold War Era: from 1946 to the present

As Soviet forces set up pro-communist governments in Eastern Europe in the weeks after the Yalta Conference, Roosevelt discovered how differently he and Stalin had interpreted its results. Before he could establish a policy to deal with the new situation, Roosevelt died of a sudden heart attack. In August 1945 President Truman ordered the dropping of atomic bombs on Hiroshima and Nagasaki. He justified the mass slaughter of civilians by saying the attack would save many other lives (both American and Japanese) because it would bring the war to a rapid close without an invasion of the Japanese home islands. The chain of events dividing the globe into the opposing blocs of the Cold War was under way. A year later Churchill said an 'iron curtain' existed between Soviet-controlled Eastern Europe and Western Europe with its American ally.

As the former allies struggled to influence the governments emerging on the borders of the Soviet Union after the war, American policy-makers became convinced that the Soviets were fanatically intent on establishing communist regimes around the world. In 1947 President Truman announced what became known as the *Truman Doctrine* in a speech to Congress during which he asked for funds to fight communist aggression in Turkey and Greece.

According to the Doctrine, the US had to follow a policy of *containment* to prevent communist expansion anywhere in the world. The Soviet ideology, inherently a threat to the US and to democratic institutions, was being spread through internal subversion as well as outside pressure. In a 'domino effect', as it was called, one nation after another would fall to Soviet domination unless the US led the 'free world' by actively intervening to prevent it. Thus the stage was set for direct American involvement in internal conflicts and wars, not only in Latin America (where the Roosevelt Corollary justified intervention) but around the world. Containment became the cornerstone of American foreign policy throughout the Cold War. Pursuing containment protected and expanded US interests abroad and its implementation contributed to the formulation of other foreign policy initiatives.

In the late 1940s the US took steps to meet the communist threat and in the process revolutionized its foreign policy. It kept its military forces near wartime levels, extending mandatory military service into peacetime and continuing its military build-up. When the Soviets rejected international inspection plans to enforce a ban on nuclear weapons, the US reacted by expanding atomic research and giving nuclear weapons a central place in its arsenal. The *National Security Act* of 1947 centralized control over all branches of the military in a new Department of Defense and created the National Security Council (NSC) and the Central Intelligence Agency (CIA).

In a sense, the Act put the country in a state of permanent military readiness by transferring enlarged powers over defence to the President and making it easier for him to take aggressive action internationally without a declaration of war. By 1950 a NSC report known as *NSC-68* defined the US stance: more than ever, America had an important mission in the world. On the US lay the responsibility to lead the free world. To that end, the nation had to quadruple its military budget so that it could take the initiative in containing communism.

Meanwhile, Secretary of State George Marshall became convinced that the US ought to fund the economic revival of Europe. The motives for the so-called *Marshall Plan* were mixed. Humanitarian concerns and ethnic ties played important roles in congressional and public approval of the Plan. Economic concerns also inspired support. Assisting Europe could absorb surpluses that threatened to cause an economic recession in the US, and a revitalized Europe would provide markets for American goods. Finally, it was believed that prosperous economies would strengthen European resistance to communism and thus contribute to the goal of containment. Approximately 15 billion dollars were spent on this programme while it was in effect from 1948 to 1951.

The vision of one world united through the Four Freedoms faded and was replaced by the sense that the world consisted of two warring camps threatening each other with nuclear destruction. Therefore, the United States reversed its historic refusal to form permanent military alliances. The first of these, the Organization of American States (OAS), was founded in 1948, and was followed by the North Atlantic Treaty Organization (NATO) in 1950 and similar mutual defence pacts that eventually covered the globe. Commitment to internationalism had irreversibly replaced the country's traditional isolationism.

When Soviet troops entered Hungary in 1956 and crushed its revolt against Soviet domination, Hungarian Americans protested strongly. President Eisenhower announced that the United States would not intervene in their homeland, however, because the Truman Doctrine did not extend to nations within the Warsaw Pact (the Eastern European–Soviet alliance organized as a counterforce to NATO). In 1968 when the Soviet Union and Warsaw Pact nations put down a popular revolt in Czechoslovakia, the US followed the same policy of non-involvement.

In the early 1950s, the fear of communism set the stage for Senator Joseph McCarthy's hunt for Americans who were involved in 'un-American activities' as spies or tools of the Soviets. In a general sense, 'McCarthyism' was nothing new, although his blatant accusations against government officials were unprecedented. Fear of communist influence and bolshevik immigrants had appeared in the 'Red Scare' of the 1920s and was part of the old distrust of the foreign that stretched, in some form, all the way back to the Alien and Sedition Acts. McCarthy and his supporters did not create the wave of anti-communist hysteria. They merely exploited the public anxieties built up by the Cold War and the threat of nuclear destruction.

The Central Intelligence Agency's covert involvement in the Bay of Pigs affair and the Cuban Missile Crisis raised Cold War tensions to new heights. However, after the Missile Crisis, relations between the two superpowers began to improve. Developments furthering this trend included the Nuclear Test Ban Treaty of 1963 and the decision that neither superpower would intervene in the Israeli–Arab war. In the 1970s President Nixon initiated the policy known as *détente* (peaceful coexistence) and the gradual reduction of nuclear arsenals that later Presidents continued. Despite unstable periods in the superpowers' relationship in the decades to come, a similar understanding between the superpowers was reached during the Gulf War almost thirty years later in 1991, when both countries condemned the Iraqi occupation of Kuwait in the United Nations and joined in contributing forces to drive President Hussein's troops back into Iraq.

In Asia the United States committed itself to containing communism in Korea, Vietnam, Cambodia and Laos. The Vietnam War, the first the US had lost since the War of 1812, produced massive anti-war protests at home and anti-American demonstrations abroad. The conduct of the war demoralized the younger generation at home as well as US combat troops. The cost of the war drained funds from President Johnson's programmes to deal with domestic poverty and inequality. The frustrations of trying to win a 'limited war' led President Nixon to authorize the secret bombing of Laos and Cambodia without congressional approval.

The Vietnam War became a traumatic experience for the American people, and has therefore coloured later involvement in other countries. During the Gulf War, the US chose to act in a multinational coalition under the auspices of the UN, even though Americans constituted the largest group of participants. Low-intensity warfare and short engagements executed with greater precision through technological weaponry have replaced the prolonged military engagement of the Korean and Vietnam Wars, and form part of America's foreign policy goals today.

An important turning point in US foreign relations came when President Nixon opened talks with the leaders of mainland China, taking advantage of a split between China and the Soviet Union, and thus reduced the apparent threat of communism. In the following years American policy was less concerned with military control, and especially since the Carter presidency, more emphasis has been put on supporting human rights in other countries. This angered the Soviets, as stories of dissidents confined in psychiatric 'hospitals' became well known through the work of Alexander Solzhenitsyn. In the 1970s the relationship between the two powers grew more tense as a result.

But the US–Soviet relationship has gone through several pendulum swings. After proclaiming strong opposition to the communists' 'evil empire', President Reagan too pursued peaceful coexistence. He accepted friendly overtures from the general secretary of the Communist Party, Mikhail Gorbachev, which led to disarmament treaties and agreements on increasing trade and cultural relations under President Bush. In 1992, however, due to internal ethnic conflicts, the Soviet Union split into a loose federation of republics. The symbol of a divided Europe, the Berlin Wall, was torn down by cheering crowds of people from both sides in November of 1989, and in the following summer the two Germanies were reunited by a treaty signed by the four allies from the Second World War. The German issue had been one that the two world leaders had never before been able to settle in their talks. On the Asian scene, President Reagan extended the *détente* policy of previous Presidents when he signed a series of agreements with the People's Republic of China in 1984.

American policy towards Latin America has varied with the temperature of the Cold War to a degree, but the commitment to containment has generally led to US support for right-wing regimes in America's 'backyard', where apparent stability has often seemed more vital than human rights. In that frame of mind, in the 1980s the Reagan administration refused to stop giving the right-wing Contra rebels aid in their guerrilla war against the Sandinista government of Nicaragua when Congress cut off funding for the Contras. The Iran–Contras scandal revealed that Oliver North and other administration officials had secretly sold weapons to Iran and used the profits to aid the Contras, in direct contradiction of congressional policy and the administration's public statements. For some commentators, the lesson seemed to be that the Cold War had produced an 'imperial presidency' that undermined the balance of power between the branches of government.

Today the political picture is uncertain. For while most nations in Western Europe have joined the European Union (EU) and are less dependent on America for their trade and military needs, the newly independent Eastern European countries are

PLATE 6.1   President Clinton with Yitzhak Rabin and Yasser Arafat at the signing of the Middle East Accord   *(Associated Press)*

knocking on the doors of NATO and the EU, and there have been repeated military conflicts within the Russian federation and newly independent neighbouring nations. It may seem appropriate for the United States and Western Europe to aid these poorer nations with their reconstruction, just as the Marshall Plan helped war-torn Western Europe, but how to do so without interfering too much in their internal affairs, or provoking Russia (which opposes their entry into NATO), is as yet unclear. The initial attempt to do this has come through the loose cooperation of the Partnership for Peace.

In the post-Cold War era, the first Clinton administration lacked direction until near its end, according to many critics. However, the President successfully pursued one foreign policy goal with considerable bipartisan support. In the 1992 election campaign, he promised to make foreign policy an extension of efforts to strengthen the domestic economy by increasing the opportunities for free trade. By 1995 both the North American Free Trade Agreement (NAFTA), between Canada, Mexico and the US and the Uruguay General Agreement on Tariffs and Trade (GATT) had been ratified by the Senate. The President has visited both Japan and China, promoting more open and fair trade and granting China most favoured nation trade status despite its human rights abuses.

At the beginning of the second Clinton administration, it seems probable that the President will continue to give consider-able responsibility to his Secretary of State. After Warren Christopher's retirement, the President appointed Madeleine Albright, US Ambassador to the UN and as such, already a member of his foreign policy 'team'. Albright is the first woman to hold the office and an ardent internationalist who argued for the use of force in international conflicts more than most cabinet members during Clinton's first term. Through her, Clinton will very likely continue the administration's general policies of open trade, reluctant intervention for humanitarian aid and strategic stability (as in Bosnia), efforts to contain the spread of nuclear weapons capacity (as in North Korea), and international cooper-ation through many alliances, trade organizations and the UN (where Albright led campaigns to oust Secretary General Boutros Boutros-Ghali and greatly reduce the organization's bureaucracy).

The foreign policy establishment debate

The governmental structures of the US are yet another factor that make the formulation and conduct of American foreign affairs distinctive. The Constitution's system of checks and balances requires the executive and legislative branches to share responsibility for the nation's relations with other countries. The nature of these branches, moreover, has resulted in opportunities for other institutions and groups to develop ways of influencing foreign policy decision-making. As a result, the official and unofficial groups that play a part in the foreign policy establishment are many and varied. There are several competing centres of power whose importance changes over time and according to the situation.

During the nation's history, the balance of power between the two branches over foreign policy has shifted. Congress was the dominant partner for most of the nineteenth century, except for the Civil War years. In the twentieth century, the President grew increasingly dominant until the US was defeated in the Vietnam War. The consensus of opinion is that the shift towards executive power resulted from the near constant international crises involving the US in the 1900s.

The President has several powers that make him the single most important figure in US foreign policy today. Each of these, however, is shared with other groups. He is the commander-in-chief, but with few exceptions has been a civilian with very limited military experience. He therefore depends on the advice of the leaders of the armed forces and other military experts to meet his responsibility for national security. Even if the President is convinced that the vital interests or territory of the US are seriously threatened, he cannot declare war. Only Congress can do that, and since the Second World War, it has been especially reluctant to do so. Consequently, Presidents have increasingly tried (rather successfully) to commit the nation to military action in other ways when they have perceived crises involving national security.

As the chief executive, one of the President's primary duties is to carry out foreign policy. But the Constitution requires the approval of both houses of Congress for the governmental expenditures that all foreign policy initiatives depend on. Not only must the President win majorities for his policies, therefore, but he can expect military leaders and bureaucrats to lobby Congress in favour of competing programmes. Further, congressional involvement does not stop there. The legislature often exercises its investigatory power to evaluate whether money is being spent as Acts of Congress stipulated and stops funding or repeals those Acts if it is dissatisfied.

The more specific foreign policy powers of the President are also limited. No other official can nominate people to ambassadorial and other high-level positions in the American foreign service, but all such appointments must be approved by a majority in the Senate. He alone can negotiate treaties with other governments, but all treaties must be ratified by an extraordinary majority (two-thirds) in the Senate. Approval from so many Senators has often seemed doubtful, so that Presidents have increasingly depended on more informal executive agreements.

Two important foreign policy roles of the President, acting as chief diplomat and ceremonial head of state, have grown greatly in importance since the beginning of high-speed air travel, electronic communication and supersonic weaponry. The possibility for extensive personal diplomacy between world leaders and the media attention it commands have made the President the visible maker of foreign policy more than ever before. During the Cold War, the threat of nuclear destruction in minutes made the greater speed of executive action a convincing argument for presidential control of foreign affairs.

The organization of the congressional and executive institutions in the foreign policy establishment create opportunities for many interest groups to exercise influence. Each chamber of Congress has a permanent committee that specializes in foreign policy with subcommittees to deal with all the major regions of the world and important international issues. Both chambers have, in addition, several other committees (with their subcommittees) that are involved in foreign policy decisions, such as the armed services, energy, commerce and intelligence committees.

The committee system makes identifying the members whom groups need to influence easier. Committee hearings during the drafting of laws or investigation of foreign affairs offer policy experts and interest groups a public platform for their views. Ethnic groups put pressure on subcommittees that recommend policy regarding their homelands. Lobbyists representing the particular economic interests of states and districts try to sway trade policy in their favour through the committees. Research institutions apply to committees for funding and influence members with their views on foreign policy issues. The national media publicize all these opinions and alternative courses of action along with the evaluations of prominent journalists.

Executive branch structures for handling foreign policy offer similar opportunities for lobbying. The Defense and State Departments, like Congress, are organized into groups of specialists that focus on particular issues of international affairs or areas of the world. These groups formulate policy suggestions that they send through bureaucratic channels to the Secretary of State or of Defense, who forwards them to the President and Congress. Although the President usually decides on major policy concerns, department bureaucrats manage the daily implementation of policy. They can also hold investigative hearings. For these reasons, the full range of pressure groups and members of Congress try to catch the ear of influential officials in the State and Defense Departments.

There has long been debate about the foreign policy establishment. According to some critics, deliberation and lobbying in roughly parallel structures in Congress and the Departments produce unnecessary confusion over policy alternatives. These observers note that the foreign policy establishment has yet another component, the personal advisers and agencies in the Executive Office of the President. The President's National Security Advisor, the National Security Agency (NSA) and the Central Intelligence Agency (CIA) often evolve a third set of priorities and policies.

'Too many cooks spoil the broth', say some. Important information gets lost in the bureaucratic maze and does not reach the Department Secretaries or the President or is delayed. Unable to sort out all the views offered, the President depends too much on personal advisers who are not accountable to the electorate. More seriously, the overlapping foreign policy establishment gives conflicting signals. It also reaches decisions so slowly that events outrun it, and US foreign policy is frequently reactive (inconsistent and piecemeal responses instead of elements in a coherent plan).

Other commentators take a more positive view of having multiple centres of policy formation. In a diverse, multi-ethnic country, they say, only a system with so many opportunities for lobbying can produce the compromise and consensus on foreign policy needed for public support. More information is likely to be considered and critical facts are more rather than less likely to percolate up to the President in such a system, its supporters claim. The issues and alternatives are at least thoroughly discussed. Most important, policy changes tend to come in incremental steps instead of wide swings, which produces greater stability in the country's foreign affairs. In historical crises, according to supporters of the *status quo*, the established structures have functioned well and taken decisive action with reasonable speed. The debate continues and polls indicate that public support for the foreign policy establishment varies with the issue and situation involved.

■ **Examine and explain the following terms:**

isolationism

Washington's Farewell Address

Monroe Doctrine

manifest destiny

Roosevelt Corollary

Fourteen Points

Four Freedoms

Truman Doctrine

Marshall Plan

Vietnam War

Gulf War

post-Cold War era

exceptionalism

Alien and Sedition Acts

expansionism

imperialism

anti-imperialists

limited internationalism

Yalta Conference

National Security Act

McCarthyism

détente

Iran–Contras scandal

■ **Write short essays on the following topics:**

1   Critically evaluate the degree to which US foreign policy is (or has been) distinct from that of other nations.

2   Summarize what you think are the important historical trends and turning points in the evolution of America's relations with the rest of the world.

3   Critically evaluate the significant changes in US foreign policy from 1945 to the present.

4   Describe the institutional structures in America's foreign policy establishment and critically discuss how well they serve as a basis for the formulation of the nation's foreign policy.

The legal system

THE LEGAL SYSTEM PLAYS A CENTRAL ROLE on the public and private levels of American society, to a greater extent perhaps than in other countries. The law is regarded very much as part of daily life and not as a remote abstraction. Legal issues and court decisions are matters of widespread interest and concern. They are also closely intertwined with the nation's political, social and economic life. Americans make active use of their legal system and are a litigious people. They are accustomed to seeking redress from the courts and have over 650,000 lawyers and judges to evaluate their cases.

There are several reasons for this cultural behaviour. First, active participation in the legal process derives from a colonial and frontier tradition of individualism in which Americans defended their own interests and rights. But legal actions can also result from group causes. The War for Independence started largely from collective legal complaints by colonists against British rule and showed that law could potentially protect both individuals and communities against oppression. However, there can also be a tension between individualistic and communal values in US society.

Second, public and private life is influenced by, and stresses a constitutionalism which stems from, the US Constitution and the later Bill of Rights (1789). These legal and political documents try to create a framework for the good society. They guarantee civil rights and freedoms for citizens and stipulate a separation of powers between an independent judiciary and the other branches of government. Americans' expectations of social and political justice thus depend, ideally and practically, on the safeguards in these documents.

Third, such constitutional features are founded on a tradition of legalism (the belief that conflicts can in fact be legally resolved) which also stems from colonial times. Civil disputes between citizens, institutions, groups and branches of government, as well as criminal cases have to be legally decided by the federal and state court systems.

Issues of justice and rights are a fundamental concern in Americans' lives. They are prepared to go to the courts for satisfaction if they feel that their civil rights have been infringed by federal or state governments, doctors, hospitals, airlines, employers, the educational system, manufacturers, commercial companies, or their neighbours. Since the US suffers from considerable crime and violence, the criminal aspect of the law also affects whole communities, particularly in the big cities, and has to be resolved by the legal system.

A very large number of civil and criminal cases are handled annually by the courts. Most are determined at state and local (rather than federal) levels. Americans have a constitutional right to have their cases quickly determined in a public trial by an impartial judge or jury (a selected number of citizens who decide the facts in court cases).

However, despite a concern with legal justice and claims that US society is humane and moral, law does not always imply justice. The ideal may not be matched by the reality, raising questions about delays and the quality of the legal system. The crucial question is one of access to the courts and some individuals may not succeed in gaining this. Access depends upon the validity and nature of a case, wealth and the level of court involved.

Critics argue that the criminal and civil systems and some police forces must be reformed and corruption removed; that the disadvantaged and poor do not receive satisfaction despite the existence of legal aid (federal or state help to those unable to afford legal fees); that the legal system is biased towards the powerful and the wealthy; and that high legal costs are an obstacle to litigants seeking help.

The law can be brought into disrepute by dubious defence procedures in both criminal and civil cases; by prosecution conduct and incompetence; by plea bargaining (which allows an accused person or defendant to avoid the heaviest criminal and civil penalties); by contingency fees (which specify payment to lawyers on the basis of results); by juries which may allegedly be biased on racial, social or political grounds; and by police procedures and conduct. The question of victims' rights and compensation has also become a contentious issue.

Legal history

The legal system is partly founded on customs brought to the US by European colonists. Many of these were English, such as the common law (judge-made case law), statutes (royal and parliamentary Acts) and the role of judges (who developed from being royal servants to independent officials). Such elements have been adapted to evolving and distinctively American features like the US Constitution, the relationship between state and federal government and the importance of judicial review (the power of superior federal and state courts to invalidate laws and actions that violate the Constitution).

When the British colonized parts of North America in the seventeenth century, the common law, statute law and judges were adopted by some colonies. But other English and European settlers had left their homelands to avoid oppressive institutions and to create a fairer and freer society. They rejected the common law and created a code system of simple rules, which started in the Massachusetts Bay Colony in 1634.

However, as life stabilized in the colonies and the population grew, such codes were insufficient to govern a more complex society; thus, English legal structures were increasingly acceptable. Significantly, colonists in pre-Independence America protested strongly that the British Crown had denied them their traditional common law rights and the Declaration of Independence (1776) contained many legal grievances.

After the War for Independence, the thirteen original states adopted the common law as the basis of their legal systems. However, as some states contained non-English settlers such as the Dutch and Swedes, the common law had to accommodate other legal customs. The same process recurred later when the US incorporated territories like California (1850). Each state thus interpreted and developed the common law in independent ways. But when the US purchased Louisiana (1803) with its existing French legal system, the common law was not adopted.

The War for Independence also involved questions about the independent role of state governments. Federal government developed later, leading to a division of authority between states and federal government. This historical process means that most laws which directly affect people today operate at the state and local level. The fifty states have their own legal systems; create their own laws in their own legislatures; and have their own police forces and law courts. All (except Louisiana) apply their version of the common law and most lawyers are qualified to practise in only one state.

Although anti-British feeling after independence led to criticism of the common law, lawyers and judges, this was reduced by new political factors. In 1787, delegates from the thirteen states at the Constitutional Convention in Philadelphia framed a Constitution for the US, which became law in 1788. This stipulated that, while individual states remained as sovereign political entities, a new federal union of the states was also sovereign in its own sphere of competence.

Article III of the Constitution created a third branch of government, the independent federal judiciary: 'The judicial power of the United States shall be vested in one Supreme Court and in such inferior courts as the Congress may from time to time ordain and establish.' The founders of the US considered the judiciary to be the weakest branch of government, restricted to applying the Constitution and the laws, but it later developed a central importance.

The Judiciary Act (1789) created new federal courts, which now have two roles: they interpret the meaning of laws and administrative acts (statutory construction) and examine any law or administrative action by national or state authorities in the light of the US Constitution (judicial review). The power of judicial review was initially contested by states' rights activists, but it was finally conceded and was an important factor in establishing a united nation.

The result of these historical developments was a legal organization for the whole country and authority was divided between state and federal courts. The states still had their own courts, common law, constitutions and statutes. Matters of state law involving citizens of a state were under the jurisdiction of the state court system. But if a state court decision violated federal laws, or involved a federal question, the US Supreme Court could ultimately review that decision and overturn it. This provided for a common jurisdiction in the resolution of some federal and state matters which could be followed from local courts to the Supreme Court. US federal laws and the Constitution thus have (in theory) a uniform application throughout the country.

The independence and status of the judiciary were strengthened over time. It is now regarded as an essential safeguard against abuse by the executive and legislative branches. Federal judges are appointed by the President, subject to approval by the Senate. There are some 900 of them who serve until retirement and who can only be removed for gross misconduct. All other judges are appointed by methods peculiar to individual states or may be elected by voters.

One further historical factor increased the standing of the judiciary and the courts. The initial Constitution contained few rights for individual citizens. Consequently, a Bill of Rights in the form of ten Amendments was voted by Congress in its first session (1789) and ratified by the states in 1791. But such rights only applied at the federal level until the 1920s. The Bill of Rights (and later Amendments) gives protection to individual citizens and guards them against imprisonment without just cause, excessive fines, or other forms of oppression. However, the courts still have to interpret these amendments in individual court cases.

Two other developments have added to the central place of law in US society. First, Congress (although granted only limited power by the Constitution) has regulated American life in many ways through successive Interstate Commerce Acts and other legislation. The authority to 'regulate commerce among the several States' (the commerce clause) and the power to write all laws 'necessary and proper' to carry out its other powers have allowed Congress to pass social and economic legislation applicable to the whole country. These activities and laws may also be examined by the federal courts, although traditionally they have not interfered overmuch.

Second, US law has become increasingly complex due to an increase in federal and state legislation. This means that businessmen, consumers and individuals are now more concerned with and directly affected by the law. They are very cautious about their legal transactions, contracts, documents and court appearances and frequently need assistance by lawyers.

Courts and judges in the US at all levels (but especially the federal) make policy to varying degrees as they interpret and apply the law. Some critics argue that the courts are therefore political institutions and the judiciary is part of the political process. But judges do not make law or policy in the explicit way that politicians do. They function indirectly in the process of resolving disputes brought to their courts.

Criminal law and civil law

The cases which come before the courts in the US are of two main kinds: civil and criminal.

Civil law involves claims for compensation (mainly financial) by an individual (the plaintiff) who has allegedly suffered loss or damage through a breach of contract or a negligent act by another (the defendant). Domestic relations actions (divorce, children and custody), automobile accidents and personal injury cases are the largest civil matters. Civil law has a service role and tries to secure social harmony by settling disputes between individuals or organizations. This is achieved by settlement during the course of litigation and negotiations, or by a judge after a trial.

Criminal law involves the punishment of those persons (the accused or defendants) who have committed crimes against society, such as theft or murder. State, local or federal authorities prosecute groups or individuals in an attempt to establish guilt, which may result in a fine or imprisonment. This is the control aspect of the legal system and the criminal law protects society by punishing those who have broken the social codes. The trial and any punishment are also supposed to act as deterrents to potential offenders.

The sources of contemporary US law

The two most important sources of contemporary US law are the common (or case) law and statutory law.

Versions of the English *common law* were accepted in all American states (except Louisiana). It is administered and interpreted by state courts and is found in court decisions of judges, who generally adopt established principles of law from previous cases. Earlier decisions create precedents which are normally followed in subsequent similar cases.

But the authority of precedent declined in the late nineteenth and early twentieth centuries. American judges now decide cases in terms of existing law and a sense of justice, so that the decision is fair and reasonable in the light of contemporary conditions. Generally, they follow the precedents unless there are good reasons for ignoring them.

Statutory law consists of laws which have been passed by state or federal legislatures. Such legislation is now very important. It grew considerably from the nineteenth century as state and federal government intruded increasingly into everyday affairs. The meaning and application of legislation are interpreted and determined by the courts.

Although much state law consists of the common law, many social, economic and family matters are now provided for by state statutes. At federal levels, statutory law is virtually the only type of law and includes the Constitution, treaties, Acts of Congress, presidential proclamations, executive orders and rules of federal departments or commissions. Federal legislation now covers a wide and influential area.

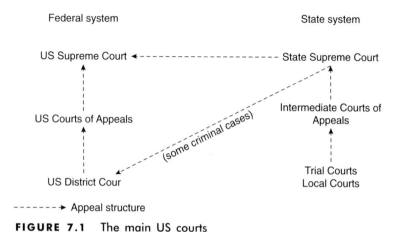

Federal system   State system

US Supreme Court ◄ - - - - - - - - - - - - - - - - State Supreme Court

US Courts of Appeals   Intermediate Courts of Appeals

(some criminal cases)

US District Cour   Trial Courts
                                                 Local Courts

- - - - - - → Appeal structure

FIGURE 7.1   The main US courts

The structure of the court system

The courts play a central and influential role in American society. They directly affect the daily lives of citizens in many areas and their decisions are widely debated. Social, as well as personal, struggles are reflected in court battles, whether civil or criminal.

US courts (see Figure 7.1) operate at separate *federal* and *state/local* levels and have their own areas of authority or jurisdiction. State and local courts handle most of the legal work and are the most immediate for Americans. The federal courts only account for some 2 per cent of cases tried annually. But the existence of separate court systems makes some litigation more complicated than in many other countries.

Parties in a case may, in certain circumstances, appeal a court decison to a higher court. An appeal is an examination of procedures and legal principles on which the decision was based in the previous trial, as well as new evidence.

The federal court system

Federal courts deal with cases which arise under the US Constitution, treaties or federal law and any disputes involving the federal government. They also hear matters involving governments or citizens of different states and thus play a part in state law. Similarly, if a case in the highest state court of appeal involves a federal question, it can be appealed ultimately to the US Supreme Court.

The federal court system forms a hierarchy. The three main levels of courts are in ascending order of appeal:

1   US District Courts;
2   US Courts of Appeals;
3   The Supreme Court in Washington, DC.

A case involving federal jurisdiction is heard first before a federal district judge. An appeal may be made to the US Court of Appeal and, in the last resort, to the US Supreme Court.

Most federal cases begin and are settled in the lower *US District Courts* and only a small minority of their cases are appealed. Some ninety-four district courts are situated in all parts of the US (with each state having at least one district court) and in various US territories such as Puerto Rico. They are trial courts in which a single judge or a jury decides each case. The majority of citizens involved in federal litigation only have dealings with the District Courts.

They try cases involving breaches of federal criminal law, such as bank robbery, drug dealing, kidnapping, currency fraud and assassination. But most of the work of the District Courts is in areas of civil law, such as taxation, civil rights, administrative regulations, disputes between states and bankruptcy. Their case-load has increased since the mid-1960s in civil matters, due to more federal legislation.

The *US Courts of Appeals* system consists of twelve courts sitting in each of eleven judicial circuits into which the US is divided, and the District of Columbia. These courts (with from three to five judges) mainly hear appeals from decisions of the US District Courts within the circuits and are not trial courts. Most of their decisions are final and set a precedent for future similar cases. Critics maintain that the Appeal Courts are the most important judicial policy-makers in the country. They are not, however, the ultimate authority because their decisions can be overturned by the US Supreme Court.

The *US Supreme Court* in Washington, DC, comprises a Chief Justice and eight Associate Justices, assisted by law clerks. It has jurisdiction in 'all cases affecting ambassadors, other public ministers and consuls and those in which a State shall be a party'. However, its main role is that of an appeal court and it hears cases from lower federal and state courts. These appeals usually involve constitutional issues, questions of federal law and conflicts between two or more of the states. Crucially, the Court has the power to review any executive and legislative action or law passed by any level of government (if challenged in a court case) and can declare it unconstitutional after judging its compatibility with the Constitution and federal law. Although not explicitly given this power of judicial review by the Constitution, the Supreme Court has developed such authority. It enables the Court to profoundly influence many aspects of American life.

Its decisions have given protection and rights to African Americans and other minorities; produced influential decisions on education and religion; and affected the death penalty and abortion issues. But, since 1790, it has ruled that only some 130 federal laws have been unconstitutional, although about ten times as many state and local laws have been invalidated. Supreme Court decisions can be overturned mainly by the Court itself, a constitutional amendment or Act of Congress.

The Court rules on some 150 cases each year and itself decides whether or not it will hear a particular case. It will usually hear cases which involve a basic constitutional principle, an important question of federal law, or a conflict between state and federal law. It does not have the power to actually make laws. However, since its authority is independent of the other branches of government, its decisions may often have a legislative/policy-making (and arguably political) force.

In general, the Court plays a restrained or conservative role, following legal tradition and previous precedent. However, historically it has had periods of controversial liberal 'activism'. Its caseload has increased over the years due to new legislation in civil rights and federal regulations, which has increased its 'political' profile.

The state and local court system

State and *local* courts constitute a large, complicated and individualistic system which covers the US. They have a wider jurisdiction than the federal courts and have much heavier workloads. They determine the guilt or innocence of persons accused of violating state criminal laws and they decide civil disputes. The great majority of criminal and civil cases, such as assaults, theft (larceny), murder, divorce and property disputes are settled within the state system.

The Constitution stipulates that the states have areas of authority (or sovereignty) outside the federal judicial system. They have their own criminal and civil legal systems, laws, prisons, police forces, courts and associations of lawyers. Court systems and laws are similar in most states. But there are differences, such as court structures and names, sentences for murder, and the ages for marriage, possession of a driver's licence and purchase of alcohol. The states jealously guard their independence and are self-contained legal units whose courts deliver judgments from which there is often no appeal. But jurisdiction can be shared between federal and state bodies if an issue has federal implications.

Local courts are the lowest state courts and have a limited jurisdiction. They hear minor civil and criminal cases (misdemeanours) that often cannot be appealed and may not have a jury. Their names vary according to locality and the nature of the case. They may be known as Police Courts, Town or City Courts, or Justice of the Peace Courts.

Trial courts are the next highest, have a more general jurisdiction and may consist of the following in different states: *District*, *County* or *Municipal Courts* which hear civil suits and criminal cases; *Juvenile* or *Family Courts* which decide domestic, juvenile and delinquency cases; *Probate Courts* which decide on wills and hear claims against estates; and *Criminal Courts* which determine criminal cases. Most of the criminal, and some civil, cases will be heard by a jury.

Some three-quarters of the states have intermediate appeal courts which hear appeals from lower courts. But the highest court is the *State Supreme Court,* which hears civil and criminal appeals from inferior state courts and can employ judicial review. Federal and constitutional matters may be appealed from this court to the US Supreme Court and some criminal cases can be appealed to the federal District Courts.

Federal and state court proceedings

American legal proceedings in both criminal and civil cases are based on the adversary system. This enables competing parties to present their views to an impartial third party, under procedural rules that allow the evidence to be presented in a fair and orderly manner. A trial under the adversary process is designed to determine the facts under the appropriate law and to resolve cases by producing a judgment. It is the impartial third party (judge or jury) who decides the case based on the evidence presented to the court.

Some Americans regard this technical process as game-playing or even corrupt. But the legal language and procedure are supposed to safeguard the rights of citizens and to ensure due process of law and equal protection under the law.

In practice, most civil disputes and some criminal cases are not resolved through court trials and many legal controversies do not result in lawsuits. The legal profession generally attempts to avoid civil and (some) criminal contests in court by arranging settlements during litigation.

Criminal proceedings

A range of rights and protections for citizens in criminal cases are provided by the Fourth, Fifth, Sixth, Seventh, Eighth and other Amendments of the Bill of Rights, which have been added to by later judicial decisions.

PLATE 7.1   New York County Court House   *(A. Devaney)*

These features stipulate that individuals shall not be deprived of life, liberty, or property without due process of law; and should be given a speedy and public trial usually by jury in the location of the alleged crime. The accused (or defendant) has the right to question witnesses; the right to compel most witnesses to appear on his or her behalf; the right to a lawyer for his or her defence (if necessary at public expense); the right (generally) to remain silent; and a right against self-incrimination.

There is protection against excessive bail (payment to secure freedom prior to trial); the police cannot force a confession from a prisoner or suspect by duress or threats; and may not hold

PLATE 7.2   Scene in a local court   *(Priscilla Coleman)*

persons for more than two days without charging them with a criminal offence. Lengthy imprisonment in isolation prior to a trial is illegal and any confession obtained by the police in these circumstances is not acceptable to a court. Some critics argue, however, that such safeguards are not always observed by the criminal legal system and that individuals' criminal rights may be abused.

Trial by jury is a fundamental tradition in America and is guaranteed in indictable (serious) criminal cases. It may also be employed in other criminal trials. Additionally, a defendant charged with an offence such as murder must have been previously indicted by a Grand Jury. The trial jury consists of from six to twelve ordinary citizens (depending on the level of the court), who make a decision based on the facts before them in court. A unanimous decision is needed in federal criminal cases and in most criminal cases in all states (although majority verdicts may sometimes be allowed).

After the trial, the Seventh Amendment guarantees that the accepted facts on which a trial was based cannot be re-examined in any appeal to a higher court and the appeal must therefore be based on other grounds. The Eighth Amendment states that there should be protection for the guilty from cruel and unusual punishment (see the death penalty debate on p. 228).

Federal district attorneys conduct federal criminal prosecutions under these rules. In state criminal cases, this role is performed by the public prosecutor, who is an elected officer with local jurisdiction.

Civil proceedings

Civil cases in federal and state courts are divided into groups. The majority deal with matters such as accident and personal injury claims. The plaintiff serves documents on the defendant and, unless the case is settled out of court, it goes to trial before a judge and sometimes a jury. In more expensive cases, a jury trial must be held. A majority jury decision is permitted in civil cases in some states.

The legal profession

Hostility was shown towards judges after independence because of anti-British feeling and in the nineteenth century attempts were made to democratize and deprofessionalize the legal system. But generally, judges are accorded considerable respect in the US, although some critics argue that they can be too political or may bow to political pressure. However, lawyers (particularly corporate, divorce and 'celebrity' lawyers) tend to be treated with suspicion or even antagonism.

The judiciary

All federal judges are nominated by the President, approved by the Senate and appointed for life in what amounts to a political selection process. They hold office during good behaviour and can be removed from office only by impeachment (proof of gross misconduct after trial by the Senate). This process has been very rarely used and never successfully against a Supreme Court justice.

State judges may now be appointed, selected or elected (by the people) depending on the practices of individual states. They may also be investigated by state commissions which may recommend their disciplining, or removal.

The judiciary has a range of functions and duties. It enforces the legitimate laws of the legislative and executive branches of government. But it also protects citizens against arbitrary acts by either the executive or the legislature. Judicial review gives the judiciary a crucial authority and judges' freedom from control by the other branches of government allows them to be theoretically 'above politics'. These factors enable American courts to follow relatively independent courses of action.

The authority of judges is generally supported and respected by most sections of the public. The justices of the Supreme Court, for example, can be very influential and their decisions can affect ordinary people's lives. Judges may, however, vary in their political inclinations from 'liberal' to 'conservative' and this may be reflected in their decisions.

Lawyers

Americans tend to distrust lawyers, although they do often need their services. This antagonism might be partly due to the large number of lawyers in society. In addition to their legal roles, they are very visible in business, politics and public life. It is estimated that one in 440 adult Americans is a lawyer and in Washington, DC the ratio is one in 64.

The legal profession is undivided and there are no formal distinctions between categories of lawyers. Its members, known as attorneys at law, counsellors or simply lawyers, exercise broad functions, although some may specialize in one branch of the law. They give legal assistance such as the drafting of contracts, trusts, or wills; settle conflicts outside court; and also present criminal or civil cases in court.

Most lawyers today will have first obtained a law degree from the law school of a university. The value of the degree varies greatly with the status of the school, although the best (such as Harvard and Yale) are world-famous. The degree gives the lawyer a general grounding in American law through academic lectures and practical case work. But lawyers also have to know the law of the state in which they will eventually practise and must pass the state bar examination.

Lawyers may work for federal and state government or in industry and commerce. But the majority are in private practice and cater for individual and corporate clients. Some work on their own and serve a range of clients, but most lawyers practise in firms. Half work in two-partner firms consisting of an office attorney and a trial lawyer, who perform different functions. The other half work in bigger firms, which have a number of lawyers and may have offices world-wide. The three categories of lawyers in big firms are senior partners and junior partners who receive a share of the profits and associates who are paid a fixed salary.

The lawyer's income is frequently a high one, at least in the medium-to-big firms and is, on average, one of the highest in the country. The top students of the best law schools are normally able to join a prestigious law firm at a good salary and may quickly proceed to a partnership.

The finances of a law firm, in addition to ordinary commercial fees, may include other features. The contingency fee (payment upon results in personal injury cases) can be charged at rates which may reach 50 per cent of the damages awarded. But *pro-bono* legal help without fees may be provided for those who cannot afford to pay for legal services and firms may participate in state and federal legal aid programmes for the poor. The provision of legal aid is an important and expensive federal programme, particularly since fees for legal services are generally very high.

The public also seem to think that lawyers are overly concerned with money and that they drive up costs and their fees.

Lawyers have organized themselves at national and state levels into bar associations (or lawyers' organizations), that supervise the profession, protect professional interests and discipline their members. The American Bar Association (ABA) was created nationally in 1878, but only about a half of lawyers are ABA members. Most states require that lawyers must be members of the state bar association, which is affiliated to the ABA. But in other states a lawyer may practise law without being a member of the state bar association.

The ABA is a conservative organization and is often criticized. But its lobbying has done much to improve the status of lawyers and it has increased its political status as an organized interest group. It has fought for improvements in the law, law schools, legal education and the legal system generally. It also serves as an important source of legal information to the general public. The expert opinion and special status of the ABA are influential in the nomination of judges and proposed changes in criminal and civil law.

Crime and punishment

Crime

Statistics (whether from official or personal experience surveys) appear to show that the US has a high overall crime rate in real terms and in comparison with other Western countries. Much of this is associated with professional crime organizations, local street gangs and drug dealing/usage. Polls reveal that fear of crime in homes and neighbourhoods is very high, particularly among women. Yet crime is spread unevenly across the country and among victims. Furthermore, some commentators on international comparisons argue that US crime statistics, apart from murder, are not exceptional and that US rates for some crimes are lower than other countries.

Although overall serious crime (violent and property offences) rose 19 per cent between 1983 and 1992, it dropped by 2 per cent in 1993, 3 per cent in 1994 and was estimated to drop in 1995. In 1993 some 14.1 million serious crimes were reported, according to Federal Bureau of Investigation (FBI) figures. Of these, the majority (12.2 million) were property crimes (burglary, larceny/theft, and motor-vehicle theft). Some 1.9 million were violent crimes against individuals (murder, rape, robbery and assault). About 24,500 of this latter figure were murders or manslaughters and firearms were used in three-quarters of these cases. The US leads the world in its number of annual murders, but this dropped by 8 per cent in 1995 and overall violent crimes dropped by 4 per cent.

The incidence of all crime is much higher in some (but by no means all) cities and in certain city areas, rather than in rural areas; many offences are unreported; and only some 20 per cent of reported crimes are solved and their perpetrators convicted. Yet it is estimated that some 60 per cent of crimes are committed by only 5 per cent of the population and that the majority of these persons have a prior criminal record.

Young people aged between 15 and 19 are the most criminally inclined age group, which will grow by 23 per cent by the year 2005. Commentators fear that this is a demographic time-bomb which will greatly increase crime statistics. In some urban areas, murder is the main cause of death among non-White males between the ages of 24 and 45 and non-Whites have a much higher victimization rate than Whites. African Americans (12 per cent of the population) disproportionately account for 35 per cent of arrests for drug possession, 55 per cent of convictions for offences and 74 per cent of prison sentences.

The reasons for crime are notoriously arguable and varied. Critics maintain that the police and courts are too lenient in their treatment of criminal suspects and sentencing patterns, while the police criticize the courts and defence lawyers. Some blame urban slums, social deprivation, poverty, bad schools, lack of educational opportunities, unemployment, lack of discipline, unstable families, drugs, organized crime and the availability of guns and other weapons.

Law enforcement

Some 553,000 officers and 212,000 civilians work in law enforcement in the US and the Clinton administration has increased the numbers. The implementation of state law is carried out by the police and detectives in the cities and by sheriffs and constables in rural areas. Federal crimes are mainly the responsibility of the FBI, which also provides technical assistance to state and local law enforcement agencies.

Crime prevention is a difficult job for law enforcement officials and the courts in the face of widespread crime. Public demands for stronger punishment for criminals create added pressure and expense. Part of this debate is the emotive question of the rights and compensation of crime victims and their families. Other factors also exist, such as overcrowding in prisons, the accessibility of handguns, uncertainties in the area of civil rights and the debated question of the death penalty. Courts and law enforcement officers consequently have difficulties in coping with the legitimate needs and demands of society and the rights of individuals.

Rights of criminal suspects

The Constitution ideally guarantees equal justice under the law for all citizens and the individual's right to freedom and security. Various Amendments and later court decisions also protect the rights of criminal suspects.

The Fourth Amendment, for example, protects citizens against unreasonable search and seizure. It is generally illegal for the police to search people's homes, persons or papers unless they have a warrant. However, the Supreme Court has created exceptions so that the police can in some circumstances search and act without a warrant. But any incriminating evidence which is gathered as a result of an illegal police search cannot be used or recognized in a criminal trial. This exclusionary rule continues to provoke controversy.

Another rule established by the Supreme Court in *Miranda* (1966) extended the protection of criminal suspects. The police must read suspects their legal rights before they are arrested or questioned. These include the right to remain silent; to have an attorney present during questioning; and to consult a lawyer before making a statement. If the police proceed incorrectly, any evidence obtained from questioning cannot be used in court. This may mean that persons who are allegedly guilty go free because of a technicality.

Many protections for criminal suspects stem from liberal Supreme Court decisions in the 1960s. Conservatives agitate for the reversal of these rulings and other provisions which allegedly over-protect suspects. They maintain that such rules hinder law enforcement and the protection of society and shift the balance of doubt towards suspects. Liberals argue that any reduction in the rights of criminal suspects may affect innocent people and leaves too much power and control in the hands of the police and the criminal legal system.

The death penalty

In 1972, the Supreme Court ruled in *Furman v. Georgia* that the death penalty amounted to 'cruel and unusual punishment' and as such was unconstitutional. This decision was reversed in 1976 in *Gregg v. Georgia*, which ruled that the death penalty was not unconstitutional in itself. It does not contravene the Eighth Amendment's prohibition against cruel and unusual punishment if it is applied in a fair and impartial manner.

Some critics argue that the Supreme Court decided the case in a narrow legal sense and ignored the moral and ethical implications of the 'cruel and unusual' clause. For them, the use of the death penalty illustrates the gap between law and justice in American society, particularly when the majority of prisoners suffering the death penalty are African Americans.

Some thirty-eight states now have the death penalty as punishment for certain capital crimes such as murder and see it as a deterrent force. Given the uncertain state of the law and opposition to the death penalty, there were few executions between 1965 and 1983. But there were 47 between 1980 and

1985; 38 in 1993 (with 30 in the southern states); and some 57 in 1995. Supporters of the death penalty (75 per cent of the public, according to opinion polls) tend to argue for its deterrent force, its use as a valid punishment for criminals and its revenge capacity. Opponents of capital punishment maintain that it is unconstitutional as a cruel and unusual punishment and does not serve as a deterrent.

Prisons

The US has a higher percentage of its population behind bars than any other country and spends some $35 billion a year on its prisons. The prison population has increased dramatically since the early 1970s; it was 1.05 million persons in 1994, an increase of 8.6 per cent from 1993 and is still growing. Prisons tend to be old and in bad condition and generally do not serve as positive examples of rehabilitation.

Imprisonment policies have been challenged since 1992, especially by the first female US Attorney General, Janet Reno. Reformers advocate improved welfare systems, better education and drug-treatment programmes, with prevention, rather than punishment and detention, being the goals.

But the Clinton administration policy, in response to public concern about crime, favours expanding the death penalty; putting more police on the streets; building more prisons; allowing some prisons to be run by private firms; stressing punishment above rehabilitation; reducing parole (conditional release of prisoners before completing their full sentence); and giving longer sentences for serious crimes and (controversially) to criminals who repeat serious crimes.

Gun control

The Second Amendment apparently guarantees to every US citizen the right to bear arms. But its wording is ambiguous and refers to a time when the British had tried to prevent the colonists from raising an armed militia. Today, however, it is very difficult to

PLATE 7.3   San Francisco police make an arrest   *(Rex Features)*

pass strong gun-control legislation, despite the fact that in 1992 handguns were used in 931,000 murders, rapes, robberies and assaults. The US Health Department reported in 1994 that guns would kill more people than road accidents within ten years. It is estimated that Americans now own some 200 million firearms of varying types.

The National Rifle Association (NRA) and other lobbies against gun control (such as militia groups) vigorously oppose restrictions on the sale and use of firearms as a violation of the Constitution. A majority (62 per cent in Gallup, 1996) of Americans favour stricter gun-control laws as a way of curbing crime. But 60 per cent oppose a complete ban on handguns and 40 per cent support a ban. A 1994 *US News and World Report*

poll showed that 45 per cent thought that protection of themselves and their homes is the major incentive behind gun
ownership and 86 per cent of men and 63 per cent of women
supported the right to keep guns in the home.

Gun-control laws were, in fact, passed by Congress in 1993
and 1994. These include the imposition of a five-day waiting
period for the purchase of handguns to permit checks into the
buyer's background; registration of all handguns; a ban on semi-
automatic assault weapons; stronger penalties for gun offences;
and tighter licensing rules for gun dealers. But these new laws are
not excessively stringent and critics argue that they do not
adequately challenge the 'gun culture'.

Self-defence

The issue of gun control is connected to questions of self-defence,
particularly at a time when victim surveys suggest that some 57
per cent of Americans have personally suffered from crime in one
form or another and to greater and lesser extents. Historically,
people's right to defend themselves, their families and their property has been a basic (and sometimes necessary) tradition in
American life.

Today, there is a widespread lack of public confidence in
the ability of the police, the courts and legislators to cope with
crime, or to adequately and effectively protect individual citizens.
People consequently feel that they must safeguard themselves
against criminals determined to commit criminal acts. Security has
become a priority for many individuals, who devise ways (often
at considerable expense) to protect themselves and their homes
from attacks, violence and burglaries. Some individuals, known
as vigilantes, may deliberately break the law in order to defend
themselves and often receive public support and sympathy in many
cases.

Attitudes to the legal system

Most Americans, according to opinion polls, feel that crime and violence are among the most serious problems in the US today; are afraid that these might directly affect their own lives; and wish for strong punitive responses to them. A 1995 *Time/CNN* poll reported that 7 per cent of Americans felt that the crime problem was improving, while 89 per cent thought it was getting worse; 55 per cent were personally worried about being victims of crime and 45 per cent were not; and 42 per cent felt adequately protected against crime by the police, while 55 per cent did not.

Yet in polls conducted by *International Social Attitudes, 1993–94* only 11 per cent of American respondents called for 'much more' public spending on the police, law and order. This figure ranked fifth after the environment, health care, education and pensions.

Attitudes to the criminal legal system vary between liberals and conservatives. Conservatives are strong on law and order; feel that the rights of criminal suspects and defendants should be restricted; favour strong criminal penalties, harsh punishment and the death penalty; and seek to overturn liberal legislation. Liberals are suspicious of the police and law enforcement agencies; are against what they see as tough criminal legislation and penalties; and favour extended civil rights for individuals.

Some critics argue that Americans have irrational attitudes to crime and violence and consequently create a self-perpetuating image that America is a violent and therefore crime-ridden society. Such attitudes are allegedly very different from those in other Western countries. They suggest a belief that American crime is actually more violent than anywhere else and that, because American criminals lack foresight as to the consequences of their actions, their crimes are more irrational. Most professionals and academics in the US, indeed, seem to agree that America's fundamental problem is one of violence itself and that a way to reduce this is to restrict access to guns.

■ **Examine and explain the following terms:**

legalism	precedent	impeachment
common law	jurisdiction	civil law
judicial review	constitutionalism	US District Courts
legal aid	plea bargaining	State Supreme Court
statutory law	ABA	the adversary system
judiciary	Bill of Rights	contingency fees

■ **Write short essays on the following topics:**

1   Why is law such an important and central part of American life?

2   Critically discuss the historical evolution of American law and the legal system.

3   What are alleged to be the reasons for the apparently high crime rate in the US?

4   Examine the arguments for and against the death penalty and gun control.

Chapter 8

Economic and industrial institutions

A GRICULTURE WAS THE main US economic activity from the colonial period to the middle of the nineteenth century. It then expanded and used fewer workers as it became more mechanized and efficient. Manufacturing and industrial output also increased greatly from the mid-nineteenth century. This growth resulted in the US becoming the world's richest country and leading industrial nation in the early twentieth century.

By the 1950s, it had achieved a global economic dominance and a large degree of self-sufficiency. Since the 1970s, the major changes have been the growth of service industries; a relative decline in manufacturing industry; a weakening in the US's world position as other countries became more competitive; and instability in some economic sectors. But, after a recession in the early 1990s, the economy recovered and grew strongly.

Economic history

America's economic expansion from the nineteenth century can be explained by its natural resources; its distinctive commercial structures and institutions; the characteristics of its people; and the principles that support economic activity.

The indigenous Native-American inhabitants of North America had varied economies, which ranged from nomadic food gathering, fishing and hunting to settled agricultural communities. A similar basic economy was adopted by later colonial Americans but this was gradually developed into a more sophisticated agricultural system based on small farms.

British settlers in the seventeenth century were often employed by British companies that had been granted trading charters by the English Crown, like the Virginia Company that established Jamestown in 1607. The colonies provided Britain with raw materials, but were not supposed to compete in manufacturing with the mother country. This relationship collapsed when Britain tried to impose taxation and trade restrictions. After the War for Independence (1776–83), the US developed its own economic policies and markets. A greater variety of goods was produced by the eighteenth century as Americans expanded agricultural production, increased their commercial interests and cultivated the prairies.

The US in 1800 was still an agricultural society. Some 95 per cent of the people lived in rural areas and the economy was based largely on self-sufficiency, with some exports. But nineteenth-century growth combined agricultural advances with expanding industrial and manufacturing bases. These were aided by government financial support and a transport revolution which established railway, canal and road infrastructures.

Agricultural productivity increased as small farmers made use of the transportation system; specialized in selected crops or animals; sold their products to a wider internal market; and developed their export potential. But this growth led to a drop in prices and by the start of the twentieth century farmers were having difficulties.

Economic progress in the nineteenth century was affected by the Civil War (1861–65) when twenty-three states of the industrial north were opposed by eleven southern agricultural states on the issue of slavery. A northern victory led to an emphasis on the nation's developing industrial base with great advances in the production of basic manufactured goods.

Between the Civil War and the First World War (1914–18), the US rapidly industrialized and became an increasingly urban country. Expansion was based on natural resources, iron, steam and electrical power. It was later helped by technical advances like the internal combustion engine, the telegraph and telephone, radio, typewriters, assembly-line production and interchangeable-parts technology. Since there were no trade restrictions in the internal US market, economies of production and distribution were possible and large-scale manufacturing developed. The export of manufactured goods became more important than raw materials. Economic activity was based on an ethos of commercial life free from restrictions, which led to a fierce unregulated capitalism. Big business became a central feature of American life.

But the industrial progress was accompanied by periodic slumps and by harsh employment and living conditions for many workers and the increasing population. These particularly affected some of the European immigrants who came to the US between 1890 and 1910. The situation often led to racial conflict between white newcomers, who were willing to work for low wages in bad conditions, and African Americans who had left the agricultural southern states in search of jobs.

The expanding economy resulted in the creation of corporations (business companies) in most economic sectors. These based their production and competition policies on marketing, advertising, advanced technology, cheap products, rationalization of the work process, efficient management organization and good service. The growth of corporations enabled the US to export many types of manufactured items and consumer goods were spread throughout the American market.

Larger corporations were formed through mergers and takeovers, leading to giant trusts and monopolies, that attempted to control competition. Trusts were identified in the popular mind with individual owners like Rockefeller in oil and Carnegie in steel, whose economic and political power influenced the whole economy. However, it was increasingly felt that government should regulate the trusts and monopoly situations, which were seen as anti-competitive.

Some anti-trust legislation, like the Sherman Anti-Trust Law (1890), had already been passed. But the trusts still controlled whole product areas. President Theodore Roosevelt (1901–8) tried to regulate them and break up monopolies. Legislation prevented restrictive deals between companies on products, prices, output levels and market shares; limited mergers that minimized competition; and improved employment conditions (such as an eight-hour working day).

But the trusts and other large corporations continued to have great power. President Woodrow Wilson (1913–20) attempted to check commercial markets. He passed a new anti-trust law;

reduced protective tariffs against foreign competition; and introduced reforms in agricultural and labour areas.

However, despite these reforms, the 1920s (the Roaring Twenties) was a period of instability and hardship for many people. Although low taxes promoted a rise in general living standards, too much money was circulating in the economic system and the consumption of goods and services increased. There was over-production by factories and farms; over-protection of US business against foreign competition through tariff barriers; and financial speculation. The economy collapsed in October 1929 with the Wall Street Stock Market and banking crash. This marked the beginning of the worst depression in American history (the Great Depression).

Demands were made for more government regulation of business activity and help to those who were suffering socially and economically. President Franklin D. Roosevelt (1933–45) argued that the Depression was due to faults in the capitalist economy and tried to remedy the situation with his New Deal. He was the first president to substantially intervene in the economy. New regulatory powers over the stock market were initiated by a Securities and Exchange Commission (SEC) and other commissions were created to supervise public utilities such as electricity. Unemployed people were given jobs in public works projects and financial help was granted to the farmers who were suffering badly. A Social Security Act (1935) was the first major federal legislation to provide security against unemployment, job-related accidents and old age. These measures aimed to stabilize the economy; regulate commercial institutions; create internal demand for American products; and prevent social and economic hardship.

The New Deal did not solve all the social and economic problems of the US, some of which have continued to the present day. Federal governments since the 1930s have consequently intervened to varying degrees in the economy either by legislation or by using regulatory powers to influence commercial life. But American governments are not generally opposed to business and have themselves invested in private sectors such as research, development, aerospace and defence.

The economy grew after the Second World War and by the 1950s had achieved global dominance. The commercial structure of large corporations, such as General Electric, Ford and General Motors, continues to dominate American business. Some have become multinational organizations owned by financial groups (rather than individuals) with diversified interests and plants world-wide. But there are many other smaller corporations and businesses, amounting to three-quarters of the total corporate market, which can be very successful and influential.

Reasons for the growth of the US economy

The US's size and plentiful natural resources are important reasons for its rapid economic expansion since the nineteenth century but they must be linked to other determining factors.

First, American traditions of pragmatism, hard work and individual initiative encourage a belief that all things are possible. These features have been attributed to the influence of Protestant religions (the Protestant work ethic) and the pioneer spirit of early settlers, whose survival lay in their own ingenuity. Many Americans find solutions to problems; retrain in other areas if unemployment occurs; create new jobs or businesses; and move to fresh opportunities.

Second, private business operates for profit at market prices; *laissez-faire* economic principles (letting things take their own course) dominate the economy and few restrictions (such as government intervention) have historically been placed on business ventures. This ethos has largely enabled people to follow their individual economic interests.

Third, governments aided economic growth in the nineteenth century. They protected US industry, farmers and manufacturers against foreign competition by erecting tariff barriers; used public money to encourage private business; and gave land and permission to private interests to develop transport infrastructures. The economy developed relatively freely and it competed successfully with European countries.

American economic liberalism: theory and practice

The founders of the US stressed individual liberty in all fields, including economic freedom. They were influenced by economic philosophers, like the Scot Adam Smith, and felt that citizens should pursue their own self-interest and profit-making activities. Greater competition and increased trade would supposedly result; society would benefit generally; consumers could buy products at competitive prices; and market forces would control the efficient distribution of goods.

Areas such as industry, health care, airlines, telephone systems, energy supplies and railways, are therefore in private rather than public ownership. Although US governments since the 1930s have promoted competition by interventionist anti-trust laws and reduction of monopolies, they have been largely confined to a regulatory role in the economy.

But a government policy of 'deregulation' (the removal of restrictions to create freer markets) has also operated since the 1970s. This has, for example, increased competition among US airlines for passengers; split the American Telephone and Telegraph company into smaller companies offering different services and prices; and allowed private companies to compete with the US Postal Service. Compared with Europe, the US has a very deregulated economy.

Nevertheless, some governments (particularly Democrats) have actively intervened in the economy and business life. For example, the Clinton administration since 1992 has increased labour market intervention and regulation with new training schemes, welfare reform, pro-union legislation and an increase in the national minimum wage (first established in 1940 with the last rise in 1996 from $4.25 an hour to $5.15).

Government regulation of economic activity can also be achieved through fiscal and monetary policy, such as interest rates, subsidies and controls on some prices. The government can exert influence as a purchaser of goods and equipment, especially in the defence, aircraft and aerospace industries. Government regulation now includes safety standards for manufactured goods;

environmental protection; labour and equal employment matters; and working conditions. Restrictions at federal and state levels curb freedom of operation for employers. They show the difference between past and present business practices and the contemporary role of government.

Economic restrictions are fiercely debated. Conservatives and many corporations argue that there is too much regulation and interference. Liberals and some citizens support an interventionist role in economic matters. While Americans have a distrust of 'big government', they also appear to dislike the near-monopolistic nature of some 'big business', which may dominate consumer choice and give bad service and products.

The US therefore does not have an absolute 'free enterprise' system, although this remains the essential feature of the market economy. Americans generally support free enterprise (as opposed to monopolies), individual initiative and the ability of a competitive market to deliver a range of necessary goods, services and resources nationwide.

Not all individuals can pursue economic success because of their differing circumstances and the influence of factors such as corporate power. Despite its traditional American value, individualism is a relative concept. It does not imply automatic success, although there is a general belief that achievement and material prosperity *may* result from individual hard work. There does not seem to be much envy directed at those who do succeed and few complain about 'the system' if they fail. There are no widespread pressures for alternative economic models. Debates are therefore concerned largely with how much government intervention and corporate power there should be in the private enterprise system.

Social class and economic inequality

The US is often portrayed as a classless and egalitarian society but there have always been social and economic differences between Americans. Arguably these constitute a class model divided into working, middle and upper classes based on job status, income, capital and (sometimes) birth.

Industrialization in the eighteenth and nineteenth centuries increased the class and wealth gaps between industrialists, manufacturers, financiers and landowners, on the one hand, and industrial and agricultural workers, on the other. Many of the latter suffered from poor social and job conditions. Commentators at the time argued that class divisions were a natural result of the freedom of competition.

In the twentieth century, workers were increasingly placed either in the white-collar service sector or the industrial blue-collar sector. It was felt that these groups fell outside the European context of the 'working class' and should be seen as 'lower middle class'.

Influenced by a mass-consumption society and rising living standards, class distinctions in the US have become less rigid. Income and occupation are now key determinants. A middle-class ideology is dominant and a large majority of Americans classify themselves as middle-class in terms of income and lifestyle. Blue-collar workers have declined, service sector white-collar workers have increased and there has been a growth in executive and professional workers.

However, some Americans might still consider themselves to be traditionally working class. There is also a considerable minority (estimated at between one-quarter or one-fifth of the population) who have historically been classified as poor. Part of this group has been recently described as an unemployable and welfare-dependent underclass.

The US is in relative terms a very wealthy and prosperous country and provides the majority of its people with one of the world's highest standards of living. The average annual income of full-time wage and salary workers was some $24,300 in 1994 and 60 per cent of families and individuals have middle to high incomes. This reveals a middle-class preponderance (defined by income) in American society.

But while the top 20 per cent of US families' earnings rose in 1993 to an average of $113,182, the bottom 20 per cent dropped to $16,970. In 1992, some 1 per cent of US households owned 30.4 per cent of the nation's wealth, compared with 36.8 per cent for the next-highest 9 per cent and 32.8 per cent for the rest. The gap between rich and poor in the US is now greater than in any other industrialized country as the rich have grown richer and the poor have become poorer. This inequality of income and wealth was emphasized in 1993 when 39 million Americans (15.1 per cent of the population) lived below the poverty lines defined by family size and single status ($14,700 for a family of four). In this total, the highest percentages were African Americans, American Indians and Latinos, whose average income is lower than whites.

Critics argue that such inequality is due to reduced wages, the decline of trade unions and low tax rates on the wealthy. More tax cuts and reductions in welfare payments may result in a society even more divided between the very rich and very poor. This situation arguably undermines America's self-image as an egalitarian classless nation. As *The New York Times* (17 April 1995) wrote: 'Even class societies like Britain . . . now have greater economic equality than the US.'

The contemporary national economy

The American economy today is a mixture of positive and negative factors. But it has since 1994 coped with internal and international pressures and is (1996) currently buoyant.

The US is the world's biggest economic power in terms of its Gross Domestic Product (GDP). This comprises the goods, services, capital and income which the country produces and in 1996 was $7 trillion. Some 3 per cent of GDP arises from agriculture, forestry and fishing; 24 per cent from mining, energy, industry, manufacturing and construction; and some 73 per cent from transportation and the service industries.

The GDP shows that the US has a very diversified economy. Its wealth reflects its abundant natural resources (coal, oil, natural gas, metals and hydro-electricity) and agricultural and industrial production are also key factors. Despite the size of the service sector, the US still produces some 25 per cent of the world's agricultural goods and manufactured products (such as machinery, automotive components and vehicles, aircraft, chemicals and high-technology hardware).

Taxation

Most of the US government's income (used for public spending) comes from taxation. The biggest sources are income tax paid by individuals and social security contributions. Income from corporate taxes (paid by companies on their profits) and excise duties are a small part of total federal receipts.

Americans pay less direct federal income tax than people in other Western countries. But they have to pay other taxes, such as property tax, sales tax and state income tax, in addition to medical, dental and pension costs. Taxation is an emotive subject for Americans. Proposed tax increases to pay for public services and government spending arouse opposition, especially from the middle class. This may determine party political policies and election results.

In 1995, the Tax Foundation estimated that the median or representative family with one income paid about 36.2 per cent of that income in taxes. The progressive nature of tax means that those with higher incomes pay proportionately more taxes. The amount of tax Americans actually pay depends on their ability to cope with complex tax forms and claim a range of deductions such as the interest on home mortgages (loans).

Features of the economy

The US is the world's biggest importer and exporter. This situation and the size of its economy mean that the US is a crucial player in global trade.

But the economy experienced difficulties from the 1970s until the early 1990s. These were due partly to international factors (like recession) and partly to domestic conditions. US prices and costs (particularly in manufacturing) did not equal those of other major

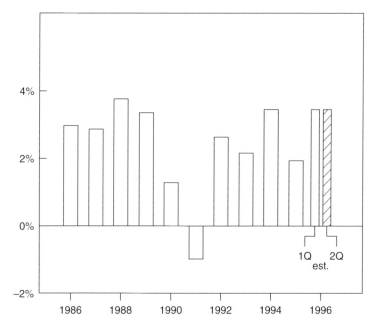

FIGURE 8.1 US economic growth, 1986–96. *(Time/Goldman Sachs and Co./Bank of America)*

competing countries (like Japan); growth rates varied considerably; inflation (increase in the average level of prices) fluctuated; and unemployment grew. The US economy did not dominate as it had done after the Second World War.

One reason for the US's relative decline is its balance of trade problem which, since the 1970s, has resulted in a deficit (importing more goods than it has exported). This amounted to $151 billion in 1994, arising from exports of $5.1 trillion and imports of $6.6 trillion. These imports are in traditionally strong American areas such as petroleum products, food and drink, machinery, iron and steel products and consumer goods such as television sets, cameras and computers which have suffered because of foreign competition.

The US's relative economic decline has forced it to become more interdependent with the economies of other countries and to

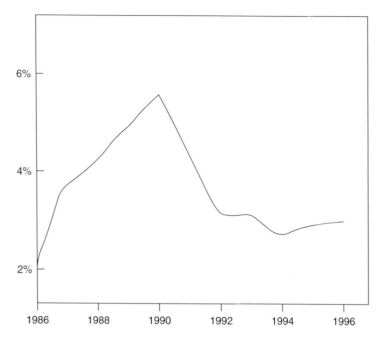

FIGURE 8.2 US inflation rate, 1986–96 *(Time/Goldman Sachs and Co./Bank of America)*

reduce its protectionism. American investment capital is an important element in the Canadian, Latin-American, European and Asian economies. After problems in the 1980s, the position improved in 1994 as foreign investment in the US amounted to $5 trillion, compared with $6 trillion in American assets overseas.

Since exports and imports account for 23 per cent of the GDP, American governments and corporations must achieve a cooperative and stable international trading environment in order to prosper. Internationally, therefore, the US was concerned to finalize the GATT (General Agreement on Tariffs and Trade) talks in 1994, which should promote freer and less protectionist world trade. Attempts by the US to balance world trading blocs also led to the creation of the North American Free Trade Area (NAFTA), ratified by Congress in 1994 but opposed by protectionists in both political parties. This is a trade agreement with

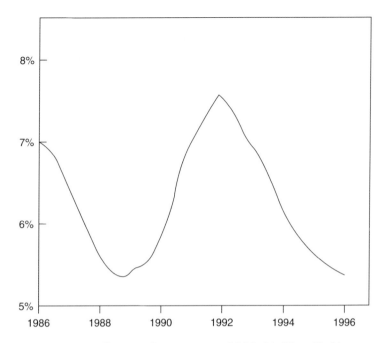

FIGURE 8.3 US unemployment rate, 1986–96 (Time/Goldman Sachs and Co./Bank of America)

Canada and Mexico and comprises the world's largest trading market. The US is also concerned to stabilize its relationships with China, Japan, the Pacific Rim countries and the Latin-American economies.

Domestically, the mid-to-late 1980s in the US saw growth and a liberal market attitude, during which many people prospered. But much of the economic growth was in the service sector which generated new but low-paid, unskilled and often part-time jobs. Meanwhile the traditional industries reduced their workforces. The early 1990s were a period of stagnation produced by the negative effects of the 1980s.

High government borrowing and spending from the 1980s and into the 1990s also created domestic problems. The result has been large annual federal budget deficits (the gap between government income and expenditure). Unsuccessful attempts to cut the budget deficit were made from the mid-1980s. Following a government shut-down in some areas in 1995–96, it was hoped to achieve a balanced budget by 2002. In 1996 the deficit was cut by some 60 per cent and was the lowest for twenty years at $107 billion. But increased public spending may result in a continuing budget deficit problem.

The budget deficit is a sign of whether the government is out of control. Critics argue that the deficit, liberal economic attitudes in the 1980s, the amount of foreign capital in the US and a high dollar exchange rate were reasons for the US stock market crash of October 1987. This affected financial markets abroad; influenced the world recession; and led to a US recession and failing economy, which lasted until 1994.

Domestic and international economic developments have challenged American business and industry. Critics argue that the poor performance of the US economy in the early 1990s was due to an overemphasis on traditional manufacturing industry. The country had not adapted sufficiently to a 'post-industrial age', in which high-technology and service industries are now a dominant part of GDP.

Critics feel that the US should improve its economic performance by modernizing factories, improving products and reducing costs and prices. It should make capital investment in service and high-technology industries and in specialist training. It is felt that government should actively promote industrial policies and Republicans believe that lower taxes and less regulation of the economy would also help. As in most countries, the future of industry and manufacturing remains problematic. Arguably, the need is to develop a capital-intensive and labour-saving industrial infrastructure which can complement the service sector.

Nevertheless, world competition has forced US industry to become more competitive by restructuring itself and increasing productivity. American workers are more productive than the Japanese and Germans because the US makes better use of its plant and machinery. Significant changes have occurred in the US economy due to advanced technology, freer trade and more ruthless corporate management.

From 1994 the US economy recovered steadily and most economic indicators were positive. Interest rates were stable (with adjustments to contain inflation). This encouraged companies to invest more and eased the burden on mortgage (loan) payers. Unemployment in 1996 was reduced to 5.2 per cent (the lowest for six years) and inflation fell to 2.8 per cent. Even widespread redundancies (downsizing) in labour and management have been offset by the preservation of smaller companies and the creation of 10 million new jobs since 1992. Between 1979 and 1996 the US created 27 million new jobs and leads the world in this area, although the quality of jobs varies. Such features have resulted in price and wage stability; productivity and growth rates (estimated at up to 4 per cent in 1996) have improved; and the dollar has been performing relatively strongly, although with fluctuations.

However, rapid economic growth can lead to inflationary pressures and result in recession. In such circumstances interest rates must be raised to control inflation. But, with the pace of growth moderating in late 1996, the American economy was experiencing a balanced, sustained expansion with low inflation, low interest rates and low unemployment.

Women and the economy

The employed workforce of 123 million (1994) has considerable mobility and flexibility. However, not all workers have gained from economic growth since 1994. Many male workers have seen weak wage growth, rising job insecurity, falling living standards for the less skilled and increased downsizing. However, the position and economic impact of women (46 per cent of the workforce) as employees and employers have improved.

More women now work and earn more. While the proportion of men with jobs fell from 80 per cent in 1960 to 70 per cent in 1995, that of working women rose from 35 per cent to 55 per cent. Male average earnings fell 7 per cent between 1973 and 1993 while those of women rose 11 per cent. In 1973, a woman's average hourly wage was two-thirds of a man's but in the 1980s women's wages gained on men's for the first time.

Well-educated women (and men) have done best. The earnings of the top 5 per cent of working women have risen by a third since 1976. However, less-skilled women have suffered, but by much less than unskilled men. This is not a matter of women taking men's jobs or pushing down male wages because low-skilled men and women have different jobs and women work more often in the service sector.

The biggest increase has been in well-educated high-income women (particularly those married to high-income husbands) who continue working after marriage. However, fewer wives of lower-skilled men have joined the workforce and the wages of lower-skilled working wives have risen more slowly than those of better-educated women. Family income has thus risen at top levels and fallen at the bottom.

There has also been a large increase in women business-owners. Their businesses are a fast-growing and influential part of the corporate economy. In 1996, it was estimated that 8 million businesses employing 18.5 million people and constituting over a quarter of smaller corporations were owned by women. Such businesses are often small, home-operated and in the service or retail sector. But women-owned businesses in the manufacturing or construction sectors are growing and more women are attending business schools.

Industry and manufacturing

Historically, manufacturing and industrial production has been a crucial factor in the US economy. The most important sectors are the manufacture of heavy transportation and automotive equipment (vehicles, aircraft and space components), non-electrical goods, electrical machinery, food products, chemicals, steel components and high-technology hardware.

The US's industrial and manufacturing heartland is the Midwest region of the Great Lakes, southern Michigan, northern Ohio and Pennsylvania around Pittsburgh. But other industrial regions have grown in the Northeast, Northwest and Southwest

(California). These tend to specialize in high-technology industries and computer manufacture. Other fast-growing industrial regions are the Southeast and Texas, where large chemical and high-technology industries have developed.

This industrial and manufacturing base is represented by leading corporations, such as General Motors (Detroit) and Ford (Michigan) in vehicles; Exxon (New York) in oil refining; International Business Machines (New York) in computers; and General Electric (Connecticut) in electronics.

Industrial and manufacturing production has been stable in recent years due to technical advances. The US is the world's leading maker of industrial goods and 18 million Americans were employed in manufacturing in 1993, although the number of blue-collar workers has declined.

Service industries

Service industries have grown faster than other sectors since the 1950s and are now the most important economic sector. This process is echoed in other industrialized countries and has encouraged discussion about 'post-industrial' societies.

Service industries vary in size from small firms to large corporations. They have developed nationwide, but particularly in the Northeast. They include government services, business and health services, banking, finance consultancy, hotels, restaurants, leisure activities, trade, personal services and communications. Service sector jobs now comprise 75 per cent of the workforce. But many of them are in unskilled and part-time positions and much of the service sector tends to be manager-intensive rather than labour-intensive.

Critics argue that the service sector is financed by and dependent upon the wealth and profits generated by technical advances in agriculture and manufacturing. The open question perhaps is whether the service sector can sustain itself and grow at a time when the industrial sector may decline, or whether complementary and balancing sectors will develop.

PLATE 8.1 Manufacturing silicon wafers
(Lonnie Duke/Tony Stone Images)

Agriculture, forestry and fisheries

Although US agriculture, forestry and fisheries have a huge productivity, they contribute only some 3 per cent to the GDP.

Agriculture

About 47 per cent of the land area of the US is farmland and is devoted almost equally to crops and livestock. The Midwest remains an important agricultural region in the country, with corn (maize) and wheat as its main crops and large-scale livestock and dairy farming in the Upper Midwest states.

The South is still a centre of traditional crops, such as tobacco (the Southeast and Kentucky) and corn and cotton (the South and Southwest). But its economy has now diversified and expanded, so that Texas and Florida are the US's main providers of cattle, sheep, cotton and rice. The West is an important region for cattle and wheat farming in the Great Plains area; fruit and vineyards in the Pacific states; and livestock herds in the Southwestern and Rocky Mountain states.

The US is the world's largest food producer and exporter; is largely self-sufficient in farm produce and supplies some 15 per cent of the global requirements of corn, wheat, beef, pork and lamb. But in 1994 only 6.2 million people lived on the nation's 2 million farms and employment was, at 2.9 million workers, about 2.5 per cent of the national workforce. Small subsistence farms have disappeared and farm labour has been reduced as competition, mechanization, technological advances and specialized farms have increased.

Despite high domestic productivity, agricultural exports declined in the early 1980s as other world markets expanded. Farmers had difficulties because of import restrictions by foreign countries and the then high value of the dollar. The importance to the US of finalizing a free-trade GATT agreement with reduced tariff barriers has been crucial to restoring the now buoyant world position of American agriculture.

Forestry

Forests cover a third of the US, mostly in the West but also in the South and the North. About 80 per cent of the forests comprise softwoods and 20 per cent hardwoods and two-thirds produce wood items and timber commercially. Some 70 per cent of forests are privately owned; the federal government owns 20 per cent and state or local government supervises the rest. In recent years, the environmental aspect of forestry has grown, with an emphasis on ecosystem management and increased recreational and wildlife uses of the public forests.

Fisheries

The US ranks sixth among world fishing nations in terms of its total catch of fish, with a value in 1994 of $3.8 billion. Fishing fleets operate from ports on the Atlantic, Pacific and Gulf of Mexico, as well as on the Great Lakes. Alaska is the leading state, with its fishing industry worth $1.5 billion a year. Louisiana has a large catch (with shellfish making up the bulk), as do Texas and California. Massachusetts and Maine, important fishing centres since the colonial era, are major players in the fisheries industry. But their traditional fishing grounds (shared with the Atlantic provinces of Canada) are in danger of depletion.

Financial and industrial institutions

American economic development, unlike that of other countries, was not accompanied by the creation of national financial institutions. Governments avoided centralizing the economic system until the twentieth century and most financial and industrial institutions had operated as private concerns.

Corporations and entrepreneurs

The corporations of the nineteenth and early twentieth centuries owned by individuals like Henry Ford (automobiles), John D.

Rockefeller (oil) and Andrew Carnegie (steel), and smaller corporations under personal or family proprietors, have decreased. Many businesses today tend to be owned by financial conglomerates, which invest in company shares for profit.

However, the actual running of the businesses is often done by professional accountants, executives or managers who may own only a small percentage of the corporation's stock or shares. The rise of an American executive and managerial culture was aided by the creation of Business Management Schools which taught business techniques to their students.

Big corporations now dominate most of American business and influence the country's consumer patterns. But smaller corporations and individual entrepreneurs account for three-quarters of the corporate system and form an important part of the business world. Such small corporations may often eventually be taken over by larger ones and large corporations expand through mergers in the pursuit of markets and profits.

Small businesses tend to be created by entrepreneurs and are often associated with the service sector. Some succeed and some fail. These businesses have been responsible for generating more new jobs than the larger corporations.

The ethos of American business, and what some might regard as an unhealthy preoccupation with making money, attracts people who are determined to succeed and are prepared to work hard to achieve material success, careers and status. But they had problems in the late 1980s and early 1990s under the pressures of domestic and international recession. Since 1994, however, the financial and business markets have improved with the upturn in the economy.

Wall Street

'Wall Street' refers to the financial centre of the US in Lower and Midtown Manhattan, New York City. It comprises business institutions, such as stock-brokers and financial companies (like Merrill Lynch), banks (such as Citicorp and J.P. Morgan), insurance corporations, commodity exchanges (dealing in coffee, cotton, metal, or corn) and the New York Stock Exchange (NYSE). These institutions deal with huge sums of money and control and invest much of Americans' capital.

Large corporations are dependent for their financing and prosperity upon stock exchanges on which stocks and shares in selected businesses are bought and sold. This system, as well as raising investment money, is an important indicator of businesses' financial standing. New York City's two stock exchanges (the NYSE and the American Stock Exchange) deal with the majority of stock sales and purchases in the US.

The NYSE (founded in 1792) comprises about 1,300 members who trade in stocks and bonds either for themselves or as agents for clients. It is a market for the buying and selling of stocks and bonds which are listed on the Exchange's trading register; these are sold to the highest bidder throughout the day and their value can go up or down. A company must have a spec-ified amount of stock and a minimum turnover of trade before it can be listed on the NYSE.

The NYSE is internationally known for its Dow Jones Average. This is a list which contains the price of stocks and bonds in selected industrial and commercial companies on the Exchange. It is adjusted throughout the working day and its move-ments are shown in points. The Dow Jones is very influential and international financiers, investors and governments see it as an accurate indicator of the US's economic health.

The banking system

Americans have traditionally been suspicious of banks. The Wall Street crash of 1929, when many banks closed and people lost all their money, still haunts the national consciousness and fears were revived during the 1987 stock market crash. US law is supposed to regulate the banking system and curb any excessive growth of individual banks.

There are about 12,000 different commercial banks in the US, which provide personal services for clients. Some banks are incorporated (or licensed) under national charter and are known

as National Banks. Others are regulated under state charters. The banking system has been increasingly deregulated to allow other financial competitors. Banks, in order to preserve business, have moved into new (and riskier) areas like securities trading, currency dealing and insurance.

There are also many non-bank institutions which function in similar ways to banks, like personal credit groups and 2,300 savings-and-loans associations. There have been recent collapses of the latter, often due to fraudulent speculation in an under-regulated sector, with resulting criticism.

Critics argue that the banking system is not as closely regu-lated at federal and state level as it should be, particularly at a time when financial institutions are expanding. Instantaneous computer-generated money transactions also suggest the need for greater supervision.

Federal Reserve System

The Federal Reserve System (created in 1913) is similar to central or national banks in other countries but its banking framework comprises twelve Federal Reserve Districts through-out the US, each with its individual Federal Reserve Bank. The system is supervised in Washington by a Board of Governors, headed by an influential Chairman. The governors are appoin-ted by the President and confirmed by the Senate. However, as independent appointees and custodians of the monetary system, they do not always agree with government economic policies.

However, the US Treasury Department (the federal financial department) does generally work closely with the Federal Reserve. It can influence the financial markets and interest rates by its supervision of the national debt and can adjust the amount of credit in the monetary sector by changing its deposits with the Federal Reserve banks.

PLATE 8.2   (previous pages) The New York Stock Exchange
(Rex Features)

PLATE 8.3   US Treasury Building, Washington, DC
(Barnaby's Picture Library)

The Federal Reserve sets the minimum financial reserves that must be held by commercial banks in order for them to operate; adjusts interest rates; controls the size of the money supply in the economy; tries to reduce inflation; issues bank notes; implements US monetary policy; and attempts to create a stable environment for corporate activity. Some 60 per cent of commercial banks are members of the Federal Reserve and are responsible for three-quarters of commercial bank deposits. Critics argue that the success of the US economy since 1994 has been due to the economic management skills of the Federal Reserve rather than the politicians.

Trade/labour unions

A national union (the Knights of Labor) was formed in 1869 to organize workers and to press for better employment and social conditions but it was not very successful. Later efforts to create labour organizations led to the American Federation of Labor (AFL), which was a collection of independent craft unions, and the Congress of Industrial Organizations (CIO), which was based on manufacturing industry. Although initially affected by conflicting loyalties among different unions, the two groups organized themselves on a wider industrial basis and in 1955 merged to form an umbrella institution, the AFL–CIO. About 84 per cent of union members are now affiliated with the AFL–CIO which has a membership of seventy-eight unions.

American unionism is more associated with manufacturing industries and construction than white-collar jobs and the service sector. Unions lost members and influence after being a powerful economic force from the 1930s to the 1950s. A minority of wage earners are now union members (15.8 per cent compared with 35.5 per cent in 1945) and in 1994 union membership amounted to 15.5 million non-farm employees.

The decline in union membership stemmed from economic trends, such as the growth of service and high-technology industries in a post-industrial economy; foreign competition; economic recession; fewer manufacturing industries; increased automation and advanced equipment; less need for blue-collar workers; and increased unemployment among union members. The failure of unions to protect the jobs of white- and blue-collar workers in the 1970s and 1980s also led to a drop in union influence. This allowed companies to restructure the labour market, sack full-time staff and employ cheap contract freelancers. The result was the creation of a two-tier workforce of skilled, highly paid staff and a poorly paid underclass with little industrial strength.

Legal frameworks for worker representation and collective bargaining between employers and employees were established by legislation only in the 1930s, after strikes and fierce struggles between union organizers, the police, government, and employers in the early twentieth century. American unions do have the right to strike but this is restricted by provisions for cooling-off periods and compulsory arbitration in certain circumstances. Strike action can be unpopular and also counter-productive for union members who may lose their jobs as a result. After a period of forty-seven years when industrial action was low, the number of strikes increased in 1994.

Although US unions have achieved pay and insurance benefits for their members, many workers regard job security as more important since there are few redundancy payments by companies to employees. Workers do not have the job security of union members in Europe, their minimum wage is low, although their average wage matches the highest European standards.

American unions are not highly organized, do not have the influence or political motivation of European labour organizations, nor have unions in the US attracted a mass membership. Critics suggest several reasons for this situation. First, the political and economic power of employers and anti-union legislation by Congress (such as the Taft–Hartley Act of 1947) and individual states have minimized union impact. Second the *laissez-faire* attitudes of the American economy, a belief in self-reliance and individualism and the lack of strict class distinctions, encourage many workers to believe in the possibility of upward mobility. Third, a high percentage of union members support the Republican Party, with blue-collar workers looking to that party for answers to their economic discontent. Fourth, the American drive for success and importance of individual effort limits a wider and more united political identification with union activity. Fifth, the 'Red Scare' of the 1920s and anti-communist agitation in the 1950s neutralized potential left-wing influences and the union membership tends to be at variance with the more politicized goals and ideology of union leaders. Sixth, immigration to the US, and the formation of ethnic groups have historically tended to detract from the solidarity aspects of trade unionism. Seventh, there have been strong divisions between skilled and unskilled workers and between different craft unions. Consequently, workers have not been closely involved in corporate policy-making

263

and there have been few substantial attempts by unions to fundamentally influence the national economy in their favour.

However, union militancy, influence and membership now
seem to be increasing. The AFL–CIO leadership is stronger; there
may be more calls for wage rises backed by the threat of strike
action; union money was donated to the Democratic election
campaign in 1996; and President Clinton may bring in pro-union
legislation (such as making it difficult for employers to replace
striking workers). The unions are now recruiting members from
a new proletariat of low-wage African Americans and immigrants
from Laos and Vietnam, workers who have traditionally shied
away from affiliation. Shortages of skilled and unskilled workers
in the expanding economy may also allow the unions to press
more for wage increases.

Attitudes to the economic system

Some traditional attitudes still seem to be held by Americans. In
terms of trusting the government on the economy, a 1994 *Los
Angeles Times* poll showed that 63 per cent of respondents
thought that government regulation of business usually does more
harm than good. Some 69 per cent believed that when something
is run by the government, it is usually inefficient and wasteful. A
1995 *Time/CNN* poll found that 86 per cent of Americans agreed
with the statement that 'People have to realise that they can only
count on their own skills and abilities if they're going to win in
this world.'

The same poll, taken at a time when the American economy
was coming out of recession, found that, of the main problems
facing the US, respondents placed the budget deficit in fourth
place, the economy generally in fifth place and unemployment
(and jobs) in sixth place; 45 per cent said that they worried a lot
about the state of the economy and 30 per cent said that they
were worried about being able to keep up with bills.

A year later (1996) and on the basis of an expanding
economy, another *Time/CNN* poll showed mixed responses. Some

76 per cent of respondents thought that their family finances were doing very or fairly well and 46 per cent thought that their overall standard of living had improved since 1992. But some 63 per cent thought that economic conditions were harsher. They agreed with the statement that 'the American Dream has become impossible for most people to achieve', although they thought that their children would have a higher standard of living than they do at present. Nevertheless, some 85 per cent were very/fairly satisfied with their jobs (as against 14 per cent who were dissatisfied) and 70 per cent were not worried about losing their jobs (as opposed to 29 per cent who were).

A 1996 American Enterprise Institute poll also found that fears about jobs and the economy had declined. However, people were concerned about taxation and the federal budget. Most Americans seemed to be doing well materially and felt better off, although they were still worrying and working hard. But the experience of poorer people was worse than the overall optimistic picture. *The Washington Post* (16 October 1996) wrote that 'The new economy has showered its favors disproportionately on workers with more experience and education'.

EXERCISES

■ Examine and explain the following terms:

AFL–CIO	Wall Street	entrepreneurs
Federal Reserve	NYSE	New Deal
Dow Jones Average	anti-trust laws	corporations
service industries	NAFTA	trade balance
budget deficit	GDP	deregulation

■ Write short essays on the following topics:

1   What is meant by the American 'free enterprise' economic system? Examine its advantages and disadvantages.

2   Comment critically on the present state of the US economy.

3   What are the strengths and weaknesses of the US trade union movement?

Social services

THIS CHAPTER EXAMINES THOSE social services which are provided for individuals and groups by the private and public sectors in the US. 'Social services' includes items such as health care, retirement pensions, unemployment payments, housing, disability allowances and welfare benefits. The latter are often associated in the public mind with government or public help to the poor, particularly African Americans and Latinos. But most social services spending by both sectors is in fact on middle- and upper-income people rather than the poor.

The existence and nature of such services differ from country to country. Their availability, as in the US, changes according to the attitudes of people and politicians. They are also conditioned by experiences with the actual workings of social institutions and the demands of social life.

Americans historically have believed in self-reliance and independence in social service areas. These have been largely seen as personal matters and the responsibility of the family or individual, rather than of state or federal institutions. The private enterprise market is theoretically supposed to supply necessary services for which individuals should pay. But, since the 1930s, there has been an awareness that some people are unable to benefit from free enterprise because of their economic circumstances. Reformers have also felt that the provision of essential social services for all should be a national responsibility. The scope of many services has consequently changed and been extended to new areas of Social Security, welfare assistance, health care and housing needs.

However, these expanded social services have not resulted in the US becoming a welfare state on the European model. It lacks a comprehensive range of centrally organized social and health care services, which are largely financed by general taxation and are available to all irrespective of income.

Americans therefore rely for the necessities of life on an uncoordinated mixture of state and federal government programmes (the public sector), help given by voluntary organizations and arrangements made by individuals themselves (the private sector). Most services in both sectors (except for voluntary bodies) are paid for out of contributory systems and benefits are gained by those individuals who contribute financially to a particular programme. Those unable to make financial contributions receive help from a range of non-contributory state and federal schemes, most of which are known as 'welfare', as well as from the voluntary services. Many affluent Americans also receive direct and indirect benefits and services because of government subsidies in areas such as education, home loans and tax breaks (or relief). The contemporary combination of public and private social services has developed largely since the 1930s and results in a complex and diversified system. Some critics argue for a unified and national system which would be more responsive to social need. Other critics and, according to polls, a majority of the population oppose such proposals, particularly in the welfare area. However, spending on social services by the public sector has increased since the 1960s and the country does provide relatively well for its most needy inhabitants, such as the handicapped and old people.

But Americans still seem to expect most other people to stand on their own two feet. Recent government policies (1996) on the restructuring of welfare programmes suggest that the US is moving further away from Welfare State models. However, some critics argue that European systems should follow the American example in order to encourage personal responsibility and reduce the increasing costs of social services.

Social services history

Some 400 years ago, the US was primarily a rural society in which most Americans worked in farming and there were few urban centres. The essence of life for the majority was self-reliance in

269

social, health, employment and housing needs. Since then, the images of the independent farmer and frontiersman have been influential in American mythology. But, paradoxically, the societies of the early agriculturalists and pioneers were also cooperative, with communal support and protection, as were many Native-American communities. Such contrasting images illustrate the tension in US life between individualism and communalism. They also affect how later Americans have responded to the issue of social services.

Industrialization and urbanization increased in the late eighteenth and nineteenth centuries and brought considerable misery to many people. But social services were still either largely private and individualistic or provided by voluntary charities, like the help given by ethnic and religious groups to their members. However, there were also small amounts of aid supplied by state and local governments. This mixture of services was conditioned, for good and bad, by the tradition of self-reliance. There was (and still is) a distinction made in the US between the 'deserving' poor who could be helped by existing resources and the 'undeserving' poor who were supposed to rectify their own condition.

Most Americans were unwilling to let central institutions organize too many of society's affairs. They jealously protected their own independence and took pride in coping and achieving by themselves. Politicians also avoided intervention in, and government spending on, social services. Consequently, no adequate national system of social services developed in the late nineteenth and early twentieth centuries.

But the system of self-reliance and fragmented aid could not cope with the economic collapse, large-scale unemployment, poverty and social problems caused by the Great Depression, which followed the 1929 Stock Market crash. The existing resources of private, public and voluntary organizations proved insufficient in the 1930s when an estimated 40 per cent of the population lived in relative poverty.

The situation improved considerably with President Franklin D. Roosevelt's New Deal in the mid-1930s. Roosevelt was concerned to rectify faults in the economy and to provide a framework for a measure of social protection. Social Security legislation was passed in 1935, which made benefits for workers and their families dependent on employment status and the payments that employees contributed during their working lives. The New Deal also provided jobs in public sector works programmes for the unemployed and tried to improve the social and economic problems of African Americans and Native Americans.

But these programmes were not comprehensive and were directed towards people who were willing to work. Publicly financed non-contributory welfare was still unpopular in 1930s' America and there was antagonism towards those who would not work or help themselves. But two important federal welfare programmes, AFDC and GA (see p. 276), were passed to help the needy, children, single parents and the handicapped.

However, after the 1930s, reformers argued that such measures needed to be supplemented by further action. Federal, state and local governments became more involved in social services. Government thinking also changed as publicly funded programmes expanded considerably after the Second World War. Individuals and groups agitated for more assistance. War veterans, for example, were given federal medical, educational and housing benefits (the 'GI Bill of Rights'). A new element of 'rights' to public social services became apparent. There was a feeling that the US should be able to care more for its citizens, particularly those who were in need.

Gradually, and on the basis of programmes like the GI Bill, the federal government became more involved in providing public social services. However, such expansion was still piecemeal and largely a response to need and public pressure, rather than a commitment to a consistent national policy. But social programmes were in fact developing under their own impetus and covered greater numbers of people.

From the 1960s to the early 1980s, more federal and state money was spent on public social services. President Lyndon Johnson (1963–8) introduced new programmes as part of his 'War on Poverty' and 'Great Society' campaigns, which were intended to alleviate need and suffering; for example, Medicare provided health care for the elderly; Medicaid supplied health care to the poor; and the Food Stamp programme gave coupons to the poor that could be used to buy food in specified shops.

Johnson also introduced a range of other initiatives (such as 'He1d Start') which attempted to attack poverty and unemployment through education, job training and regional development. But, valuable though they were, these policies were not directed towards the establishment of an American welfare state. They were intended more as opportunities for those people who were prepared to work and better themselves.

Nevertheless, the Johnson reforms formed the basis for future public social services. A range of agencies were also established to implement the new programmes. But, increasingly in this expansive climate, some of the poor and needy came to regard non-contributory welfare and health care as a right and the number of claimants grew.

Public spending on social services increased through the 1970s. There was also a move away from defence and military spending to expenditure on social programmes. However, Presidents after Johnson differed in their attitudes to social service and welfare schemes. It also became difficult to persuade Congress to allocate further public money to such services. Domestic economic problems by 1980, such as rising inflation, curtailed new social legislation.

President Reagan (1981–8) tried to reduce the cost of welfare and public programmes during his administrations. He wanted Americans to be responsible for their own lives through self-help and to depend less on government aid. But, despite such aims, the cost of Social Security, welfare schemes and unemployment compensation to the federal budget increased. Public social programmes had thus grown relatively rapidly. But Republican administrations have not been keen to raise income taxes in order to pay for them, particularly welfare.

The Bush administration (1989–92) attempted to reduce social and public spending, but was forced to meet increased demand by tax rises. The Clinton administration (1992–) tried to introduce proposals for universal health care financed mainly by individual and corporate contributions. But this reform collapsed and the return of Republican majorities in Congress at the 1994 mid-term elections led to proposals for greater curbs in social services spending.

Under pressure from a Republican Congress and public opinion, President Clinton in 1996 fulfilled his 1992 campaign pledge to change American welfare policy by cutting and restructuring federal public spending. Some critics argue that this marks an unravelling of New Deal programmes, returns the US to the old mentality on social services and negatively affects large numbers of the population, such as children. Others maintain that the welfare reforms signal a move from a system of non-contributory benefit entitlement to one of personal responsibility.

The organization of contemporary social services

Some 30 per cent of total US payments for items such as health care, retirement provision, employment protection and housing derive from the private sector. This means that individuals make arrangements for their own needs from a range of commercial organizations, such as insurance businesses. Companies, trade unions and other bodies also use private sources to insure their workers and members. The voluntary sector is often included in the private sector. It comprises a range of charities, local bodies, national foundations and religious groups. They are dependent upon individual donations and provide many forms of assistance for the needy and poor.

The public sector today amounts to some 70 per cent of all social services and health care payments. It comprises, first, federal Social Security benefits under a contribution system for all employed people and their families and, second, non-contributory welfare programmes, health services and housing organized by state, local and federal governments.

Social Security, health care, education and welfare in the public sector now represent a very large budget item for American governments but the quality of public services varies from state to state. This is because of 'matching-funds' policies (whereby the states have to equal federal funds in some cases); the wealth of individual states; their prioritization of programmes; differences in states' cost of living; and the need to produce balanced budgets.

The main public sector organization is by federal, state and local programmes. Budget responsibilties are allocated between Washington, DC, and the states. However, the states generally have the primary and immediate task of implementing and delivering their public social services.

At the *federal* level, public social services are administered through government programmes and many different departments. It is the Department of Health and Human Services that administers or supervises most of the schemes. Its establishment (originally as the Department of Health, Education and Welfare in 1953) was a crucial acknowledgement of responsibility for, and the importance of, social services.

This federal organization can become uncoordinated due to the varied departments and responsibilities involved. Some critics argue that there should be common implementation by one inclusive national body. Others prefer a more specialized approach centred on separate departments for each activity.

Public social services at the *state* and *local level* are also usually divided between separate bodies but, in some states, there are umbrella agencies that combine health, welfare and other related programmes.

Public social services

It is convenient to divide public social services into two main sections. The first is the contributory Social Security system, through which benefits are earned and distributed. The second includes those people receiving assistance based on financial need. This is awarded on the basis of means or income, but is not tied to a contributory system. It is the area generally known as 'welfare'.

Some citizens count on the existence of a social safety net based on public funds. Others debate its bureaucratic complexity and inefficiency, incompleteness, effects on the morals and initiative of welfare clients, abuse and cost. Public sector services (particularly in health care and welfare) have become central issues in American politics.

Social Security benefits

Governmental provision for Social Security is a large and expanding part of public social services, which is administered from Washington and in 1996 amounted to $347 billion of the federal budget. Social Security contributions produce 32 per cent of all federal income and Social Security payments amount to 20 per cent of federal spending.

Social Security derives from the programmes contained in the 1935 Social Security Act. It now refers to three main areas: the old age, survivors, disability and health insurance programme (OASDHI); Medicare; and Unemployment Compensation. Employees and the self-employed contribute financially (some 7 per cent of earnings) to these programmes during their working lives. They (and their families) receive benefits from the system as a result of their contributions. It is therefore a social insurance programme. The benefits include pensions on retirement, which are relatively low at about a quarter of average earnings; medical care for the elderly and disabled under Medicare; disability payments; illness and accident provisions; and unemployment payments.

The Department of Labor supervises the system of Unemployment Compensation, but each state administers its own programme. The majority of workers are covered; unemployment benefits last for between 26 and 39 weeks; and the general compensation is about a quarter of the worker's earnings.

However, since Social Security may not cover all the bills, provision for old age, illness and unemployment often has to include additional private resources for many Americans, such as savings, investments and insurance policies. Most employers and unions also provide additional retirement, unemployment, health care and life insurance services for employees. These are mainly paid by employers or unions, but can also include financial contributions from workers.

Welfare programmes

Public concern about poverty resulted in federal legislation from the 1960s. This provided financial help to the needy and poor; work, training and rehabilitation programmes under various government departments; resources to house and feed the homeless; and health care for the sick who lack financial provision. But the total cost of programmes for the poor and needy amounts only to some 6 per cent of the federal budget and many people (perhaps a half) do not take up the public benefits to which they are entitled.

The cost of welfare programmes has been traditionally shared by federal, state and local governments. Generally, federal funds are distributed to the states, which should spend equal (or matching) amounts of money to the federal funds. But some northern states provide a lot of welfare help to their citizens and some southern states give relatively little. Each state devises and organizes its own programmes. It defines, on the basis of a balanced budget, which families and individuals qualify for assistance in terms of needs.

Until 1996, the main federal welfare programmes, or non-contributory aid to the needy, consisted of Medicaid, Aid to Families with Dependent Children (AFDC) and Food Stamps. But there are other programmes under the General Assistance (GA) scheme which provide income support, cash grants, aid for housing, school meals, Supplemental Security Income (SSI) for the elderly poor and help with other basic necessities.

Medicaid is a health scheme and is the largest direct federal aid programme for citizens under 65, amounting to $92 billion of federal spending in 1996. It is supposed to provide health care for those who do not have private insurance or the financial ability to pay for a range of medical requirements.

The second largest programme of federal aid to the poor was (until 1996) AFDC. Payments to the disabled and families with children were based on need and the official poverty line (see p. 278) was used as a guideline. AFDC payments varied between the states, with southern states generally paying less than northern ones. By 1996, AFDC assistance amounted to $25 billion for some 15 million persons, of whom two-thirds were children.

AFDC was abolished in 1996. Welfare responsibility was passed to the states, which receive federal grants to run their own programmes. There is a five-year lifetime limit on welfare benefits (two years initially) and most recipients will have to enrol in workfare schemes (see p. 279).

The third programme derives from the 1964 Food Stamp Act. It provides coupons that are used by eligible needy people, who lack an adequate low-cost diet, to buy food in approved shops at an average national rate of some one-third of its normal price. The Department of Agriculture (as part of its programme to cut surplus food stocks) organizes the distribution of food and food stamps through state and local governments. The number of people using the scheme rose between 1970–80 and its cost in 1994 was $24.5 billion. Eligibility for the programme was reduced in 1996.

This welfare system does provide a degree of help for the most needy. But people who are unemployed for long periods may receive little help from the government. Employment is, therefore, a crucial factor for most Americans, from which stems their ability to provide for themselves. Without work, they can obtain little public assistance unless they fall into the welfare categories. The restructuring of AFDC benefits in effect means that after two years on welfare an individual *must* find a job. Certain hardship exemptions are available for the very poorest 20 per cent who cannot find work when the benefits end. But for most people it will be sink or swim and they will be dependent on how much individual states are prepared to spend on their welfare programmes.

The needy and the poverty line

Welfare payments are therefore made to people who do not have the resources to live at an appropriately decent minimum level (by American standards). The eligibility for such assistance is based on the 'official poverty level'. This is calculated annually (to take account of inflation) by the Federal Social Security Administration. It determines earned income levels below which a household and single people are classified as 'poor'. The poverty-line income is equal to three times the cost of a nutritionally adequate diet and depends on the number of people in a household. In 1993 it was about $14,763 for a family of four, although other categories (such as single people) live below this level.

The number of people living in poverty has fluctuated. In 1993, 39.3 million Americans (or 15.1 per cent of the population) were below the poverty line. Of these, 12.2 per cent of Whites, 33.1 per cent of African Americans and 30.6 per cent of Latinos were below the poverty levels. This suggests that the last two groups are disproportionately represented among the poor. Additionally, children remain over-represented among the poor with a poverty rate of some 23 per cent of all children.

Poverty consequently remains a reality for a sizeable minority of Americans. The poorest people tend to be concentrated in inner city areas which suffer the greatest deprivation. Poverty is also a feature of rural regions. Most poor homes are those where householders have a low or no income. Sometimes these may be single mothers or fathers with young children, or where individuals may be above employment age or are disabled.

An important tax aid designed to lift the working poor with dependent children above the poverty line is the earned-income tax credit (EITC), established in 1975. Instead of facing higher taxes as their incomes increase, individuals with one dependent child (for example) can qualify for a tax credit of up to $2,094 (1995) and up to a maximum wage of $24,396. This means that they will receive lump-sum payments or refunds from the Inland Revenue Service (IRS).

Although fewer Americans are poor today than they were in the past, the debate on the 'poverty question' continues. Critics argue that the federal government should provide funds to eradicate poverty. Others feel that welfare programmes are expensive, inefficient and ineffective and do not give incentives to the poor to help themselves. Some observers maintain that an 'underclass' has developed that is dependent on welfare ('the dependency culture') and which constitutes a serious social problem of disaffected people who may have opted out of national life. The 1996 limitation of federal welfare programmes may arguably be seen as an attempt to break this cycle of permanent dependency.

Single-parent families

Of the 97 million American households in 1994, 68.9 million (71 per cent) contained families; but 12.4 million (18 per cent) of these families were headed only by a woman (divorced, widowed or single) and 2.4 million were headed by a man. Some 22 per cent of all children were being brought up by a single mother and 3 per cent by a single father.

Such families are connected in the public mind with the problems of the needy, the poverty line, welfare programmes and minority groups. Critics argue that a disproportionate number of female-headed families are among the needy and amount (with children) to half of the total poor. According to official statistics, they also comprise 50 per cent of food stamp users and 80 per cent of people on earlier AFDC schemes. But some one-parent families do have incomes above the official poverty level and their children receive a minimum of welfare payments such as free school meals.

Workfare

Some states in recent years have started innovative and relatively successful 'workfare' (work + [wel]fare) programmes. Generally, states require that welfare recipients, such as single parents, should be prepared to work (often in special public-service jobs), take part in job training schemes, or attend educational courses. Care facilities are also provided for families with small children. It was hoped that such programmes would encourage welfare recipients to move off welfare and into secure jobs.

With the 1996 abolition of federal AFDC and the introduction of welfare limits, more people will be obliged to undertake workfare and training schemes as part of their state welfare entitlement. Since more jobs will be required, the question is, who will create them and at whose expense?

Voluntary services

Given the level of poverty in the US and the inability of federal and state governments to meet all the social requirements of the people, the existence of charitable voluntary organizations who help those in need continues to be important. They are usually included in the private sector of social services but they should strictly be seen as a complementary third sector to the private and public sectors.

There is a wide range of social services organized by local and national bodies, which help and campaign on behalf of the disadvantaged. Financial contributions by Americans to such bodies and campaigns are frequently generous. At the national level, institutions like the Rockefeller and Ford foundations and other smaller foundations perform an important role in care research and in health and welfare programmes.

But, at a more grassroots level, religious and other charitable voluntary organizations and unpaid volunteers are often crucial for many people in local communities. They provide a mixture of professional and non-professional aid; supply services for sick or elderly people; operate hospitals, care centres, clinics, retirement homes and shelters for the homeless; and visit old, handicapped and needy people in the community. On these levels, they provide what is often much-needed assistance and comfort.

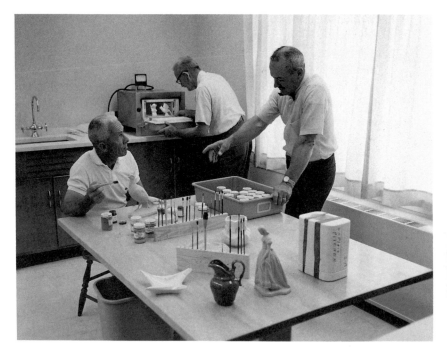

PLATE 9.1 Virginia Methodist retirement home
(David W. Corson/Barnaby's Picture Library)

Health care services

Some Europeans have negative reactions to the American health care system. They feel that it lacks a publicly funded and comprehensive National Health Service since federal funds pay for only 40 per cent of all health care. This aid covers some people of all income groups, but not all the population.

American critics (and popular opinion) also itemize the system's alleged limitations and present a diverse picture of medical provision. They suggest that available and adequate care may depend upon the wealth, gender, residential and ethnic background of the patient. White males living in affluent neighbourhoods and some of the poor and elderly may be relatively well covered by private and public facilities respectively. But people under 65, those of average income, females generally, those from a non-White background and people who live in rural areas or inner city locations may have difficulties in obtaining satisfactory health care.

American health and medical services are divided between the private and public sectors. Private hospitals, clinics and surgeries are in general well equipped and efficient and may be run by a variety of commercial organizations or religious groups. Many of those in the public sector, financed by state and federal funds, tend to lack resources and adequate funding. Doctors, particularly those in the private sector, generally have high incomes and constitute an influential professional interest group.

Most employees and their families (together with the affluent) are normally insured for health care through private insurance schemes. These may be organized individually, by employers or by labour unions against the cost of health treatment and loss of income if workers fall ill. Insurance premiums, which tend to be expensive, are made by deductions from wages and salaries or by individual contributions.

But, generally, no one health insurance policy covers all possible eventualities and many individuals may have to subscribe to several policies in order to protect themselves adequately. Nevertheless, they may still themselves eventually have to pay for some treatment which is not covered by the insurance policies. A considerable number of Americans (estimated at 37 million people) have no health insurance cover either because they cannot afford it or for other reasons (although they may have the income to buy insurance). The irony is that while the US has high quality and extensive medical facilities, particularly in the private sector, gaining access to them remains a problem for a substantial proportion of the population.

People's anxieties about possible illness are conditioned not only by relatively high insurance premiums, but also by the cost of treatment, which (especially for serious illness) is very expensive. There is some hostility towards the medical profession, whom the public often suspect of pushing up medical costs for its own profit. It was this situation that the Clinton administration tried to address by its proposals for a universal health care scheme. These failed, to some extent because of opposition by employers and employees to high compulsory contributions to the programme. It is therefore not only doctors and insurance companies who are opposed to public (or 'socialized') medicine in the US.

In the public sector, health care is available to those requiring it, but who lack money and insurance to pay for the service. The federal non-contributory Medicaid programme provides federal grants to states for the free treatment of the poor and needy, blind and disabled people and dependent children. However, because of matching-fund policies, the scope of Medicaid varies among the states and some provide more aid than others. Medicaid apparently covers only about 40 per cent of the poor nationwide.

Nevertheless, state and local governments provide a range of public health facilities for many categories of people from the poor to war veterans and the armed forces. They operate or support hospitals, mental institutions, retirement homes and maternity and child health services. Public facilities may also be supplemented by voluntary organizations, universities and other bodies, which provide free health care for the local population. But, ultimately, public medical and care services suffer from varying standards, inadequate coverage of the needy and differences in the amount of money spent on them. This means that a large majority of Americans under 65 are dependent upon private medical insurance schemes and the private sector.

A second federal health programme, Medicare (formed in 1965), covers much of the costs for the medical treatment of elderly (over 65) and disabled people and amounts to some 8 per cent or $195 billion (1996) of federal budget spending. This is dependent upon Social Security contributions during an employee's lifetime. Additionally, because of the incomplete coverage of Medicare, many elderly people may not be able to cover the full cost of some types of treatment, particularly the most expensive. They usually have to depend on additional private insurance or savings for the balance of their medical fees.

Some 13.4 per cent of GDP derives from the provision of US private and public health care services, which constitute a very large business sector. This GDP figure is considerably larger than in most other industrialized countries. Much of it stems from the high incomes of the medical profession (with doctors having an average annual salary of $170,000), management or administrative costs and the expense of equipment and drugs. Critics argue that the American public is not receiving the full benefit of such expenditure, particularly when medical services can vary greatly, as in rural and poor areas. Compared with other countries, the US spends more on health care but helps fewer people.

Critics have commented on other serious developments in recent years which have added to health-care costs. The first is well-publicized lawsuits for damages by patients against doctors and hospitals because of alleged inadequate or wrong treatment. Lawyers can profit considerably by fighting personal injury lawsuits on a contingency fee basis. But the rise in such cases forces doctors to insure themselves against the risks of being sued. Medical care and vital decisions can be consequently influenced by these considerations. Drug companies may also have to pay high compensation when medicines damage patients. Lawyers' fees, expensive insurance policies and higher drug prices increase the overall cost of treatment which is passed onto the patient or insurer.

A second reason for escalating health care costs is the number of AIDS (acquired immune deficiency syndrome) and HIV (human immunodeficiency virus) patients in the US. In 1994 there were 44,052 deaths from AIDS and the rate of new cases doubled in 1993 to 103,500. These illnesses have increasingly affected sections of the population which lack health insurance. Cases continue to grow more rapidly among women than among men and African Americans and Latinos are disproportionately represented in the totals.

The problem of paying for the treatment of these patients, who must be helped because of health threats to the population, has become urgent. The number of patients who receive treatment under Medicaid varies between states but while states and

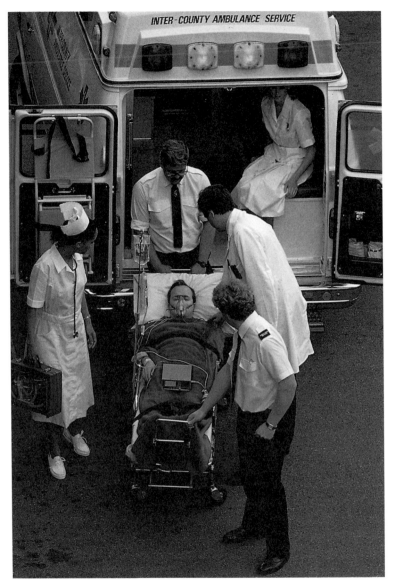

PLATE 9.2   Man on ambulance stretcher
(Julian Calder/Tony Stone Worldwide)

cities have increased their funding to cope with the problem, increased federal finance is also needed.

However, despite the limitations of the American health care system, life expectancy in 1994 was 72 years for men and 79 for women. Deaths resulting from serious diseases and illnesses, like heart problems, have declined in recent years. These improvements are partly due to better diets, increased exercise and greater health awareness in the population, as well as better medical care.

Housing

Homes and houses are very important for many Americans and their families. They give a sense of possession and material satisfaction, personal identification and individual lifestyle, around which family activities take place. But the average American may also move home many times and home-ownership is very much associated with socio-economic mobility. A young family unit will move frequently in the early years from apartments to houses and up the housing market. There may be further moves in middle age from urban situations to the suburbs. Some people may restrict themselves to a particular location, but many Americans move large distances throughout the country.

Most Americans want to own their own homes, after usually renting in the early adult years, and two-thirds prefer to live in suburban areas. Many achieve this ambition, and home-ownership (of houses or apartments) is very high at two-thirds of the housing market (107 million housing units in 1993). But some people do not succeed. Mobility is influenced by poverty, deprivation and unemployment. The housing market in the US is consequently divided between the private sector for those who are able to buy or rent and the public sector for those who require assistance in obtaining low-rent property.

Some two-thirds of the housing units in the private sector are 'single-family dwellings', often of a detached type and usually having front and back yards or gardens. Other people live in apartments (whether purchased or rented) and the rest occupy a variety of different housing units.

Private houses and apartments are in general reasonably priced across a broad band, although they are subject to price fluctuations in the housing market. They are usually of good standard and comfortable, with many amenities. Most owners borrow money (a mortgage) which is secured by the value of their house and income in order to pay for them. In 1995, the median (or representative) house cost $109,000 and had an average mortgage of 8 per cent. This entailed a monthly repayment on the mortgage of $643, which amounted to 19.9 per cent of average family income. House prices rose faster than incomes in the 1980s, but the housing market then suffered from the economic recession of the early 1990s.

Public sector housing in the US is meant to provide for the minority of Americans who are unable to buy property or to afford private high-rent accommodation. Such housing has been historically affected by the bias towards private provision and self-reliance. Individuals have been expected to make their own housing arrangements, rather than expecting these to be a public responsibility.

But the growth of urban slums and substandard housing in the nineteenth century, together with social misery and threats to public health, resulted in the creation in 1934 of the Federal Housing Administration. This department provided loans to those organizations which were willing to build low-rent accommodation for needy people. Local and state governments also built public housing, and implemented stricter building codes, health codes and public sanitation regulations to deal with slum conditions.

However, attempts to create more low-cost public housing with federal funds in the cities and other areas (which were relatively successful in the 1960s and 1970s) have frequently been opposed by property owners and sometimes by state and local governments. Although racial and religious discrimination in renting such housing has been curtailed, it still exists, often in veiled forms. While many states and cities have implemented fair-housing laws and fair-housing commissions, a large number of low-income people and minority groups in large urban centres continue to live in barely habitable housing. Bad housing conditions are also experienced by people living in small towns and rural communities.

The homeless

Local, state or federal governments in the US, as in other industrialized countries, have consequently failed to provide sufficient amounts of low-cost rented accommodation for low-income groups and the federal government has reduced subsidies for such housing since the 1980s. Since the number of poor Americans also increased in the 1980s and 1990s, this situation has resulted in a greater number of homeless people throughout the nation. Estimates of their numbers vary, ranging from unofficial figures of up to 3 million and official figures from the Department of Housing and Urban Development of about half a million.

Voluntary organizations attempt to help the homeless by providing shelter and food for limited periods. Most of the funding for these bodies comes from private donations, although some finance is also provided by local and city governments. However, federal government finance for the homeless continues to be very small.

Attitudes to social services

While most Americans today are successful, independent and provide for themselves, some do not succeed, have varied problems and need help. This was even more true in the past. At the beginning of the twentieth century, it is estimated that between 50 to 60 per cent of the population lived in relative poverty. This percentage decreased to some 22 per cent in 1959 and about 11 per cent in 1973. But it increased again at the end of the 1980s and reached 15.1 per cent in 1994.

Occasional Gallup opinion polls on the causes of poverty consistently show that one-third of Americans feel that people are poor or become poor due to their own lack of effort; one-third think that people are poor because of circumstances beyond their control; and one-third believe that poverty stems from a mixture of both reasons.

On one level, the social services debate in the US is concerned with the problems of the needy and poor. As the polls above indicate, it is divided between traditional notions of self-reliance and the question of whether society should do much more in this field. It may appear that Americans lean too far in favour of individuals providing for themselves and do not give enough thought for those in need. A common expression in this context, which is frequently heard, is 'The Lord helps those who help themselves'.

The virtues of self-reliance are stressed by people who are already able to provide for themselves. Americans can sometimes be uncharitable to those citizens who are less successful or fortunate and may be unsympathetic to their position. Many feel that welfare has detracted from traditional virtues of responsibility, thrift and hard work and has contributed to a dependency culture. Until the 1960s dependency upon welfare was widely perceived to be shameful and shaming.

But the debate is not only about the poor and needy. It also involves the question of whether the US should adopt a nationally organized European-type 'welfare state', which would provide comprehensive social and medical schemes for all, funded out of general taxation. Historically, the biases against a centralized system have been considerable and the influence of private enterprise economics is felt in the social services sector. Arguably, the provision of a national system depends on political will, public acceptance and the power of vested interests. Proposals for change involve questions of the organization, level and extent of services and how much public responsibility should be embraced.

There does seem to be a scepticism about centralized control in the US. A *Los Angeles Times* poll in 1994 found that 69 per cent of those interviewed thought that the federal government controlled too much of the people's daily lives. *International Social Attitudes 1993/94* (Jowell *et al.* 1993) asked respondents whether there should be a definite government responsibility to

PLATE 9.3   Graffiti in Harlem   *(Jacky Chapman/Format)*

provide certain social services. Of the US respondents, only 40 per cent wanted this for health care, 40 per cent for decent pensions, 21 per cent for decent housing and 14 per cent for decent unemployment benefits. These percentages were considerably below the responses in European countries. There seems to be an unwillingness to contribute financially to national plans and a preference for personal decisions on how to spend one's money.

Nevertheless, public social services in the US have expanded relatively successfully since the 1930s; absolute poverty has declined; living standards have risen generally; greater public expectations have been created; and social institutions have developed.

But relative poverty and need still exist and the number of people on welfare has grown since the 1950s. The population has increased, people are living longer, the elderly require more health care, society has become more complex and the demands upon social institutions and services have increased. It is inevitable perhaps that social services costs will continue to rise in real terms and that all societies will contain a number of individuals who must be provided for at public expense by a social safety net. Some critics argue that the US is politically unwilling to take on the kind of social responsibility and commitment for the whole community that this situation supposedly requires. In the meantime, the Social Security and Medicare systems are increasingly put under pressure as larger numbers of people reach retirement.

Historically, American public social services have expanded in the face of opposition but some recent developments seem to be regressive. In 1996, the Clinton administration cut federal welfare programmes and restructured AFDC. In 1993, it also controversially tried to introduce universal health care, which would cover all the population and improve the delivery of health services by controlling costs. It was to be funded by increased income taxes and larger insurance contributions from workers and corporations. It would also depend on the support of employers and private medicine for its success. But the plans collapsed. They were probably too ambitious; their costing was ill thought out; corporate interests, insurance companies and private medicine were opposed; and the proposals did not find favour among many ordinary Americans.

Yet when a 1995 *Time/CNN* poll asked how well respondents could cover the cost of medical care if their family was affected by major illness, 40 per cent said that they could cope easily, 44 per cent with difficulty and 14 per cent said not at all.

EXERCISES

■ **Examine and explain the following terms:**

welfare	AFDC	one-parent families
Medicaid	workfare	'War on Poverty'
medical lawsuits	poverty level	OASDHI
food stamps	GI Bill of Rights	Medicare
self-reliance	the New Deal	mortgage
Social Security	non-contributory	
unemployment	benefits	
compensation		

■ **Write short essays on the following topics:**

1   Critically discuss the provision for health care in the US. Should there be a National Health Service?

2   Examine the American division between public and private sectors of health, social provision, and housing.

Education

High expectations

Since the colonial period, Americans have expected a great deal from their educational institutions. Just teaching the usual subjects has rarely satisfied demands on the schools. Americans have also wanted learning to serve other social institutions, ideals and goals.

Such expectations invite disappointment and controversy. Combined with the circumstances of the country's history, they have also led to a very distinctive educational system. With its fusion of church and state, Puritan New England aimed at religious indoctrination, making even learning the alphabet a series of theological lessons, though maxims of 'good sense' for getting on in the world also received attention. American optimism shines through in much later pedagogy. The Founding Fathers hoped schooling would discover natural merit in citizens and nurture an elite to defend the republic from tyranny. People on the frontier dreamed education would be the 'great leveller', a compensator for their alleged inferiority to coastal society and a guarantee of democratic equality.

Well into the twentieth century schoolbooks fairly glow with faith in the possibility of endless self-improvement for boys dedicated to American ideals. The schools taught girls to play a supportive role, Blacks to know their place, Indians to be civilized, and immigrants to be American workers. Until recently, only a few private institutions and schools outside the mainstream provided correctives to this hierarchy. But since the mid-1950s, civil rights movements (starting with African Americans' demands for educational equality) have made schools a centre of contention over which traditions and ideals, what order in society, and what means of reaching those goals Americans should support.

Educational institutions become the bearers of each age's values. In part because expectations and the rate of change remain high in the US, education is a focus of intense debate.

American educational history

The colonial period

Local control over education developed early in America and remains characteristic of its educational institutions. During the colonial period, the British authorities did not provide money for education, so the first schools varied according to the interest local settlers had in education. The common view was that parents were responsible for children's education. In the southern colonies, schooling often came from a private tutor, if the family could afford one. Each town tried to build a school in colonial New England and Pennsylvania.

The colonists expected the schools to teach religion, and reading skill was highly valued because it allowed people to read the Bible. Puritan Massachusetts founded the first American public school under a law entitled the 'Old Deluder Satan Act'. Reading, writing, and arithmetic (the so-called three 'R's') were the core subjects, and through them, pupils were prepared for local religious, economic and political life.

Higher education also began early in the colonial period. In 1636 Harvard College was founded, only six years after the Puritan migration to America had begun. By the Revolutionary War, nine colleges prepared a small elite of men for the ministry and leadership in public life. Although these colleges encouraged religious toleration, rivalry among them was evident, in part because all but two (Columbia and the University of Pennsylvania) represented one of the major Protestant denominations. At this point, church and state were not separate, and essentially private institutions of higher education regularly received public funding.

Building a society along the frontier also motivated the early development of schools. Because they were few and the wilderness vast, the settlers discovered that law, order and social tradition broke down unless people cooperated to establish the basic institutions of society. Thus, 'school-raisings' became as much a standard part of cooperative community building as 'house- or barn-raisings'.

Before the Civil War

None the less, only five of the thirteen original states included provisions for public schools in the constitutions they wrote during the War for Independence (1776–81). In 1830, none offered state-wide, free public education. But support for common schools was strong. Thomas Jefferson and other Founding Fathers insisted that universal public education was essential to produce the informed citizenry on which a democracy depended. In the 1870s the federal government passed laws providing for education and land for schools in the future states of the Great Lakes region.

Jefferson envisioned replacing Europe's aristocracy of birth with a school-bred *meritocracy* of talent. But in the 1830s, President Andrew Jackson's Democratic Party opposed that ideal as elitist, and supported public schools as an equalizer that would give every man a chance to rise in society. Around the same time, reformers in the Northeast, such as Horace Mann, publicized the notion that public schools could reduce the growing crime, poverty and vice of the cities by helping to assimilate their growing immigrant population. Towards those ends, Mann led a movement to lengthen the school year, add 'practical' subjects, raise teachers' salaries and provide professional teacher-training.

By the Civil War, all states accepted the principle of tax-supported, free elementary schools. Every state had such schools in some places, but most teachers were poorly trained, and the quality of the schools was considerably lower in the South and West. Most children went to school sporadically or not at all. In the North only one out of six White children attended public school in 1860. In the South, the figure was one out of seven, and it was illegal to give slaves schooling.

At the time, public opinion rejected the idea of mandatory school attendance, mainly because most people believed parents, rather than governments, should be responsible for education. Moreover, most parents needed their children's work or wages to make ends meet. Public *secondary* education was available at some 300 'free academies' across the nation, for those who could spare their children's contributions to the family economy.

As the states abolished established religions after the Revolution, church and state became separate. Only gradually, however, did Protestant instruction disappear from public schools. In the North and Midwest, immigrant groups began to establish *parochial* (private, church-related) elementary and secondary schools in the 1840s to preserve their ethnic heritage and avoid pressures to assimilate in public schools.

The pattern of higher education was transformed before 1865. The Supreme Court distinguished between public and private colleges in 1819 and freed private institutions of higher learning from state control. Thereafter hundreds of private experiments in higher education appeared, even though public funding dropped to very low levels. During the Civil War, the Morrill Act (or Land Grant College Act) set a revolutionary precedent by laying the foundation for the *state university*. The beginning of the federal government's involvement in public higher education, the Act gave each state huge land areas for higher education. The result was dozens of Land-Grant Colleges, which developed into state universities. Equally important, it promoted the higher education of larger numbers of students and called for college-level courses in agriculture, technical and industrial subjects, in order to attract students from the working classes. The first colleges to admit African Americans and women also opened before the Civil War.

1865–1945

The rapid pace of urbanization, industrialization and immigration brought a turning point in American education after 1865. In the popular print media, the immigrant slum child became the symbol of the dangers of these processes, and the public schools were asked to remedy the situation.

Assimilation through the schools seemed increasingly necessary as immigrants from southern and eastern Europe and several Asian nations arrived in large numbers. The schools were expected to Americanize these exotic newcomers by teaching them English, the principles of American democracy, and the skills needed for the workplace. Just as important, the schools would get immigrant children out of unhealthy tenement housing, off the streets, out of factories, and away from gangs. To accomplish these goals, *compulsory school attendance laws* were soon adopted in the states. By 1880 almost three-quarters of school-aged children were in school.

These laws also applied to racial minorities. After the Civil War, the federal government's Freedmen's Bureau and other Northern organizations founded many schools in the South for the former slaves. But whether African-, Asian-, or Native-American, minority students everywhere were placed in separate schools. In 1896 the Supreme Court's *Plessy v. Ferguson* ruling gave legal backing to the segregation that already existed.

Politicians quickly put children in school, but they did not as quickly appropriate money for hiring more teachers and erecting new buildings. Overcrowded, poorly maintained schools and staff shortages were typical of American public schools between the 1880s and 1920s. Opening teaching to women (often the daughters of immigrants) provided the new teachers, and 'normal schools' to train them grew rapidly in number.

Around 1900, public school teaching was not considered a profession. The average annual salary for teachers was lower than that of an unskilled worker, and many teachers had no more than a high school education themselves. Yet real progress was made in teacher preparation in the decades after compulsory attendance laws were passed. States set standards for teaching licences, which increasingly included a college degree with courses in pedagogy. After the 1920s, 'school marms' and 'schoolkeepers' were members of a profession called 'educators'. Salaries for teachers, however, remained low, and the profession was regarded as one of the least prestigious.

In the same period, reformers assigned the schools new prior-ities and duties. John Dewey and others held that curricula and teaching methods had to be changed. Instead of moralistic piety and rote memorization, the schools had to give pupils practical skills suited to their environment and the habit of discovering knowledge for themselves. 'Learning by doing', personal growth, and child-centred rather than subject-centred teaching became the goal.

Public schools were to become community centres and the means of social progress. About this time, *progressive education* introduced physical education, music and fine arts, and vocational subjects (training in skilled occupations) as electives (optional courses). These educators also developed the after-school extra-curricular activities, such as team sports, that became a typical part of American education. In 1917, the federal government offered financial support to any public secondary school that emphasized vocational education. Some immigrant parents criti-cized progressive education because they felt less demanding electives took time away from academic subjects. They also objected to the frequent assumption that immigrant children did not need academic studies, since they would not go on to higher education.

After 1865, private church-related colleges, often founded by European immigrant groups, rapidly increased in number, espe-cially in the Midwest. Coeducational higher education (colleges open to both men and women) became the norm there during the Civil War, when fee-paying women were necessary to replace the men who had joined the Union armies. Coeducation continued to spread, and by the 1920s almost half of American college students were women. Further east, however, the so-called Ivy League uni-versities (Harvard and other prestigious schools from the colonial period) remained men's institutions, and hence, benefactors estab-lished separate women's colleges in that region. Racial segregation extended to higher education during this period, when colleges for African Americans, such as Howard University and Hampton Institute, were founded in the South after the War. In 1890 a new Morrill Act provided the region with land for Black public colleges that emphasized manual and industrial education.

After 1900, graduate and professional schools became more common. Advanced degree programmes began to transform some well-established universities into research institutions, and engineering schools, business colleges, law and medical schools were founded in growing numbers. For all but a small elite, however, a college degree seemed a luxury. Even in 1940, less than two out of ten college-age people attended institutions of higher learning. Instead, as parents less often had farms, handicrafts, or family businesses to pass on, they secured their children's future through further education at vocational, office, secretarial, or management schools.

The post-war period

The Second World War was a watershed in American higher education. To ease the return of war veterans to civilian life, Congress passed the Servicemen's Readjustment Act (the so-called 'G.I. Bill') in 1944. Under the Act, the federal government paid tuition and living costs for veterans in higher education and directly funded the expansion of study programmes for the first time. Within two years, half the people in college were veterans, many of them from working-class families with little education. More students graduated than ever before, and the typical student ceased to be a member of the upper-middle or upper classes. By 1971, when the programme ended, nearly 2,500,000 veterans had benefited from its provisions. Higher education in the US had become mass education and was regarded as a right rather than a privilege.

The launching of the Soviet satellite *Sputnik* in 1957 spurred another increase in the federal government's role in public education. Now the schools were enlisted in the Cold War and called on to meet the challenge of Soviet technology. The National Defense Education Act (1958) provided federal money for research and university programmes in science and technology, as well as loans to college students. The legislation also allotted federal funds for teaching science, mathematics and foreign languages in high schools.

After 1958, federal money was targeted for college-level foreign language teaching, the equipping of language laboratories, and eventually for the humanities in general. In the 1950s, state after state required teachers to sign 'loyalty oaths' to the US, and Senator Joseph McCarthy (among others) attacked the universities as hotbeds of communism. Education became a patriotic obligation as well as a right.

The Supreme Court's *Brown* decision struck down the principle of separate-but-equal educational facilities for the races in 1954. One year later the Court ruled that public school districts all over the nation had to present plans for achieving 'racial balance' in their schools. Federal school policy began to show a profound change in national priorities.

For almost twenty years, from 1955 to 1974, the Court tried to desegregate America's public schools. It settled on *busing* as the most effective way to integrate the schools. Until very recently, one universal rule in America was that pupils attended the school closest to their homes. Since Blacks and Whites live in different residential sections of US cities, they attend different school districts. Residential segregation produces segregated schools. Therefore, the Supreme Court decided to 'bus' students to other districts until 'racial balance' in all city schools had resulted.

In city after city across the nation, parents, school authorities and politicians of both races protested and resisted. But the Court held firm, with the result that Whites fled to the suburbs in greater numbers, and the small percentage who could afford to, sent their children to private schools. Federal authorities decided that busing plans could produce integrated schools only if they included the 'lily-White' suburban schools around major cities. After such plans began transporting Whites into city schools, the public outcry grew louder. By 1974, the nation's mood had become strongly anti-busing, and when asked to decide whether a city-and-suburbs busing plan was constitutional, the Supreme Court backed down, saying no tradition in American public education was more deeply rooted than the local control of schools. Thus busing stopped being effective for school desegregation.

In the 1990s, about 30 per cent of the schools are still mostly or entirely Black. An even larger percentage are 'racially segregated' if the definition includes schools that are predominantly Latino and Black. Most of these schools are located in the North or Southwest, because the Court integrated Southern schools first and did not support busing between the suburbs and inner cities of the North after 1974.

Since the 1960s, the federal authorities have fought the effects of prejudice and the related problem of poverty through involvement in educational programmes. In 1963, Congress began providing money for college and university buildings. In 1964, it decided that federal funding was available only to educational institutions that could prove they did not discriminate on the basis of race, religion or national origin. The Higher Education Act of 1965 helped minority and 'disadvantaged' students get college loans. State and federal grants to poorer public schools have generally come in two ways. First, laws made the income levels in local districts the basis for distributing public funds. 'Low-income' areas qualified for extra grants and special programmes to attract good teachers. Second, governments more than tripled their contribution to the general budgets of cities with social and educational problems.

In general, federal government policy has aimed to implement the principle of *affirmative action* that President Lyndon Johnson expressed in his commencement speech at Howard University in 1965:

> You do not take a person who for years has been hobbled by chains and liberate him, bring him up to the starting line of a race, and then say, 'You are free to compete with all the others', and still justly believe that you have been completely fair.

Affirmative action programmes to improve women's and minority groups' access to education have proliferated since the early 1970s. On the primary and secondary levels of public education, affirmative action first led to a redesigning of teaching programmes and textbooks. Discriminatory references to women and minorities have been replaced with even-handed treatments, or more often, with 'positive role models' and examples of how women and minorities have contributed to American history and culture. History and literature books, especially, have changed as a result of this effort.

The hiring of staff on all levels has also been affected because governments have required educational institutions to become equal opportunity employers. That has meant hiring more teachers from minority groups at elementary and secondary schools and more women professors at universities and colleges. By law, educational institutions must encourage minority group members to apply for teaching positions. They must be sought out and interviewed or the school might lose government funding. Finding qualified women and minority group members for positions has been somewhat easier since the 1970s because of affirmative action plans for teacher-training programmes and the increased number of students from these groups who have completed university degrees.

Two affirmative action programmes are designed to help 'disadvantaged' pupils succeed in primary and secondary schools. Head Start provides pre-school tutoring to children in educationally deprived families to help them begin formal schooling at the same level as those in more fortunate families. Upward Bound supplies remedial teaching, private tutoring and work-study programmes for older children. While Upward Bound has suffered funding reductions, Head Start is considered a success and has received additional congressional appropriations. It benefits close to a million children today.

Affirmative action programmes in education have, however, provoked a number of US Supreme Court decisions. These have not called for the end of affirmative action, but have changed the methods used to put it into effect. The best-known court cases in this area have involved complaints from White males denied admission to university programmes, in their opinion, because female and minority-group applicants were given preferential treatment. In the *Bakke* decision (1977), for example, the Supreme Court ruled that it is unconstitutional to increase the number of students from racial minorities in university programmes by setting numerical quotas. In 1996 California voters ended the state's affirmative action programmes by supporting Proposition 209.

In the early 1980s, Diane Ravitch, a well-known authority on US schools, listed the accumulated expectations Americans had for their educational institutions. It was hoped that education would reduce social inequality; improve the economy and economic opportunity for individuals; spread the capacity for personal fulfilment; civilize and uplift the nation's cultural life; raise the level of and participation in its political life; and lessen alienation, distrust and prejudice by increasing the contact among racial and socio-economic groups. Perhaps understandably, a mood of disappointment with educational institutions has been evident in the US since then, because most of the social dilemmas the schools were supposed to solve remain serious problems.

Elementary and secondary schools

Local control over schools was the tradition during the colonial period. The Constitution makes no mention of education, which reserves power over education to the states or people, according to the Tenth Amendment. All fifty state constitutions have quite specific provisions about education. Generally, these clauses (and state education laws) define the state's role and delegate primary responsibility for schools to local governments. As these are created by the states, their powers over education can be altered by the states.

Local authorities set up *independent school districts*, whose elected local boards of education make most decisions regarding public elementary and secondary schools. Generally, the districts organize their schools into kindergardens for 5 year olds; elementary schools for 6 to 12 year olds; middle schools (or junior highs) for pupils from 13 to 15, and high schools for students between 16 and 18 years old. In the 1990s school year there were some 15,500 of these school districts with a total enrolment of over 40 million pupils.

PLATE 10.1 Kindergarten play *(Janine Wiedel)*

Only when specific powers given to the federal government in the Constitution are involved, such as the protection of rights guaranteed in the Bill of Rights, do the federal authorities become directly involved in educational issues. In practice, the federal government seldom interfered with local schools to protect civil rights until the 1950s. The national government has also provided land for school sites, funds for special educational projects, and influenced local school policy by making federal grants for education dependent on following non-discriminatory practices.

The federal government's involvement in education remains quite limited. Its administrative agency for overseeing and formulating educational policies was formed late and is still understaffed compared to that in other developed countries. Not until the early

1950s did Congress set up a federal Office of Education in the Department of Health, Education and Welfare. A separate Department of Education was not established until 1979. Ronald Reagan received considerable support then, when he promised to eliminate the Department if he was elected. Even today the federal government provides on average only about 4 per cent of the funding for public primary and secondary schools.

Until the 1950s almost all state governments limited their involvement in education to two areas: establishing public state universities and setting general guidelines for public primary and secondary education. A *state board of education*, appointed by the governor, formulated the guidelines, and the state's agency or department of education was to see that they were carried out in local districts.

The state board of education commonly sets only general minimum standards. It determines the number of days in the school year; the procedures for licensing teachers and administrators; the school-leaving age (usually 16), the 'core curriculum' that pupils must complete at each level of school; and minimum requirements for academic progress at different grade levels. To graduate from secondary school, for example, students must pass a core curriculum that usually includes four years of courses in English, three in social studies, and two in mathematics and science.

These common requirements serve several purposes. By establishing a degree of uniformity among diverse school districts, they allow educational leaders to keep the schools in line with standards in other states and developments in pedagogics. Hence, the core curriculum also facilitates the evaluation of individual schools and makes it easier for pupils to move from one district or state to another and gain admission to colleges and universities around the nation.

In recent decades, state boards have increasingly implemented testing programmes to make individual districts more accountable for reaching a certain level of academic achievement at specified points in pupils' schooling. The same tests are often used in many states, and the results for districts and states are publicly available. The state board and parents are therefore better able to judge the relative success of the local schools in meeting educational goals. During the 1980s, growing numbers of state boards won approval for state-wide tests to measure teachers' mastery of core subjects and educational methods.

There are three important kinds of localism encouraged by the delegation of state authority to local school districts. *Financial localism* generally refers to the delegation of responsibility for funding schools to local districts. In the 1980s, state spending on education increased by as much as 70 per cent, and federal contributions to public schools grew significantly as well. Yet, local real-estate taxes currently raise 46 per cent of local school budgets. (The average school district receives half its funds from the state and the rest of its financial resources from the federal government.) In other words, local money still makes a very significant difference for public schools.

In a rich district with valuable homes and businesses 46 per cent represents the resources for better teaching salaries, buildings and equipment than those in most other districts. In the smaller school budget of a poor district, 46 per cent represents less money, and that has just the opposite effect on resources for its schools. Each district is free to decide how high it wants to set property taxes for education. But even though poor districts approve higher tax rates than wealthy districts, they raise less money for schools because local property has so little value. Thus, financial localism (in combination with the causes of the great economic differences between school districts) is still the reason for wide variations in the quality of American public schools.

State plans to redistribute local property taxes aim to reduce the educational inequality resulting from financial localism. *Redistribution plans* collect the real-estate taxes in the state and place them in a fund for public education. This money is then redistributed to even out the differences in school budgets across the state. Such plans can bring drastic changes in the school budgets of both rich and poor districts. Generally, they have taken money for education from the suburbs and given it to inner-city areas. Hence, there has been less money for schools dominated by White pupils and more for schools with many Blacks, Latinos, and Asian Americans.

As expected, redistribution plans have met opposition. Some suburban groups have tried to preserve the advantages of their schools through private donations or special local education taxes. At least one state (New Jersey) has responded by ruling that any increase in the school budgets of richer districts will result in an automatic equal increase in the budgets of poorer districts. Recently, state courts all over the nation have begun to demand redistribution programmes.

Increased state contributions to local school budgets and redistribution plans have given state boards of education greater leverage in enforcing state-wide standards. However, state authorities often show a reluctance to use their power. Like the public they serve, they still believe that in a democracy, education should not be imparted by central authorities, but designed by the people in the governments closest to them. Such thinking and the opposition of suburban voters have limited the effects of redistribution plans. The result is that the money spent per pupil in predominantly White suburban schools is commonly one and a half to two times that spent in racially mixed city schools. American traditions of financial localism in education remain strong.

Political localism is chiefly exercised through the members of the *local board of education*. They have more power over the schools than members of the state board do and are nearly always elected. Anyone who lives in the district can be a candidate for the board. The majority of those elected are parents, teachers and local business people. The school system's chief administrator is usually an *ex officio* member of the board with no vote but great informal influence over decisions. Recently it is more accepted to elect a student to the board. While some boards have difficulty reaching agreement because members represent opposing political views, often the board as a whole reflects the district's predominant conservative or liberal political attitudes.

The local board is powerful because it makes a range of important decisions. It determines the size and content of the school budget and controls the hiring and firing of teachers and administrators. The choice of subjects, programmes and educational goals beyond the state minimums is the board's, as is the definition of school disciplinary rules and routines. It must approve the selection of library and textbooks, and it has the final word on how educational facilities should be designed, constructed and maintained. Local boards make decisions on whether the district should apply to the state or federal government for aid under specific programmes. Boards that are most resourceful in applying for these funds get more help. In practice, that means districts with well educated populations (and usually higher incomes) often succeed in getting more money from the state and federal governments.

Another important source of political localism is the PTA (the Parent–Teacher Association). The PTA is a voluntary organization, whose officers are elected by the members. It has no legal authority to make school policy, but its discussions often frame the issues debated and decided by the school board. Moreover, people who have been active in the PTA are often the local residents who get elected to the board.

The third kind of localism in American education, *social localism*, refers to the distinctiveness of districts' educational priorities and goals that results from differences in their populations' social attitudes. These attitudes generally reflect the local population's dominant socio-economic class and mix of occupations, religions, races and ethnic groups. It can be argued that social localism produces differences in the public schools that are quite as significant as those caused by differences in districts' ability to pay for schooling. School board members and PTA leaders, who may or may not be representative of the local population, cannot afford to ignore these attitudes and the population characteristics from which they spring.

Social localism is significant because local boards make important policy decisions. It has led to public schools emphasizing agricultural methods, industrial arts, commercial studies, or college-level 'advanced placement' courses. It has inspired religious, White supremacist, and assimilationist policies in some districts, and opposing policies in others.

Recently, extreme examples of social localism have resulted in replacing evolutionary theory with the biblical story of creation in science courses; removing literary classics from school libraries; sex education lessons and the presentation of alternative lifestyles and sexual orientations in elementary schools; a district policy of teaching that American society is the world's greatest; and decisions to refuse the children of illegal immigrants public schooling. Many such extreme social policies are struck down by judicial rulings or changed after public reactions.

The goal of Americanizing immigrant children has been discarded. Today, after the civil rights movements of the 1960s and 1970s, support for equal educational opportunity and *pluralism* is standard in the rhetoric (though not as often in the practices) of most American school districts. In fact, equal opportunity today means that both state and federal governments sometimes deem it necessary to intervene in the affairs of local school districts to ensure that minority students are given an education fitted to their special needs and problems. Pluralism produces even more various public schools as some local districts tailor their curricula to suit Blacks as well as Latino and Asian immigrant children and add ethnic studies courses and bilingual education programmes.

Today pluralism in the public schools means debate over the core curriculum. Led by scholars in college education departments who question the traditional content of required subjects, districts, states, and even the federal government have tried to redefine common standards and the canon (accepted principle content) of subjects.

Committees of recognized experts in many fields meet (sometimes for years) in the hope of agreeing on a national curriculum. In the US, however, that can only consist of suggested guidelines, because states control educational programmes. Consensus has not been very difficult to achieve on the canon of mathematics or science. But in 1996 heated debate prevented agreement on the required content of history curricula, not least because they concern deciding who and what are the essential parts of the nation's heritage and identity. Meanwhile, the views accepted in many districts and states have caused publishers to redesign basic textbooks in history and most core subjects for all school levels.

Private elementary and secondary schools

Pluralism means not only permitting great variety in the public schools but also allowing a wide variety of private schools. About 12 per cent of the school-age population attends one of the nation's more than 24,000 private schools. Private educational institutions show even more variety than the public schools; four of five are parochial schools (run by religious groups). By far the largest number of these are Catholic institutions, but fundamentalist sects, a range of other Protestant denominations, orthodox Jews and some Asian religious groups also run parochial schools.

Non-sectarian private schools have a weak religious allegiance or are entirely secular. They are quite diverse but frequently promise a high standard of academic excellence, adherence to a particular theory of education, the ability to instil discipline and maturity, or some combination of these qualities. The Montessori schools offer a specific method of learning. Elite college-preparatory boarding schools (so-called 'prep schools') have exceptionally well-qualified faculties whose goal is to help the children of the wealthy gain admission to prestigious universities like those in the Ivy League, and eventually take their place in the country's upper class. A variety of military academies specialize in dealing with 'problem children' whose parents can afford to reform their habits by subjecting them to the rigours of a regimented life away from home.

Private schools depend heavily on endowments (private donations), investments and income from fee-paying students to meet their expenses. Public funding amounts to less than 10 per cent of their budgets. The courts have limited the public funding available to parochial schools to programmes that benefit school pupils in general, rather than particular institutions. Thus, all children can receive government aid for some medical services, nutrition supplements and transportation to school, but not grants to pay tuition.

Some private educational institutions offer financial aid to attract students from a variety of social backgrounds, while others follow a restrictive *admissions policy* to maintain a more homogeneous student body. Exclusivity has always been an important attraction of most private schools. Busing programmes to end segregation contributed to increased enrollment at all-White private institutions. The Supreme Court's ban on group prayers and religious instruction in general in the public schools has caused others to turn to private education. Dissatisfaction with the public schools' academic standards, lax discipline, drug abuse, or crime has convinced yet other parents to pay for private education. These problems are certainly more avoidable in private schools, since the expulsion of pupils who cause them is much simpler for private institutions.

Higher education

High school graduates enter higher education through a process of mutual selection in a system that is decentralized, diverse and competitive. Colleges and universities select a student body according to criteria set by the individual institution rather than by a central authority. The federal government has only an indirect influence on these standards through equal educational opportunity programmes, civil rights laws and constitutional rights. State approval is necessary for institutions of higher learning to operate and grant degrees, but once that is gained, state involvement is usually minimal.

This large degree of institutional independence has encouraged grass-roots experiments and innovations in higher education and the resulting diversity is enormous. The public sector includes the national military academies, fifty state university systems and hundreds of local technical or 'specialty' schools, *community colleges*, and city universities. In the private sector there are thousands of institutions, ranging from specialty schools to small church-related colleges to major universities with separate undergraduate, graduate and professional schools.

Thus entrance criteria reflect the particular character of the institution and the competition it faces from institutions of a similar sort. High school graduates try to gain admission to a school that suits their individual needs. Students' requirements also vary greatly because the population is so heterogeneous, and secondary schools so different in type and quality.

In such a system, devices are needed to help institutions and students make informed choices in the selection process. There is no battery of nationally designed and evaluated examinations that pupils must pass to receive a high school diploma. That fact and the great variation in the programmes and quality of US secondary schools make evaluating applicants' academic achievement difficult for colleges. To provide a basis for comparing pupils' skills, private agencies have developed competitive college entrance examinations that are given all over the country on the same day. Almost all colleges and universities require applicants to take the best known of these, the Scholastic Achievement Test (SAT), and many prestigious schools also require pupils to submit their scores on other national tests.

In addition, institutions have admissions departments that visit and evaluate secondary schools, interview applicants and review pupils' application forms. Secondary schools have guidance departments with counsellors who evaluate colleges and universities for students and recommend programmes suited to their abilities and test scores. Regional organizations called accrediting bodies monitor the quality of secondary schools and institutions of higher education.

A closer look at some of these institutions of higher learning illustrates the choices students have. Post-secondary *technical* or *'specialty' schools* offer training for specific occupations, such as accounting, computer programming, laboratory work, or business management. These institutions have become particularly numerous since the Second World War because of rapid changes in technology. Today, a few specialty schools are as prestigious as well-known universities.

Community colleges give courses covering the usual requirements for the first two years of college, at little or no cost to the student. After that, students may graduate with an *associate in arts* (AA degree) or transfer into the third year of a full college or university programme and continue towards a *bachelor of arts* or *science* (BA or BSc degree). Community colleges are run by local authorities and offer many shorter certificate programmes suited to the occupational needs of a local area. As a result, many of their students are mature adults who study part-time.

Community colleges first appeared in the 1930s but did not become commonplace until around 1970. One of the more important recent developments in American higher education, community colleges fulfil a number of public expectations. They give reality to the consensus view that a basic college-level education should be available to the general population virtually free of charge. They satisfy the nation's commitment to 'life-long learning', the belief that retraining and continuing education are vital to the individual's and the nation's international competitiveness. Finally, they reflect public opinion that currently favours even more local control of education. Community colleges have opened the possibility of almost unlimited local control over courses of study and have also proved particularly adept at organizing cooperative programmes with local businesses and labour unions.

Although a clear majority of colleges and universities in the US are private, four-fifths of high school graduates choose public institutions. One important reason for this situation is that tuition (the cost of instruction) at city and state universities is often a small fraction of the fee charged at a private institution. Location also reduces the cost. City or state residents pay much lower tuition rates than students who come from other places. Some public systems have purposely built campuses in many parts of the city or state so that students can live at home while they study.

Public systems also attract more students because many have open admissions policies or minimal acceptance requirements for area residents. The majority of secondary school graduates who have average grades can thus avoid rejection in the intense competition for acceptance at more selective schools. Most of those are private, but city and state systems also have an enormous range of standards and programmes. Many 'branch' campuses of public universities are much like community colleges, but some concentrate on excellence through advanced courses in a limited number of fields. State university systems usually have a main campus that maintains higher overall standards. The best of these, the Berkeley campus of the University of California and the Madison campus of the University of Wisconsin, for example, have reputations that equal those of such elite private universities as Harvard, Yale, Princeton and Stanford.

Private higher education in the US is typical of American pluralism, the belief in allowing many alternatives and centres of decentralized power. A private sector that educates a fifth of university-level students is large compared to that in other Western nations. Yet private institutions could expand their size greatly if they wished. On average, private colleges and universities accept only one in ten applicants.

There is no single or simple reason for this restrictive admissions policy. Inability to pay school costs is rarely the main reason for turning down an applicant. Good private institutions have little difficulty finding enough fee-paying students. Stipends, scholarships, low-interest loans, part-time work-study programmes, or a combination of these are made available to people the institution wants. Private colleges and universities recruit as much as a third of their students among well-qualified poor, minority, and foreign groups. Even the most prestigious institutions offer some of these recruits extra help (so-called *remedial courses*) as a form of affirmative action, because they believe studying with people of varied backgrounds is a vital part of a good education.

The reasons most private institutions have for remaining relatively small are related to their concept of a quality education. A few concentrate on high academic standards as their single definition of quality. Many more combine that goal with the ideal of a special community of learning. The ideal of community is often served by requiring students to live on campus and by having relatively few students per teacher to encourage the close contacts between students and faculty. A sense of community is also often established by bringing together staff and students who share a

PLATE 10.2 Stanford University campus
(Barnaby's Picture Library)

religious or ethnic background or socio-political orientation. Most American racial, nationality, and religious groups have founded at least one private college or university.

Some institutions are common to both public and private higher education. The four-year *liberal arts college*, which about two-thirds of American students attend, is the most important of these. One of several units in a university or an independent organization, its purpose is to provide basic courses in a broad range of humanities and sciences. Liberal arts students usually do not specialize until their third year. That 'major', the capstone of their undergraduate education, is a requirement for the BA or BSc degree.

A primary goal of the liberal arts college is making its graduates so-called 'well-rounded' individuals (generally well informed and cultured people). By requiring a core curriculum, these

colleges help maintain a common culture in the US. Until around 1980 few questioned this canon of study and research, which aimed to expose students to the fundamental values of American and Western culture. Since then, the definition of the canon has conflicted with the ideal of pluralism.

Debate over the canon has become so intense in the academy and educated public that Americans speak of the 'culture wars'. Nothing less than a redefinition of American identity or realizing *cultural* equality has been attempted. By the late 1990s, many scholars had successfully argued that the canon of many subjects must be widened to include the work of women and the non-Western cultures of many Americans. Debate continues, but the core curriculum is already much changed.

A liberal arts degree is required before students can enter *graduate schools*. These may be professional schools, such as law or medical schools, or advanced liberal arts schools that offer masters degrees (the MA or MSc) and doctorates (the PhD). To be admitted to graduate schools, students must normally take a competitive examination, either an entrance test for the professional school or graduate record exams (GREs) in liberal arts subjects. A hallmark of the best universities, America's high quality graduate schools are internationally famous centres of research.

Higher education in the US is a competitive struggle. Over 60 per cent of high school graduates (some 12 million people) entered colleges or universities each year in the 1990s, but only half of these students completed a degree. City and state universities normally 'weed out' one-third to one half of the freshman class through tough introductory courses and exams that must be passed if a student is to stay enrolled. All American institutions of higher education use the system called *continuous evaluation*. It requires students to take mid-term and end-of-term examinations, write essays and term papers, and complete additional tasks the instructor chooses to give. Course grades result from a weighted average of the student's marks on these assignments. A minimum overall grade average is necessary to continue one's studies.

Recent problems and policy debates

'State of the nation' evaluations have become a regular part of public debate about American education. Federal commissions and the US Secretary of Education, associations of the states, organizations of educators and private foundations regularly identify problems and suggest policy changes.

Concern over the quality of schooling at all levels is the common theme in expert reports and public opinion polls in the 1990s. Efforts at reform in the previous decade appear to have stabilized falling test scores on national public school tests and college entrance examinations but have not raised them significantly. Average achievement levels in language skills, mathematics and science remained lower in the US than in many other developed nations, according to comparative studies of secondary pupils, which also show that American students spend less time doing homework. Reports on the condition of higher education lament a steady decline in the basic skills of college graduates.

The *causes* of unsatisfactory quality in education are a matter of much debate. Some commentators on public elementary and secondary schools claim that only the achievement levels of inner-city districts are a problem and that their poor results skew the national averages. There is agreement, however, that continued White flight to the suburbs and private schools produce increased racial segregation and inadequate funding in urban areas. Others think the problem of quality is nearly universal in the public schools. Polls show that the public link lowered quality to drug abuse and the lack of discipline.

At all levels, analyses of the causes of decline focus on curriculum changes. Some critics assert that students neglect basic skills because they are allowed to choose too many excessively vocational or undemanding electives. Such criticisms provoke heated responses, especially when they are linked with allegations that pluralism, the introduction of women's or non-Western 'multicultural' components, has weakened the core curriculum in schools. Revision of the academic canon is on-going, as many institutions adjust their sense of the essential, evaluate suggested national curricula, add remedial programmes and implement stricter standards of proficiency.

Proposals for policy changes in public elementary and secondary schools show conflicting attitudes towards decentralization. In Gallup polls, large majorities support requiring local schools to follow a standardized national curriculum and conform to national achievement standards. But the same polls reveal strong support for *school choice programmes*, which often involve further decentralization.

School choice allows families, rather than school authorities, to select the schools their children attend. Choice programmes began with the decentralizing of school districts by giving individual schools the autonomy to design their own curricula. The first autonomous public schools were so-called *magnet schools* in inner cities. These institutions were allowed to specialize in particular subject areas (such as the fine arts or science) and were given the funds and staff that, it was hoped, would bring voluntary desegregation by attracting students from other districts.

By the 1990s, magnet schools had multiplied, especially in large urban school systems, and school choice programmes now aim to maintain high standards by putting these schools in competition with each other. In increasingly large areas, *universal choice* completely breaks the connection between place of residence and the public school a pupil attends.

School choice advocates say the increased number of high quality programmes give students more chances to develop their abilities and point to reductions in racial segregation. Opponents argue that school choice relegates most staff and pupils to institutions that are weaker than ever before because they lack leadership and positive role models. They also criticize the concentration of the best faculty and pupils in magnet schools as an elitist approach that contradicts the ideals of American democracy. In the late 1990s, around a million children in the US were being taught at home because their parents had decided to opt out of institutional schooling altogether.

■ **Examine and explain the following terms:**

'school-raisings'   meritocracy

Horace Mann   Morrill Act

compulsory school attendance laws   John Dewey

progressive education   'G.I. Bill'

coeducational education   *Sputnik*

affirmative action programmes   busing

independent school districts   social localism

state board of education   pluralism

state redistribution plans   parochial schools

community college   state university

private higher education   liberal arts college

graduate school   admissions policy

continuous evaluation   magnet schools

school choice programmes

■ **Write short essays on the following topics:**

1   What do you view as major developments in the
    historical evolution of American education? Defend
    your views.

2   Debate the advantages and disadvantages of
    localism in public elementary and secondary educa-
    tion.

3   Describe the private sector in American elementary
    and secondary schooling. Is it good public policy
    for the US to allow such alternatives to public
    schools?

4   Discuss the issues of current debate in American education. Why are these questions important or difficult in the US?

5   How can entering American higher education be described as a process of mutual selection in a system that is decentralized, diverse and competitive? Discuss the pros and cons of such a system.

The media

THE TERM 'MEDIA' MAY INCLUDE ANY form of communication by which people are informed, educated and
entertained. In the US, it refers primarily to the print media (newspapers, books and magazines) and the broadcasting media
(television and radio). But some of these forms have also become
profitable parts of the film, video and computer industries as
multi-media corporations have been established in recent years.

The media have evolved from simple methods of production and distribution to their present sophisticated technologies.
They now provide a communications system which conveys
words, messages and images to a mass audience; offers a wide
diversity of consumer choice; covers homes and places of business; is an inevitable part of daily life; and is powerful, influential
and controversial.

Americans are very aware of and considerably conditioned
by the media. It is estimated that the average full-time worker is
exposed to various forms of the media for some nine hours a
day. But there is also concern about and resistance to their dominant and pervasive roles. Government has frequently tried to
muzzle the media (to little real effect) and pressure groups attempt
to promote reform.

The media clearly influence some public opinion and shape
attitudes and values by setting agendas and deciding what is newsworthy. Radio and television, for example, have been responsible
for minimizing cultural and regional differences across the US but
they have also reflected social diversity as they search for new,
profitable markets. Access to power may also be gained through
media and information sources. Politicians use these to influence
voters and political life and events have consequently become
more immediate for Americans. However, the abundance of information and television images may also confuse and desensitize
audiences, leading people to reject the media.

Although non-commercial media do exist, most US newspapers, magazines, book publishers and radio and television stations are privately owned. They are commercial businesses operating for profit and are closely tied to commerce, industry, advertising and sponsorship. The media industry now ranks as the country's ninth largest. Commercial and manufacturing companies use it to encourage consumers to purchase their products through national and local advertising. Total advertising revenues account for a considerable part of the nation's economy, although critics oppose the alleged negative influence of advertising on the media.

While commercial control is significant, the audience's opinions also influence the media industries. These must respond to their audience's wishes for a varied range of entertainment, information and news, if they are to be profitable. The ratings system for radio and television (statistics on audience approval) and print media circulation figures are important determinants of success or failure.

Developments in mass communications and entertainment, such as computer technology, cable and satellite television, printing advances and video recorders, have expanded the scope of the media society and helped to shape the country's cultural life. The growth of media outlets has widened this market; reduced the dominance of traditional formats; appealed to more diverse segments of the population; and increased participation by viewers, readers and listeners. The availability of American television series, books, periodicals and satellite programmes (such as CNN) abroad has also internationalized the US media's influence.

Media history

Books and newspapers were the first media to emerge in early American history due to a public need for news, education and information. Book production increased when a printing press was set up in 1638 in Cambridge, Massachusetts. But presses and the print media were controlled politically by the colonial authorities through a licensing system. Although the first news-paper, Benjamin Harris' *Publick Occurrences Both Foreign and Domestick*, was published in Boston in 1690, it was banned because it did not have a licence.

The eighteenth century

Newspapers developed quickly in the eighteenth century. They gained influence and readership as they were freed from licensing control and responded to political events and the demands of a growing population. The first, relatively comprehensive news-paper, the Franklins' *New England Courant*, was published in Boston in 1721. Later, papers became a unifying force in the fight for independence from the British and spread news of east-coast revolt to western settlers.

Magazines were the last print media to emerge and were partly influenced by middle-class wishes for entertainment. Andrew Bradford's *American Magazine* was the first magazine, appearing shortly before Benjamin Franklin's *General Magazine* (January 1741).

As the population grew and the frontier expanded west-wards, the social role of the print media was emphasized. Printers transported their equipment across the country and established presses and printshops wherever they settled. They normally first published a book of local laws, followed by a newspaper and magazine. But, after the War for Independence, newspapers declined in quality. They became abusive and biased propaganda tools of political parties with vehement editorials in support of special causes and political programmes.

Nevertheless, newspapers gained the protection of the First Amendment of the Bill of Rights in 1791, which guaranteed freeedom of the press. Americans were aware that papers had generally supported them against the British before and during the War for Independence. They were determined that Congress should not have the power to infringe press freedom. This crucial development formed the basis of 'prior restraint' (the doctrine that the authorities cannot muzzle the press before publication).

Newspapers also made greater attempts at objectivity in order to gain and retain readers.

The nineteenth century

By the mid-nineteenth century, the print media had become even more important and influential as a social and cultural force. There was an increase in literacy rates and an expansion of schools and libraries, which created a new mass market of readers. Revolutionary high-speed presses were manufactured to satisfy the market demand for news, entertainment, education and information. Many new magazines and newspapers emerged after 1825 and the publication of textbooks, general information books and children's books increased.

There was also a strong demand for novels, which sold in large numbers, and many were written by women. Novelists were aided by the introduction of paperback books in 1842. This development is still influential today, because paperbacks are part of publishing firms' structure and are relatively cheap purchases for consumers. They began as 'supplements' to newspapers and were later printed by orthodox book publishers.

Newspapers became a cheap and genuine mass medium and rapidly increased in number. They were mostly owned and edited by powerful and influential individuals who were personally involved in their papers. They introduced new publishing methods and forms of communication. James Gordon Bennett established the first modern American newspaper, the New York *Herald*, in 1835. He employed reporters to gather news; appointed the first foreign correspondents and a Washington press corps; and delivered the news before his competitors by using the telegraph and fast transportation.

Bennett was followed by Horace Greeley with his New York *Tribune* (1841), whose editorial page was very influential nationwide, and by Henry Raymond, who published *The New York Times* (1851). These and other owners improved news-gathering methods and developed innovative newspaper structures.

At the end of the nineteenth century, Joseph Pulitzer and William Randolph Hearst, with the *World* (1887) and the *Journal* (1895) respectively, dominated US newspapers. They were fierce rivals in a struggle for bigger circulation figures and produced newspapers which contained a mixture of sensational news reporting ('yellow journalism') and social crusading. They also introduced Sunday papers and the comic strip. But a significant development occurred when E.W. Scripps founded the first newspaper chain from 1889 (a collectivist structure which became important in contemporary newspaper ownership).

Newspapers and other print media were now established as the primary means of communication for the population and had very large readerships. But journalism also became big business for some news organizations, which focused less on social crusading and more on maximizing profits.

The twentieth century

Personal newspaper ownership continued in the early twentieth century. Joseph Patterson printed the New York *Daily News* in 1919 (the first modern tabloid) and Robert R. McCormick published the Chicago *Tribune* from 1910.

But newspapers generally became more conservative because advertising, on which they now depended financially, replaced circulation figures as the main source of income. Advertisers originally aimed at a middle-class market, but later divided the population into other class and income groups. This resulted in different types of newspapers, which reflected varied lifestyles and consumption levels. Most newspapers still tended to be concentrated in local areas and cities and were owned by individuals or companies. But economic pressures by the middle of the twentieth century forced many personal owners to sell their papers or join large chains and conglomerates which then dominated the media business.

Meanwhile, the market for novels increased in the early twentieth century. Books expanded into other formats as publishers organized the industry into its modern structure.

Magazines and newspapers were similar in form and content and often embarked on crusading investigative journalism, which President Theodore Roosevelt called 'muckraking' (exposing scandal and corruption). Investigative reporting had previously been largely political but it now also included criticisms of the general social system and attempted to gain public support for specific campaigns. Such investigative journalism became a feature of the print industries and was to spread to radio and television later in the twentieth century.

However, the print media were challenged by Hollywood's silent films and later sound motion pictures which became the dominant entertainment sources of the 1920s and 1930s and an alternative attraction for audiences. These media forms also had to compete with radio broadcasting in the 1920s. Radio provided a new national and world perspective for many Americans. It unified country and city, minimized rural isolation and contributed greatly to cultural standardization.

Commercial television was introduced at the New York World's Fair in 1939, but the Second World War prevented its early progress. After the war television began increasingly to dominate the other broadcast and print media. Its immediate information service affected the traditional news function of newspapers and its entertainment role challenged magazines, books and films. But the other media coped with this competition and continued to grow. Today, the US media are relatively decentralized with a great number of newspapers, magazines and radio and television stations. However, many of these are in fact owned by multi-media conglomerates.

Freedom of the media

The First Amendment to the Constitution states that Congress shall not make any law that interferes with or abridges the freedom of the press. This freedom from government control and censorship has been vigorously defended over the years.

The media today, including the broadcasting media, claim equal treatment under the First Amendment and there is no overt government censorship of content or form. But freedom from prior restraint is not absolute. The Supreme Court has indicated that injunctions preventing publication could be granted if material clearly jeopardized national security and exceptions to prior restraint have occurred in less serious areas such as school newspapers. There are also licensing and anti-monopolistic regulations by agencies such as the Federal Communications Commission (FCC), which make the broadcasting media less free than the print media. Critics additionally argue that while the media appear to be constitutionally free, they are in fact subject to and conditioned by advertising, concentrated ownership patterns and economic pressures.

The media, in following their constitutional rights, have often pursued a confrontational or adversarial line towards public authorities and individuals. They see themselves as a 'Fourth Estate', or fourth branch of society after the law, government and religion. They have published official secrets; revealed classified documents; and exposed corrupt practices, unethical behaviour and injustices in American life. This has led to tension between the media and public authorities. For example, the *Washington Post* and *The New York Times* published the 'Pentagon Papers' in 1971. This was a classified US Defense Department paper containing details of the American role in the Vietnam War. After appeals by the government, the Supreme Court ruled that the newspapers had a constitutional right to publish the information. The *Washington Post*, in another famous case, investigated and disclosed the Watergate scandal (resulting in the resignation of President Nixon). Media sources revealed the facts and extent of the My Lai massacre in Vietnam and the later Iran–Contra affair. Contemporary investigations continue into the activities of politicians, institutions and public figures.

The question of the media's role, influence and power is controversial and debatable. Critics argue that the media (particularly television) have become too powerful and influential and that their freedom should be curtailed. The news media are accused of bias, distorted journalism, invasion of privacy, manipulating events and with actively trying to shape public opinion by setting particular agendas. But actions for libel and obscenity, contempt of court charges to force the identification of journalists' sources and injunctions may be used against the media. These can protect individuals and organizations in certain circumstances and arguably prevent absolute free expression by the media.

There is in fact a close (and for some critics unhealthy) relationship between the news media and public authorities (symbiosis). Each side needs the other and uses each other to mutual advantage. Each needs the sources and opinion-forming roles of the other, so that the media are dependent on public authorities and vice versa. This is particularly true of television news, but is also increasingly true of the talk format radio stations. The relationship is consequently both adversarial and symbiotic and arguably each side loses part of its absolute independence and freedom.

The contemporary print media

The press (newspapers)

In 1995, some 1,548 daily newspapers (mornings and evenings during the week) were published in the US, with a circulation of 59 million. There were also some 891 Saturday and Sunday papers with a circulation of 62 million. In addition there are about 7,000 weekly, semi-weekly and monthly local newspapers.

Newspapers cater for different readerships. Some are characterized as 'quality' or 'serious' papers and have in-depth international and national news and feature coverage. Others are 'popular' or 'tabloid' publications, which emphasize crime, sports, comic pages, sex and scandal.

It is often argued that the US does not have a national press (centred in one city) or newspapers with a mass circulation which are available in all parts of the country on the same morning. This is due partly to the nation's size and different time zones, but also because of a concern with local issues and identity. However, the national influence of some large quality metropolitan newspapers, such as *The New York Times*, the *Washington Post*, *The Los Angeles Times* and *The Wall Street Journal*, together with *US Today*, is considerable. They are read throughout the country, in part through the use of computer and satellite technology which facilitates local printing. These newspapers, and others such as *The Christian Science Monitor*, *The (Baltimore) Sun*, *The St Louis Dispatch* and *The Milwaukee Journal*, have an international reputation.

Newspapers have experienced fundamental changes and developments in recent decades, which have resulted in certain features being characteristic of the contemporary industry.

There has been a considerable decline in the readership of all (but particularly large city) papers since the mass circulation years of the early twentieth century and the total number of newspapers has decreased. Critics maintain that this is due to people moving to the suburbs from the large cities and developing new media habits; mergers between existing papers because of economic pressures; competition from radio, television and other media sources; and circulation battles between different print formats (such as magazine supplements). But smaller dailies and weeklies have increased in numbers and circulation in local areas. Generally, newspapers have been forced to adapt to changed markets in order to expand their readership and circulation levels.

Newspaper declines have been accompanied by a reduction in competition and a lack of variety in publications. Ownership is now held by a few publishers and corporations (media conglomerates). Unlike in previous decades, the number of cities with competing newspapers has been reduced and many cities with daily papers have a single publisher. A large number of papers are owned or controlled by nationwide chains, which have some 70 per cent of all daily sales.

Concentrated ownership of newspapers by large groups supposedly results in economies of size, efficiency and rationalization and gives greater profitability. But it also causes monopolistic conditions, a similarity in content and format and

TABLE 11.1 Average circulation of main daily newspapers (1994)

Newspaper	Circulation
The Wall Street Journal (quality)	1,780,442
USA Today (popular)	1,465,926
The New York Times (quality)	1,114,905
The Los Angeles Times (quality)	1,062,202
Washington Post (quality)	810,675
(New York) Daily News (popular)	753,024
(Long Island) Newsday (quality)	693,556
The Chicago Tribune (quality)	678,081
(Detroit) Free Press (quality)	554,606
(Chicago) Sun-Times (quality)	518,094
The San Francisco Chronicle (quality)	509,548
(Boston) Globe (quality)	506,545

Source: 1995 Editor and Publisher International Yearbook

raises questions about objectivity and accuracy. While some quality papers are in fact local monopolies, critics argue that a greater diversity of newspapers would result in the counterbalancing of potential error and bias.

Newspapers have experienced significant technological changes in recent years, such as automated composing rooms and the use of computer and electronic technology to process news. Some news is still gathered by individual reporters but in fact most newspapers, radio networks and television companies worldwide now obtain their news directly from two US-based news services or agencies: Associated Press (AP) and United Press International (UPI). They are independently owned and collect national and international news items which are sold to newspapers and other media sources. This means that a few sources of news dominate in the US market and results in comparatively homogeneous international and national news.

But the big American papers themselves still provide a large number of their own news stories and sell copyrighted news and features to international and smaller national papers. This allows the wide dissemination of news throughout the US and contributes to the influence of the larger papers. Similarly, the articles of independent syndicated columnists appear simultaneously in many newspapers. The stories in the big papers often influence local newspapers and television news programmes in their choice of newsworthy items.

Critics argue that, since the emergence of competition from television with its immediate news, newspapers generally have become more responsible; make their news columns as fair and accurate as possible; attempt to be objective and detached in news reports; and try to separate news from opinion (which is usually confined to editorial pages).

But the competition with television has led to different emphases in newspapers, particularly in the area of investigative journalism. Although small local newspapers concentrate largely on local news, they are also involved in wider issues (such as pollution) and have revealed cases of political corruption. But it is usually the large city papers which are most active in investigative journalism and are able to devote resources to in-depth coverage. However, it is important not to over-emphasize the amount of investigative reporting carried out by the US media. Few journalists engage in such work and most rely on common sources rather than their own independent investigations.

Investigative journalists argue that they are promoting important social change with their exposures, quote their constitutional rights, maintain that they perform a necessary public and democratic service and see themselves as servants of the public rather than of the government. As in the past, some critics are opposed to investigative reporting, arguing that it constitutes a serious invasion of privacy in many cases and gives newspapers too much political influence.

Magazines and periodicals

Some 11,000 magazines and periodicals are published in the US at varying times from weekly and monthly to quarterly and half-yearly. They cater for most tastes and interests. Some have small and others have large circulations. About ninety-one magazines sell between 850,000 and 5 million copies each issue and a smaller number have huge circulations. Some of these have international editions or are translated into other languages. But only six magazine companies account for half the total magazine revenue, indicating a high conglomerate concentration and influence. The list in Table 11.2 reveals that the best-selling magazines in 1994 dealt with retirement (*Modern Maturity* and *NRTA/AARP Bulletin*), television information, general reading, travel and women's interests.

Mass circulation magazines declined from the 1950s because they had to compete for advertising and sales with television and newspapers. Rising costs of production and paper led to smaller formats and fewer magazines. Popular publications like *Life*, the *Saturday Evening Post* and *Look* did not survive. A shift to specialization in specific areas has occurred, as magazines try to establish market positions.

But general magazines (such as *Reader's Digest*) continue to be an important element of American cultural life. They were originally designed for entertainment purposes but they could also be influential in social and political areas. Today, general magazines are mainly informational and are concerned with very varied aspects of social life. They are aimed at readers in specific age, interest or economic groups.

The more specialist magazines are targeted at people with particular professional occupations and interests and serve as an important means of communication among them. In fact, the majority of all magazines and periodicals are 'trade' or specialist publications. They cover business, professional, technical, industrial, scientific and scholarly areas.

American news magazines are very successful when compared with the experiences of other countries in this field. *Time* (4,036,146 in 1994), *Newsweek* (3,158,617) and *US News and World Report* (2,240,710) dominate the news magazine market. They sell well in the US; have international editions; and sell some of their news material to publications world-wide.

TABLE 11.2 Top ten US magazines: average circulation 1994

Magazine	Circulation
NRTA/AARP Bulletin (retirement)	21,875,436
Modern Maturity (retirement)	21,716,727
Reader's Digest (general interest)	15,126,664
TV Guide (specialist)	14,037,062
The Conde Nast Select (travel/fashion)	12,850,436
National Geographic (specialist)	9,203,079
Better Homes and Gardens (specialist)	7,613,661
Good Housekeeping (women's interest)	5,223,935
Ladies Home Journal (women's interest)	5,048,081
Family Circle (women's interest)	5,005,301

Source: Audit Bureau of Circulations, 1994

Some influential periodicals specialize in coverage of educational, political and cultural topics, such as *The Atlantic Monthly, Harvard Educational Review, Saturday Review, The New Republic, National Review, Scientific American, Foreign Affairs, Smithsonian* and *The New Yorker*. These, together with other specialist professional journals, supply the more serious end of the magazine market and some of their material is reprinted internationally.

The leisure or hobby end of the magazine market is catered for by magazines which deal with sports, popular pastimes, motoring, fashion and leisure activities. Some, such as *Cosmopolitan* (2,527,928 in 1994 in the US) and *Vogue* (1,181,313) also sell internationally.

Book publishing

There was concern in the mid-twentieth century that radio, film and television might reduce the appeal of reading and the sales of books. But book purchases have increased and the US leads the world in the number of books read per head of population. American books cover a comprehensive range from fiction to technical works. They have become an important leisure, as well as an educational and professional, activity.

Critics give several reasons for this situation. US schools generally have encouraged reading and a love of books; public libraries have actively sponsored book usage in local communities nationwide; and there are no restrictive laws which control book selling and book prices. There is an open market in new and used books, which are widely sold in a variety of sales outlets in addition to standard book shops.

There are 2,500 major book publishers in the US, which publish hard cover and paperback books and differ in size and variety of publications. But six of them account for more than half of total book revenues. Many thousands of new books are published each year and a large export trade has contributed to the world-wide influence of American books, especially in the scientific and technological fields.

About a quarter of the publishing structure deals with books intended for a general audience, such as fiction, bestsellers, biography, art books and children's books. But three-quarters of the publishing business is divided among textbooks, reference works, subscription book clubs and scientific and technical publications.

The contemporary broadcasting media: television and radio

The US broadcasting system is characterized by its great diversity and division into commercial and non-commercial sectors. The commercial sector is largely financed by money from businesses that pay to advertise goods or services before, during and after programmes, or by subscriptions from cable and satellite users. Advertising is a large and profitable industry and its connection with the media is controversial because of its alleged influence.

The non-commercial sector, like the Public Broadcasting Service (PBS), is largely non-profit-making, educational or cultural in nature and run by organizations such as colleges and universities. It is funded by individual subscriptions, corporate sponsorship and grants from foundations, private bodies, educational sources and the government. But it has to survive on limited budgets. Although public television does not carry advertising, its credits to corporate sponsors do look like the format of television commercials.

All radio and television stations must be licensed to broadcast by the Federal Communications Commission (FCC). This is an independent federal agency, financed by Congress, whose members are appointed by the President. It controls the stations by granting limited-period licences to applicants and has a supervisory and regulatory role. But the FCC does not control the actual reception of broadcast programmes through the air. This means that there are no licence fees in the US for owning equipment such as television sets. Broadcast reception is therefore freely available in most cases, except for cable and decoded satellite services.

There is no direct government censorship of broadcasting content. But the FCC, with its licensing power, does regulate media ownership by ensuring that there are no monopolies and that a variety of services and programmes are provided throughout the country. Its Fairness Doctrine also requires stations to give equal time to opposing views and commercial stations must show free 'public service' announcements, such as Red Cross blood drives and Alcoholics Anonymous programmes.

Television

Television is the dominant and most controversial national medium. In 1995 some 98 per cent of American homes had at least one television set, which may be switched on (if not continuously watched) for an average 7.2 hours a day. Children on average watch television for four hours a day and adults for three hours a day. Surveys suggest that television is the most important and reliable source of news for most Americans. It can be influential in forming opinions and consumer choice and critics argue that it is potentially capable of affecting the outcome of political elections.

The Federal Communications Act of 1934 established local television stations as the bodies legally responsible for all their output, no matter where their programmes originated. In 1994 there were 1,520 'broadcast' television stations (those which broadcast over the air), which vary in size and have separate identities and characteristics. Some 350 were non-commercial or independent and 1,170 were commercial stations.

Most of the commercial television stations are affiliated with and receive many of their programmes from the Big Three private national television networks, which buy most of their programmes from independent production companies. The Big Three are the American Broadcasting Company (ABC: 1943), the National Broadcasting Company (NBC: 1926) and the Columbia Broadcasting Service (CBS: 1928).

The networks compete against each other to attract the highest audience ratings and advertising revenue. Thus, most of the programmes that most people watch are the same across the country and are shown at the same time during prime time (7.30/8.00 p.m. to 11 p.m.). This structure has traditionally given the Big Three networks great influence. Until the 1980s, they dominated American television, having a combined share of 90 per cent of the total television audience.

In addition to their entertainment role, the networks have news-gathering organizations in the US and world-wide. They broadcast nationwide news and current affairs programmes throughout the week, such as CBS's *60 Minutes* and NBC's *Meet the Press*. Local commercial television stations also have news teams, reporters and film crews to provide local news programmes as well as the national network news.

However, the largest television network (in terms of the numbers of its stations) and an alternative to commercial television is the commercial-free PBS. This system was established in 1967 by the Public Broadcasting Act and has 350 stations sharing programmes. The recent growth of these television stations has been considerable, although they have a much smaller audience than commercial television. The high quality of their news, educational and entertainment programmes (such as children's

TABLE 11.3 Top ten prime-time commercial television programmes, 1994–95

Title	Format
Seinfeld	(situation comedy)
E.R.	(hospital series)
Home Improvement	(situation comedy)
Grace Under Fire	(situation comedy)
NFL Monday Night Footbal	(sports)
60 Minutes	(news and current affairs)
NYPD Blue	(police series)
Friends	(situation comedy)
Roseanne	(situation comedy)
Murder, She Wrote	(crime series)

Source: Nielsen Media Research

programmes, imported drama series and films) attract very selective audiences.

Independent, cable and satellite television

Since the 1980s, the power of the Big Three networks has declined because of new competitors. A first challenge came from independent television stations, which were originally unaffiliated with the networks and broadcast syndicated programming, comprising mostly repeats of earlier network series. They have built larger audiences nationwide by expanding the quality and range of their services and by using broadcast technology and cable and satellite facilities.

Cable television is the second key element in the relative decline of the networks. Cable stations originally provided television programmes to subscribers in communities which could not receive air broadcasts, largely because of geographical limitations. There are now many different types of schemes, systems and programmes. Cable companies transmit cable and other network, affiliated, independent and public television services. There were

PLATE 11.1 CNN coverage of the Gulf War

some 11,200 cable television systems in the US in 1995 and the number of households with cable facilities was 60.4 million in 1994 (or 63 per cent of those households with television sets). The top two cable networks in 1995 were ESPN (sports) and CNN (news).

Cable companies charge a fee to subscribers for the cable service and are financed through this revenue and advertising. Viewers opt to pay additional sums for specialist channels and live broadcasts of special events. There has been a considerable development of ethnic cable channels nationwide with networks for African-American, Latino, Jewish, Chinese, Japanese, Portugese, Greek, Hindi and Korean interests.

Satellite television is the third threat to the dominance of the Big Three. It originally offered programmes to rural populations who could not receive cable systems. It enables those people with a satellite dish and who pay subscriptions to benefit from a wide range of television channels.

A fourth threat to Big Three supremacy is the home video market, with videos either for sale or rent. By 1995 there was at least one video-cassette recorder (VCR) in 85 per cent of American homes.

The fifth threat to the Big Three networks is the growth of a fourth network, the Fox Broadcasting Corporation, owned by Rupert Murdoch's News Corporation. This began broadcasting in 1986 with limited two-nights-a-week programming. It has now expanded its offerings and viewing times to seven nights a week and is a serious rival to the Big Three.

Traditional network television has thus faced competition to retain its audience as viewers have increasingly changed to other services. Cable, satellite and independent television stations are very attractive because they offer many different channels and provide a wide range of specialized alternative choices. In 1994, household viewing shares were 52 per cent for the Big Three networks, 21 per cent for independent stations, 4 per cent for public television, 26 per cent for basic cable and 5 per cent for specialist/pay cable systems.

Attitudes to commercial television

American commercial television programmes have a somewhat dubious reputation both in the US and abroad. A variety of opinions about and criticisms of commercial television have been levelled by consumers and public officials.

It has been attacked for its bias towards commercial and mass entertainment programmes (soap operas and quiz games), which sell goods and services through advertising. Advertising companies and station owners may also interfere in programme content in the pursuit of profit. Some consumers criticize such programming, which is directed at the lower end of the television market, and argue that television companies should be more involved with quality educational and news programmes.

But news broadcasting is also controversial because it can either appear to trivialize events by its reporting techniques, or affect public opinion by the biases in its news coverage. Commercial television is attacked for its portrayal of violence and for the alleged impact of violence and explicit sex upon both children and adults. The debate over possible links between violence and sex on television and its occurrence in society continues, although such programmes are not now shown in the early evening and new 'V-chip' technology will allow parents to censor children's viewing.

There is a considerable amount of citizen involvement in other issues, such as groups campaigning for better quality children's television and others which attack the alleged explicit language and immorality on television. Minorities and women are also concerned with television programmes and object to the representation of ethnic and gender stereotypes. Commercial television (and the advertising companies) are often sensitive to such criticisms, since it can affect their profits. Some critics maintain that objections have made commercial television into a more conservative institution and there are indications that advertisers and owners may be paying more attention to the public's wishes.

Nevertheless, attitudes to American commercial television are not solely a list of complaints and negative comments, nor is it all of poor quality. It can perform essential educational and informational functions. Documentaries and in-depth news presentations can be of high quality. It provides live coverage of important events, both domestically and world-wide. It has the capacity to closely examine politicians and their policies, so that viewers may make up their own minds about a range of issues. Politicians and advertisers in their turn are very aware of television's power and influence and this may help to moderate their behaviour.

Radio

Radio had a revolutionary impact following its commercial introduction to the US in the 1920s. Critics argue that it (and its
immediate news function) helped to unify the population of the
cities and the countryside; increased the national and world awareness of Americans; and informed them about the events of the
Second World War. But radio was overtaken by television in
the 1940s and has had to develop new markets and emphases
to survive. It has become divided into formats and specialities
which are directed at specific consumer markets and this has
increased the diversity of radio offerings. Radio is still important,
particularly on the local level, for its news, participatory and
entertainment roles. Some 89 per cent of American homes had a
radio in 1995.

There is no one national radio station in the US. Instead,
cities and local areas may have several independent stations and
all are regulated by the FCC which grants them operating licences.
They may often have different approaches. Small-town stations
carry local news and community interest items, as well as national
and international news derived from larger stations. Big cities are
served by a large number of local stations and have many different
formats.

There were some 10,160 radio stations nationwide in 1995,
most of which are commercial organizations and the remainder
are non-commercial. Commercial radio ownership tends to be
concentrated in the hands of a relatively few conglomerates.
Commercial stations obtain their funding mainly from the advertising on their programmes, which are purchased from many
different sources, although they do make their own programmes.
The public radio stations are generally owned and operated by
educational institutions and religious groups, with a similar high
reputation to PBS for their documentaries, news and debates. The
National Public Radio Network (NPR) is an umbrella organization of most non-commercial radio stations.

Diversity of choice is the key element of radio in the US
and many stations provide 24-hour services to satisfy their
customers. Most commercial radio stations are organized around

and follow a specific format, which is designed to attract particular audiences. Permission from the FCC is necessary if a station wishes to change its format.

Some stations consequently provide music programmes (mixed or specialist) such as country and western, popular music, rock and roll, light classics, classical music and jazz. Others concentrate on news, studio interviews and discussions, talk shows and interviews, phone-ins (audience participation by telephone) and religious programmes. Stations with a talk format account for 10 per cent of stations and the number of listeners and active participants has increased considerably. Some stations broadcast only news for 24 hours a day, while most others provide five-minute summaries hourly or half hourly. Others offer a variety or mixture of the above.

Attitudes to the media

In terms of Americans' faith in their institutions, a survey in *The Good Life and Its Discontents* (Samuelson, 1996) reported that only 13 per cent of respondents had a great deal of confidence in the media, compared to 29 per cent in 1966. But Congress (8 per cent) and the Executive branch (12 per cent) did worse.

Attitudes to alleged bias (or partiality) in the US media are revealing. According to a survey by the Roper Organization (1984), 41 per cent of the public thought that the media are biased against sections of society. Groups such as business executives, workers, liberals and conservatives thought that the media are against their own particular organizations and interests. Such varied findings, which might indicate that the media are in fact doing a good job, are echoed in other countries and point to difficulties in assessing media bias.

The media themselves decide what are newsworthy political issues and public events on which to concentrate. This choice reflects journalists' personal opinions, although the media insist that they try to be objective, present all sides of a case and use self-censorship in order to avoid overt bias. But American research suggests that there is a definite positive bias towards established institutions and values in the US media, although (perhaps surprisingly) not much partiality for particular political candidates and political policies.

Critics argue that there is therefore a general media bias or scepticism aimed at all politicians and policies. The tendency is towards negativism rather than positivism and this produces an unfortunate undercurrent in reporting. Television is seen as more critical than newspapers and magazines and the national media are more critical than local media.

The commercial bias of the media (except for PBS) is more obvious for critics and the public. Most media are private businesses and must sell subscriptions and advertising in order to make a profit and survive. Larger audiences create greater advertising revenue, so that advertising can shape media content and may result in the media printing or broadcasting what advertisers want.

On the other hand, commercial bias also means that the media must give the public what it wants in order to retain the audience. The media (particularly television) can become entertainment rather than information or education and employ emphases, such as human interest stories, conflict, action, melodrama, the visual and the superficial. Some critics argue that such emphases lead to a lack of quality, particularly of news, and detract from the media's information role.

In terms of news and general media content, *Understanding American Government* suggests that

> The media have to be responsive to the people to make a profit. They present the news they think the people want. Because they believe the majority desire entertainment, or at least diversion, rather than education, they structure the news towards this end. According to a number of studies, they correctly assess their consumers. For the majority who want entertainment, network television provides it. For the minority who want education, the better newspapers and magazines provide it. Public radio, with its hour-and-a-half

nightly newscast (*All Things Considered*), and public television, with its hour nightly newscast (*MacNeil/Lehrer News
Hour*), also provide quality coverage. The media offer something for everyone.

(Welch *et al.*, 1995, p. 244)

EXERCISES

■ **Examine and explain the following terms:**

yellow journalism	William Randolph Hearst
ratings	muckraking
newspaper chains	networks
New England Courant	advertising
formats	conglomerates
Washington Post	Watergate
syndication	cable television
PBS	FCC
bias	UPI

■ **Write short essays on the following topics:**

1   Should the freedom of the American media be curtailed?

2   Analyse the contemporary significance of American newspapers in terms of their historical development.

3   Discuss the structure and influence of television in the US.

Chapter 12

Religion

MANY WESTERN COUNTRIES have experienced twentieth-century declines in religious observance and increased secularization. Such developments have been variously attributed to the influences of industrialization, consumer cultures, self-seeking pleasure principles and universal education.

However, the US seems to be, in comparison with these countries and despite its materialistic image, relatively religious in terms of denominational identification. Surveys indicate that 82 per cent of Americans regard themselves as members of specific religious groups. Public opinion polls also show that a majority (including a large number of young people) are very interested in spiritual matters and acknowledge that religion is important in their lives. But they nevertheless feel that the influence of religion is decreasing. Some critics also argue that faith is being trivialized in modern America and that religious beliefs are increasingly treated as arbitrary and unimportant.

As in other countries, belief and formal membership of religious denominations are not always translated into active participation. Although high in Western terms, polls suggest that only some 40 per cent of Americans actually go to a religious service at least once a week. There may therefore be important differences between personal religious beliefs and active attendance at services; between orthodox observance and religion as a social activity; and between institutional worship and the effect of religion upon the larger society. Consequently, the extent of American religiosity should not be exaggerated. It may sometimes be more activist and socially directed than devout or contemplative. It may involve a reaction to and a disillusionment with present conditions and a vague unstructured striving for self-definition.

Nevertheless, religion in whatever form does play a role in US life. It is clearly illustrated in the large variety of religious groups which reflect personal, communal and ethnic identities for citizens; in its influence on national institutions and morality; and in the country's history.

Religious history

The contemporary diversity of US religious life has its roots in Native-American religions, colonial history and the successive waves of later immigrants into the country. The historical development of religious practices needs therefore to be emphasized in order to appreciate the present.

This history is characterized by certain features. First, religious pluralism (many faiths) in US society stems from some settlers seeking freedom from European churches and wishing to freely practise their own forms of worship and by others bringing their existing beliefs to the US. Second, religious activity of an evangelical (conversion-based) type has been an important feature at various times in US history. Third, there has often been an emphasis on the social aspects of religion. Fourth, religion has been closely linked to a belief in democracy and freedom. Fifth, religious identities have often been connected with social class and ethnicity.

Throughout American history, all or some of these features have been reflected in periodic religious movements (known as Awakenings or Revivals), which have varied in intensity and scope; religious activism; missionary work; utopian ideals; an interest in ecumenism (cooperation between different faiths); and various forms of fundamentalist belief.

But there have also been denominational conflicts; widespread and consistent religious discrimination and intolerance; periods when American interest in religion was very low; and an increasing secularism.

The colonial period

Colonial settlement led to a wide variety of religious denominations. These included different types of established European

351

Christianity because some colonists wanted to practise (and some-times spread) their faiths. Other dissenting groups wished to create communities where they could practise their individual religions without interference or persecution. Religious faith was central to these people and it influenced their commercial and everyday lives.

Most early colonists were Protestants and Protestant Christianity was to have a dominant influence on US society. But, since there were many Protestant and other denominations, conflicts persisted between the various faiths. For example, in the early seventeenth century, Virginia's population was largely composed of members of the established Anglican Church of England. But when dissenters from the Church of England settled in the colony, the Anglican Church taxed them. Quakers were banned and Baptist ministers were arrested, although French Huguenots, German Protestants and Scots-Irish Presbyterians were allowed their own congregations.

Meanwhile, two groups of Calvinist settlers (later called Congregationalists) had arrived in the New England area, who were different from the Virginia Anglicans. The first group (Pilgrims) came to Plymouth, Massachusetts in 1620 from England and Holland to found their own church. They were separatists who had left the Church of England because they disapproved of its doctrines and had suffered persecution. The second, larger group arrived in Massachusetts Bay in 1630 and were Puritans who wanted to purify the Church of England.

Neither group was religiously tolerant. They expelled Church of England members and initially confined membership to people who had personally experienced conversion. They believed that God had chosen or predestined specific individuals to achieve salvation. Hard work was a means of pleasing God and any resulting prosperity was a sign that He regarded them favourably. Critics argue that this Puritan (Protestant) work ethic is a conditioning factor in a general American ambition to succeed materially in life.

Religious diversity was most evident in the Middle Colonies. These were settled by Protestant groups such as Welsh and Dutch Calvinists, Scottish Presbyterians, Swedish and German Lutherans,

PLATE 12.1 A well-tended church in Richmond, Virginia
(S. Wright/Barnaby's Picture Library)

Baptists and English Quakers. Protestants and Roman Catholics established themselves in Maryland (formed originally as a haven for Catholics), with religious toleration for all Christians. But Puritan pressure during the English Civil War resulted in toleration for Roman Catholics becoming limited and it ended in 1692.

However, the first Catholics to arrive in America in the sixteenth century outside the original thirteen colonies were missionaries from Spain, Portugal and France. They established churches and missions in the south and west of the country in present-day Texas, California, Florida and New Mexico.

A few European Jewish traders also settled in the English colonies, despite an official ban on Jewish immigration and some Sephardic Jews arrived in New Amsterdam in 1654. Newport, Rhode Island, became the main colonial centre of Jewish life, with other groups in New York, Charleston and Philadelphia.

Most of the original thirteen colonies had an official established church from colonial times until the War for Independence. The Anglican Church served Virginia, Maryland, the Carolinas, Georgia and parts of New York and the Congregational Church was established in New England. But other groups, such as the Presbyterians, Lutherans and Baptists, did not become the established church in any colony.

The eighteenth century

There was a change of emphasis in the eighteenth century. Although many early colonists and settlers had been motivated by religious beliefs, the majority of immigrants now travelled to America for material advancement, free land, or commercial adventure. There was a decline in religious influence and it is estimated that in 1750 only 17 per cent of the population formally belonged to a religious group. However, many people might still have retained nominal adherence to a faith.

But large numbers of immigrants continued to arrive in the eighteenth century, often with distinct religious identifications such as Scots-Irish Presbyterians from northern Ireland. Some of these settled in New England, where they shifted the Congregational (or Puritan) church towards Presbyterianism, and in New York. Others went to New Jersey, Pennsylvania and western Virginia. German Lutherans continued to immigrate and Jews in the eighteenth century arrived from Germany and Poland. But the main emphasis was still on Protestant Christian denominations.

Two major events affected colonial communities in the eighteenth century and produced more active religious responses: first, the Great Awakening (religious revival) and second, the American War for Independence. The Great Awakening affected the colonies in the 1730s and 1740s and was the forerunner of modern evangelical activities. It was an emotional reaction to the increasingly formalistic and dry nature of most religious practices. It began in Massachusetts among the Congregationalists and spread along the East Coast from Maine to Georgia and the western frontier to include Presbyterians, Methodists and Baptists.

Revivalist preachers tried to convert people by stressing God's power, a personal experience of salvation and a human capacity for repentance and rebirth. The Great Awakening created friction and churches were split, as ministers either supported the revivalists or opposed their emotionalism and conversion practices. But it was something of a unifying force as clergy travelled through the colonies and its radicalism in part influenced the coming War for Independence.

The War for Independence was a traumatic event for American religion with loyalties divided among the churches. Scots-Irish Presbyterians, Lutherans, Baptists and Congregationalists were mainly on the American side of the struggle, while the Methodists remained neutral. Some Anglicans supported the British and others the American cause, as did Catholics in Pennsylvania and Maryland. But pacifist religious bodies, like the Moravians, Quakers and Mennonites, were often persecuted during the war because of their beliefs.

The Methodist and Baptist churches were the first to recover after the War. But the Anglican Church lost much prestige due to its ties with England. Attempts to retrieve its position failed and the creation of a new American Protestant Episcopal Church in its stead proved necessary.

However, despite the Great Awakening and the War for Independence, religiosity at the end of the eighteenth century was weak and most Americans were not active church members. The Great Awakening had not had a lasting or deep effect; the new Episcopal Church was largely inactive; and other religious groups had become either austere and intellectual, or were departing from their original religious doctrines. Protestant Christianity appeared to be declining with the abolition of most established churches after the War for Independence.

The nineteenth century

But religious groups recovered and consolidated themselves in the nineteenth century as further revivals occurred; the population expanded westwards; immigration increased; missionary activities grew; and the churches involved themselves more actively in social concerns as a result of industrialization and economic growth. However, the Civil War (1861–65) was a testing time for American religion.

A Second Awakening came at the beginning of the century on the East Coast and spread westwards along the frontier. It sometimes led to superficial emotionalism and divisions within the churches but it also increased the number of evangelical groups west of the Appalachians, such as the Baptists, Presbyterians and Methodists. This expansion was to influence future religious development and the creation of modern evangelical and funda-mentalist movements. A further influence, if restricted largely to literary intellectuals, was Transcendentalism, which stressed the individual and nature as a reaction to traditional Puritanism.

However, religious groups were increasingly subject to conflicts among themselves and with other churches. This was particularly true of the period of 'Protestant sectionalism' (1830 to 1860), which was characterized by theological quarrels, divi-sion of churches and formation of many sects.

For example, attempts to unite the Congregationalists and Presbyterians resulted in division and conflict. There was also tension between the High and Low Church wings of the Episcopal

Church. The East Coast High Church was dominant, but the Low Church wing increased its membership on the western frontier. Similar splits occurred among the Lutherans, but the arrival of conservative German immigrants after 1830 prevented the liberal wing from dominating the church. Norwegian and Swedish Lutherans immigrated in considerable numbers about 1840 and supported the conservative wing.

New religious movements or sects were formed as a reaction to existing faiths in the nineteenth century, such as Spiritualism, Millerism (Seventh-Day Adventism), Mormonism, Perfectionism and Shakerism. These had very different theological beliefs to the traditional churches. Many other religious groups, often with a strong social emphasis, were also established from the 1850s and reflected a continuing American concern with social issues.

Meanwhile, the Roman Catholic Church was greatly strengthened by Irish, French and German immigration from 1830 and by immigrants from eastern and southern Europe later in the century. The church, after earlier internal conflict, was now controlled by its bishops. It attracted the new immigrants and Irish settlers in particular were to influence the church in future years. But Catholic newcomers suffered considerable prejudice and hostility from the dominant Protestant groups.

Indeed, some of the more extreme Protestants attempted to maintain strict Puritan traditions and to oppose the influence of Roman Catholic immigration. For example, the Woman's Christian Temperance Union (1874) tried to stop the use of alcohol and campaigned to maintain the Puritan Sabbath.

Between 1840 and 1880 the Jewish population expanded from 15,000 to 225,000 because of repression and persecution in Germany. Some Jews were Orthodox, but many became members of the new Reform movement. This adapted traditional practices to modern conditions and helped Jews to assimilate more easily to American life. But Jews experienced a general anti-Semitism and discrimination in society, particularly from Protestants.

However, despite religious tensions and the emergence of new sects, a more liberal spirit in and among the churches developed during the course of the nineteenth century. Churches became interested in education and schools and colleges were created with distinct religious identifications. From 1820 increasing immigration promoted new outlooks and activities among the churches. Influential inner-city missions were formed on the East Coast, which actively addressed the new problems of a wealthier and bigger population. Critics argue that it was the example of these mission movements and their activism rather than the two Great Awakenings that saved American Christianity and increased religiosity.

However, slavery and the Civil War were divisive influences on religion. The anti-slavery position was based on humanitarian, democratic and biblical impulses. But there were conflicting interpretations of slavery from both anti- and pro-slavery religionists. Some churches, like the Episcopal Church, tried to be neutral, while others were divided. These waverings resulted in post-war America experiencing a period of religious uncertainty and inaction, as churches tried to recover from the effects of the Civil War.

After 1880 the US increased its wealth substantially, due to the effects of industrialization and a booming economy. But divisions developed between rich and poor and there was much social misery and inequality. There were conflicts between employees and employers, leading to strikes, unemployment and industrial unrest. The churches responded to these problems. Some emphasized social and moral commitment; supported the workers; provided for their social and economic needs; and many of the clergy played an active role in dealing with community problems. This social concern is still a feature of many contemporary religious groups in the US.

The twentieth century

The variety of religions in the US increased at the end of the nineteenth and during the twentieth centuries as large numbers of immigrants arrived from central, eastern and southern Europe, Latin America and Asia.

This particularly strengthened the Roman Catholic Church, but it also included a range of Asian religions, such as Hinduism, Sikhism and Islam, as well as considerable numbers of Jewish immigrants fleeing persecution in Europe. Eastern Orthodox churches were also established by Greek, Russian, Armenian and Syrian immigrants. Such groups tended to concentrate in the bigger cities and retained their own languages in religious and daily life. This produced tight-knit communities with strong ethnic identities, but it also distanced them from many Americans. The result was often intolerance (based upon ignorance and Protestant dominance) directed against the new arrivals.

Critics argue that the diversity of new and established religions has led to competing pressures in US religious life in the twentieth century between pluralism and ecumenism (closer relations between faiths); social action and spiritual renewal; and secularism and religious growth.

Religious *pluralism* (diversity) can be a sign of vitality and lead to greater toleration of different religions but it may also be divisive. The dominant religious majority in early US history had been White Protestant. It had established basic national characteristics, but often treated the later Roman Catholic, Jewish and other immigrants with suspicion and hostility. However, this situation gradually changed in the early twentieth century and considerably from the 1950s, due to further immigration, population growth in ethnic communities, changing social attitudes and the reduction of the Protestant majority. Three major faiths (Protestant, Catholic and Jew) have since then shared American religious life with many other churches, groups and sects.

The pluralistic nature of US religion has been partly offset by *ecumenical* movements among different religious groups. The faiths have become less divisive and have been more tolerant towards, and cooperative with, other religions. Traditional churches divided by historical disputes, like Congregationalists, Lutherans, Presbyterians and Methodists, have arranged mergers. Cooperation occurred at local and national levels between Protestants, Catholics, Jews and Orthodox groups with the creation of ecumenical organizations. For example, the Anti-Defamation

League (1913) and the National Conference of Christians and Jews (1928) reduced anti-Semitism and tension in the early twentieth century. There was also a growing assimilation of immigrant groups into the larger society as old-world languages diminished and 'national' churches/synods tended to merge. Internationally, American Protestants helped to found the World Council of Churches in 1948 and ecumenism was treated positively by the Second Vatican Council (1962–65), which encouraged Catholics to be more open to other religions and modern developments.

But by the 1970s, ecumenism had declined. This was due mainly to concern that individual church beliefs might become weaker in the ecumenical climate and to an increased conservatism that resulted in divisions in some church groups. Nevertheless, Protestants, Catholics and Jews have become less divided and anti-Catholicism and anti-Semitism are not as virulent or as widespread as they once were. Catholics and Jews have achieved greater status and recognition in American life and a growing number of religions such as Islam, Buddhism and Hinduism have been increasingly accepted. The emphasis has turned perhaps to co-existence, rather than ecumenism.

Critics have remarked on other areas of tension, which have been reflected in the opposing views represented by *social action* and *spiritual renewal*. The conflicts between the two trends are important for understanding religious developments in modern America, particularly in recent decades.

Social action stresses religion's public role and follows American traditions of liberal theology and social commitment. Many churches have promoted ecumenism and been involved in programmes for social change. Some have actively intervened in the social problems and moral concerns of the twentieth century like starvation, poverty, racial inequality, refugees, the Vietnam War and industrial relations. This swing towards liberal positions in social matters has also often involved new theological interpretations of belief and practice.

However, some conservative groups within Protestantism emphasize *spiritual renewal* and reflect a desire among many Americans for more personal religious commitment and simple faith. Spiritual renewal movements are founded on a close reading of the scriptures and literal interpretations of the Bible (fundamentalism). They are traditional and orthodox in their beliefs; stress the importance of personal salvation; are suspicious of social action; and oppose liberalizing trends. Their emphasis on fundamental beliefs and fellowship has led them to reject evolutionary theories (Darwinism), new interpretations of the Bible and what they consider to be corrupt forms of modern life. Many Protestant churches in the early twentieth century consequently experienced a series of battles between liberals, modernists and fundamentalists.

Some fundamentalists left their churches to form new groups, where they could practise their beliefs. Others, from the 1960s, have joined evangelical churches. These, and fundamentalism, are connected to the eighteenth- and nineteenth-century traditions of revivalism and evangelicalism with their espousal of conversion, emotional experiences and personal salvation. Evangelical Christian groups have become a powerful force in the US in recent decades; have attracted much media and popular attention; and have grown strongly.

The terms 'evangelical' and fundamentalist' tend to be used interchangeably. 'Fundamentalist' can be applied to specific Protestant and other religious groups. 'Evangelical' involves fundamentalist Christian beliefs and is applied to many denominations with very varied titles, but which are often based on converting people to their beliefs in a born-again experience. They believe in the Bible as the authoritative word of God and in a personal relationship with Christ. Their anti-modern, anti-secular conservative message is based on moral issues, the role of the family and education. They provide moral and simple certainties for many Americans and stress individual responsibility and commitment.

Evangelical ministers and movements use television and radio to spread their message and have become very skilful in their use of the media. They own or control some 1,300 radio or television stations. The preachers can become very popular celebrities and their media performances attract large audiences and advertising revenues, so that religious broadcasting has become very profitable. After a fall in popularity and influence in the late 1980s, the evangelical churches recovered strongly from the mid-1990s.

The vogue for spiritual renewal since the mid-twentieth century has also led people to join a wide variety of sects, cults and churches. Common to them all is an attempt to create close emotional fellowship. The more extreme groups, such as the Moonies and some guru-led organizations, have aroused hostility among many Americans. Their techniques of recruitment, alleged brainwashing of members and religious fanaticism are heavily criticized.

Some Americans in the search for personal spiritual growth and answers to modern problems have joined eastern religions such as Islam, Hinduism and Buddhism. Others seek religious satisfaction in a wide range of alternative beliefs such as the occult or Native-American religions.

But some critics argue that the emergence of so many religious and pseudo-religious groups and the possible diffusion of national identity in this amorphous situation, have led concerned Americans to embrace a 'civil religion' centred on US political traditions. This is a mixture of religion, morality and nationalism which emphasizes symbols, emblems and traditions, such as the national motto ('In God We Trust') and the pledge of allegiance to the flag ('One nation under God'). Critics maintain that 'civil religion' overarches the different varieties of belief and gives the US a distinct moral character and sacred mission. But although this may be a source of national integration, it can also be divisive and its contemporary influence, while formerly evident in the public school system, is debatable.

There has also been an increased *secularism* in twentieth-century US life which has conflicted with these expressions of *religious growth*. Personal decisions can be made without reference to religious teachings or interpretations. Secularism particularly affected education. Some private schools and colleges had previously been created by churches specifically as a way of promoting religious belief. But, in the twentieth century,

PLATE 12.2 Mosque, Michigan *(Rex Features)*

educational institutions were increasingly secularized by state and other authorities. A more relaxed and informal American society, together with increased leisure opportunities and forms of entertainment, have also contributed to the growth of secularization.

But, despite the overall trend towards secularism, more Americans were involved with religious groups and activities in the mid-twentieth century. This coincided with greater interest in religion after the Second World War. Since then, there has been decline in some churches and growth in others.

Church, state and politics

Church and state in the US are supposedly separate. The First Amendment of the Bill of Rights (1791) states that 'Congress shall make no law respecting an establishment of religion, or prohibiting the free exercise thereof'. First, this prohibits the establishment of a national church or state-supported religion. Second, it protects individuals' right to practise their own religion and their freedom from others' religion. Religion, or the lack of it, is a private matter and the First Amendment reflects the liberty to organize one's own life, for which Americans have historically fought.

There were official established churches before the War for Independence and Massachusetts had an established church into the 1830s. But eventually all churches were separated from the state and religion from government. This permitted a diversity of religious practices, which has continued. There are no church taxes in the US; the churches receive no state support; there are no legal or official religious holidays; and no political party is affiliated to a particular denomination. Any congressional act which attempted to impose legislation in these areas would be regarded as violating the Constitution. Since the 1960s, the Supreme Court has also forbidden government from aiding one religion over another or even from aiding religion over non-religion.

Religious groups are therefore independent organizations and self-supporting. They depend upon their members' financial contributions for their continued existence and payment of expenses. Americans' donations to their churches are very generous with 45 per cent of all charitable donations in 1995 going to religion. The fundamentalist and evangelical churches tend to attract the greatest amounts. The local religious building and its congregation are the crucial strengths and centres of American religion. They also provide a variety of social, cultural and community activities outside religious services; supply relief services for the poor and needy; and engage in missionary work domestically and overseas.

However, as society has become more complex and govern-ment more pervasive, church and state have interacted and sometimes interfered, with each other. For example, states in the past restricted the free exercise of religion by prohibiting Catholics and Jews from voting or holding public office. The law has also indirectly interfered with those minority religions which require special working practices, such as Mormons and Seventh-Day Adventists. In these cases, however, the Supreme Court and Congress have often invalidated such restrictions by permitting exceptions. But the Supreme Court has also occasionally restricted adherents' free practice of religion if their behaviour is against the public interest. Arguably, therefore, the division between church and state is not absolute and both Congress and the Supreme Court in some cases have reached decisions which appear to contradict the First Amendment.

Although religion is supposed to be a private matter, public and private life are not inseparable. It is perhaps inevitable that religion should influence US public and political life to some degree, given the diversity and prevalence of religious groups. Religion is very much a part of American society and moral and political issues (such as the abortion and death penalty debates) may be influenced by religious beliefs. Leaders of all the churches do in fact actively campaign on social, moral and political issues.

A religious sensibility is reflected in national symbols and emblems, like the seal of the US, the currency and in the pledge of allegiance to the American flag. US Presidents have often belonged, at least nominally, to a religious group and politicians frequently refer to God and the Bible in their speeches. Newly elected US Presidents swear the inaugural oath of office on the Bible; sessions of Congress commence with prayers; and both houses of Congress have official chaplains.

But formal religion generally has little real influence in national political matters or institutions, beyond rhetorical expres-sions. Politicians are very conscious of the constitutional position and its restrictions upon government action, as well as the restraints of religious tolerance. However, personal beliefs may affect the way in which some individuals react to political issues and actually vote in elections. There has, for example, been a recent increase in the number of evangelicals and Catholics who vote Republican.

A source of national debate and concern in this area of religion and politics has been the role of evangelical groups and their leaders. Many of them are very visible, actively propagate their beliefs and attempt to influence public opinion, social institutions and political processes. They do not restrict themselves to moral and religious matters, but are involved in and campaign on political issues such as anti-abortion legislation and the restoration of prayers in public schools. The evangelical right, sometimes known as 'the Moral Majority' or the 'Christian Coalition' (because of their moral absolutism and so-called American values), has supported conservative politicians in election campaigns and some of its leaders have also attempted to gain political office.

Contemporary US religion

Religion in the US underwent significant changes following the post-Second World War revival. The influence and membership of traditional mainstream Protestant churches declined in the permissive atmosphere and liberal social climate of the 1960s and 1970s. The active membership of Catholic and Jewish congregations has also fallen following earlier growth. But increasing pluralism has led to new religious groups such as fundamentalist and evangelical churches which attract large numbers of members, a variety of sects and cults and eastern religions like Islam, Hinduism and Buddhism.

However, despite these changes, the large majority of religious Americans today are still within the so-called Judaeo-Christian tradition. US religion consequently consists of three main faiths: Protestantism, Catholicism and Judaism.

Protestants

Protestantism is the largest and most diverse of the American faiths. Although some 79 million Americans might consider themselves as 'Protestants', they are divided into a great number of different churches and sects, with varying conservative and liberal outlooks. This pluralistic variety means that there is no one umbrella denomination for all Protestants. Each church is independent, supports itself financially, employs its own ministers, constructs its own buildings and follows its own beliefs.

The Presbyterian (4.3 million members in 1995), Lutheran (8.4 million), Episcopal (2.5 million) and Reformed churches (2.1 million), together with small Congregational churches, constitute mainstream Protestantism from early US history. But the large memberships of the Baptist churches (36.3 million) and Methodists (13.6 million) are now generally considered part of this mainstream Protestant grouping (despite their evangelical history). The largest mainly White Protestant denomination is the Southern Baptist Convention, followed by the United Methodist Church, while the largest Black Protestant denomination is the National Baptist Convention, USA, followed by the Church of God in Christ.

Protestantism is divided between mainstream churches and fundamentalist/evangelical churches with conservative beliefs. But mainstream churches also have different emphases. The more traditional ones tend to have somewhat liberal theological and social attitudes; are composed largely of middle- or upper-class people; and have formal worship and service patterns. Other churches, like the Southern Baptists, may consist of lower-income groups and encourage emotional responses to religion, such as 'born-again' conversions.

While mainstream Protestant churches have lost members since the 1970s, evangelical/fundamentalist Protestant churches, such as the Seventh-Day Adventists, the Church of the Nazarene and the Assemblies of God, have increased their membership. They offer absolutist moral instruction and traditional values and appeal to those Americans who want moral direction. The mainstream Protestant churches have responded by retreating somewhat from their earlier 'liberalism' in order to attract members.

Roman Catholics

Although there was a large Catholic immigration into the US in the nineteenth and early twentieth centuries, American society continued to be predominantly White Protestant in religion and national attitudes.

However, the Roman Catholic Church today is the second largest religious group after Protestants, but the largest in terms of a single denomination or church body. It had about 20,000 churches and 59.9 million members in 1995 and is also the largest predominantly White denomination. Just under a quarter of Americans consider themselves to be Catholic, whether practising or not.

Catholicism was historically confined to ethnic groups such as the Irish, Polish, Italians and Germans in the big cities and was initially largely working class. This urban concentration enabled Catholics to achieve considerable political power at the local, if not the national, level. But after the Second World War, Catholics greatly improved their educational standards, income and class status and many affluent Catholics moved to the suburbs. The Roman Catholic Church built more churches and schools for its growing population, although parochial schools have now declined in number and influence.

But the movement of Catholics from tightly knit urban communities to the suburbs has arguably meant a consequent loss of Catholic identity. Catholics are now more eager and willing after years of discrimination against them to mix with non-Catholics socially. Non-Catholic hostility towards Catholics has largely disappeared and was illustrated by the election of Catholic John F. Kennedy as President in 1960. American Catholics are also influential in international campaigns and domestic social projects and tend to be more ecumenically-minded today than they have been in the past.

However, religious and social change has meant that the Catholic community has experienced internal tensions. Although increasing in population terms, Catholics are not as active in church activities as they were and attendances at weekly mass have declined. The Church is also divided between liberals and conservatives with opposed opinions on birth control, abortion, the celibacy of the priesthood and the question of potential women priests. These concerns have also provoked clashes with conservative Vatican views.

The Jewish community

Jews historically have tended to settle mainly on the East Coast in the big cities. After immigration, their religious practices changed somewhat and now range from traditional Orthodox to moderate Conservative and liberal Reform groups. But all groups have been concerned to preserve their Jewish heritage and traditions. As the Jewish population grew, they established Hebrew schools and contributed to Jewish charities. The creation of the state of Israel in 1948 was an additional focus for Jewish identity. Although anti-Semitism increased in the early twentieth century, this has now been reduced because of general changing social attitudes, ecumenism and sympathy for Jewish suffering in the Second World War. Jews have assimilated more into American society; they are more tolerated and accepted than they once were; and intermarriage between Jews and non-Jews has increased considerably. The Jewish faith had some 4.3 million members in 1995, or some 2.2 per cent of the total population.

Other religious groups

There are other significant US religious groups in addition to the three main faiths, such as the Buddhist Churches of America (230,000 in 1995), Eastern Orthodox Churches (3.5 million), Hindu (910,000) and Islam (5.5 million).

Religion and education

Administrative and financial organization of public schools is carried out by local communities, and school boards composed of elected citizens from each community oversee the schools in each district. They establish school policy for their area and often actually decide what is to be taught. It is at this level that battles between fundamentalists and modernizers over the school curriculum have been fought, such as the debates involving the teaching of evolution and creationism.

The constitutional separation of church from state means that public schools can teach about religion, but they cannot promote it. Religious education is supposed to be neutral. However, some critics argue that, in practice, most public schools were for a long time active proponents of Protestant Christianity, by means of the morning prayer and other activities. This reflected a historical Protestant dominance in US society. But such an emphasis was no longer valid when Judaism and Catholicism were recognized as two of the three great American religions after the Second World War.

In 1962–3, the Supreme Court reflected this new fact of religious and social life. It ruled that laws requiring the reciting of the Lord's Prayer, Bible verses or prayers in public schools were unconstitutional because they violated the principle of separation between church and state by fostering religion. In 1984 the US Senate rejected two constitutional amendments that would permit prayers in public schools. Such decisions have thus banned public school prayers, although the practice does continue, particularly in the rural South.

In 1984 President Reagan signed a law prohibiting public high schools from barring students who wished to assemble for religious activities outside school hours on school property. Supreme Court rulings have also allowed state university property to be used by students for religious purposes as long as that property can also be used by others for other purposes. But in 1992 the Supreme Court banned clergy from offering prayers at graduation ceremonies for public elementary, middle and high schools. These cases distinguish between state recognition of religion by the participation of officials at public ceremonies and the participation of students in voluntary religious activities on state property.

Critics argue that public schools have continued to imbue patriotic attitudes into American schoolchildren by means of civil religion, such as the oath of allegiance to the flag (with its phrase 'One nation under God'). However, the Supreme Court ruled in 1842 that no child should be obliged to take part in the flag salute and since then it has further restricted this practice. But such traditional religious symbols as the words 'In God We Trust' on US currency have not been invalidated by the Supreme Court.

On the other hand, the private sector of education accounts for 15 per cent of total student enrolment. Some private schools are still run by churches or religious groups at both primary and secondary levels, with Catholic parochial schools being in the majority (40 per cent). Such schools are often intended to supply religious orientation and education. But some other private schools, and particularly those founded in the 1970s and 1980s, have no religious identification.

The question of whether private schools should receive public money is vigorously debated. The private sector (church-supported or not) generally receives no funding from federal or state governments. However, rising costs resulted in Congress (1965) granting parochial schools free lunches, transportation, textbooks and health and social services. But the Supreme Court has struck down most other forms of aid. Thus, two 1985 decisions prohibited public school teachers from going into private religious schools to teach courses with funds supplied by public sources.

Attitudes to religion

A *World Values* survey (1990–93) found that 82 per cent of Americans thought of themselves as religious. A 1995 *Time* report on a University of Akron *National Survey of Religion and Politics* showed that Americans identified their religious affiliations as: evangelical Protestants (25.9 per cent), mainstream Protestants (18 per cent), African-American Protestants (7.8 per cent), Roman Catholics (23.4 per cent), other Christians (3.3 per cent), Jews

(2 per cent) and other religions (1.1 per cent). The latter were Muslims (0.4 per cent), Hindus (0.2 per cent), Buddhists (0.2 per cent) and others (0.3 per cent). But 18.5 per cent of the respondents regarded themselves as non-religious.

Various US polls (*The Economist*, 1995) consistently report that 95 per cent of Americans believe in God; four out of five believe in miracles, life after death and the virgin (Mary) birth; 65 per cent believe in the devil; 75 per cent believe in angels; and nine out of ten own a bible.

According to a 1995 *Time/CNN* poll, respondents answered 'yes' to the following questions. Have one of your prayers been answered specifically (65 per cent)? Have you felt the direct presence of God (53 per cent)? Have you witnessed what you considered to be a miracle (37 per cent)? Have you been visited by an angel, the Virgin Mary or a saint (8 per cent)?

The same poll reported that in answer to the question 'Do you think that the ethical and moral standards of Americans today are as high as they should be?', 11 per cent said 'yes'. But 88 per cent thought that they should be higher. An *American Enterprise Institute* poll in 1996 found that a high proportion of respondents thought that morals were one of the top ten problems facing the country.

■ **Examine and explain the following terms:**

secularization	Protestantism	evangelicalism
'civil religion'	pluralism	school prayers
Puritans	fundamentalism	Congregationalists
social action	sectarianism	ecumenicism
Great Awakenings	denomination	the Episcopal Church

■ **Write short essays on the following topics:**

1   How is the diversity of contemporary denominations reflected in, and due to, American religious history?

2   Describe and examine the ways in which American religion has been characterized by division and conflict.

3   Analyse the growth and present position of one of America's main faiths: Protestantism, Catholicism or Judaism.

The arts, sports
and leisure

THE DIVERSITY OF CONTEMPORARY US society is reflected in how Americans organize their artistic and sporting/ leisure lives. These features reveal a series of varied and different cultural habits at all levels of society, rather than a simple image of one unified national culture. They involve a mixture of the amateur and the professional on public and private levels and are divided between participatory and spectator-based activities.

However, there are some distinctively American aspects to this picture in areas such as sport, painting and modern dance, which in some respects convey a particular national identity, even though it may not be shared by all Americans. Some critics argue, for example, that baseball and American football (irrespective of their disputed origins) are uniquely and representatively American in their combination of baseball's individualism and football's teamwork ethos.

But there are also more specific European and global influences and many other forms of 'ethnic' expression (such as Jewish theatre, Native-American crafts and Asian-Indian films) in the US, which rely upon their culture of origin rather than a purely American identification. On the other hand, many distinctive American features, such as Hollywood films, jazz, country and western music and the musical, have helped to create an internationalized mass culture.

A general American work ethic, competitive ethos, ambition and drive for success and achievement also noticeably embrace sporting, leisure, and artistic pursuits. These are taken very seriously (some might say too seriously) at both professional and amateur levels. Those Americans who play sports, either professionally or on an amateur basis, often do so because they are concerned to win, as well as to achieve the large amounts of money available in the professional games. Even holiday activities for some may have a competitive edge and a deliberately planned and goal-oriented context.

Other allegedly American values, such as self-improvement and self-definition, may be echoed by those people who go to concerts and the theatre or pursue other artistic activities. They indulge not only for fashionable reasons, but because they feel that the arts are self-improving and that culture is an admirable and positive thing in itself. Many Americans also exercise, take part in keep-fit classes and diet, at least initially, to improve themselves by becoming healthier and fitter in body and mind.

But not everyone is a fitness fanatic, a culture vulture, professionally ambitious or obsessed with goals. Many people are spectators rather than participants, as shown in the figures for college and professional football games, although a large degree of team identification is also evident here. The very high figures for television viewing (particularly of sporting events) and the dubious quality of many of the entertainment programmes shown suggest that the US also has its fair share of passive viewers and those who are not overly concerned with high culture, self-improvement, or achievement. But even simplistic television quiz games may have a vicariously competitive thrill to them and mindless entertainment can be a relaxing escape from competitive everyday life and work.

Sporting, leisure and artistic activities in American life are increasingly important for many people and central to their lives. This is reflected in the large amounts of money spent by Americans on entrance fees, equipment, various forms of musical instruments and recreational or cultural buildings. A huge advertising expenditure is also devoted to them, mainly through newspapers and television. In 1994, 'entertainment' (broadly defined) was fourth in total advertising fees ($4.4 billion) after cars, retailing and business and consumer services. The advertising of sporting goods and leisure equipment was also prominent in the list at $1.1 billion.

Yet American history in these areas has its darker side. A range of sports, leisure and artistic activities have suffered from discriminatory practices, so that African Americans, Native

Americans, Jews and women, among others, have experienced considerable racism and exclusion. This applied not only to performers (if they were allowed), but also to spectators who were segregated and to actual sports which were divided along colour lines. In the early twentieth century, there was a gulf between America's segregated society and its democratic ideals, which placed civil rights firmly on the public agenda.

While overt racism and discrimination have been largely reduced they still influence contemporary pursuits. Stereotyping exists so that, for example, African Americans find it difficult to advance in professional tennis and golf with their White upper-class images. The impact of women's sports has increased greatly since the early twentieth century. But discriminatory factors remain, which echo those in the wider society. However, it should also be emphasized that the breakthrough of minorities and women into, and acceptance by, the larger US society frequently came initially through sports and the arts.

The arts

The US is often stereotypically perceived as a society in which low-quality television, sports, film and other forms of popular or mass entertainment take precedence over, and therefore minimize, the more 'highbrow' arts. Europeans, in particular, may some-what snobbishly regard America as lacking what they would term a sophisticated and traditional 'high culture'.

In practice, however, according to opinion polls, official statistics and commentators, Americans today are increasingly attending dance performances, classical or symphonic concerts, music recitals, opera and visiting a varied range of museums. These activities suggest a higher and more acceptable cultural profile for the arts today than in the past. Artistic activity has developed momentum from the late 1960s and there has been an increased participation by amateur and professional individuals and groups in the arts across a wide range of painting, music, modern dance, theatre, ballet and film.

The number of arts-related companies or organizations has also increased since the 1960s. Throughout the US there were some 102 opera companies with annual budgets of $500,000 or over in 1994; ninety-nine symphony orchestras in 1992 with annual budgets in excess of $1 million; and 400 ballet and dance companies in 1994. Many of these are first-rate with world reputations, international conductors, directors and soloists. Increasing numbers of cultural buildings are being built throughout the US, with lavish styles and facilities.

However, some of these activities are probably still connected with their traditional associations of 'high culture'. On the other hand, larger numbers of people are following other more popular pursuits. The number of people who attend film cinemas (1.5 billion in 1990) and theatrical performances has risen considerably, suggesting that an increasing number of people (particularly the young) are returning to these and other cultural forms in preference to television, which has become the province of older viewers.

The media, particularly the television networks and Public Service Broadcasting, have helped to establish an increasing interest in and support for the arts through their promotion, advertising, sponsorship and coverage of cultural events. Participation in the arts has spread to greater numbers of people in all age groups and most social and economic classes throughout the country.

This cultural development is significantly being carried out with a relative minimum of direct financial support for the arts from central government sources. However, the government's and states' roles in supporting, financing and sponsoring the arts have increased. A federal agency, the National Endowment for the Arts (NEA) was created in 1965 and has become more fully involved in encouraging and developing artistic ventures.

The NEA obtains federal funds and then distributes these to various arts sources. Much of the money goes to state programmes and to administrative costs. But a range of activities such as music, media arts, museums, theatre, arts in education, dance, opera, visual arts and literature benefit from NEA aid.

However, although federal appropriations to the NEA have risen considerably since 1970, they were reduced by the Clinton administration to some $154 million in 1995.

The arts in America have therefore traditionally depended for their survival and promotion upon the private financial contributions of individuals, foundations (such as Ford and Rockefeller) and commercial corporations. There is tax relief or deductions (tax-breaks) for those individuals and companies which donate to the arts.

In addition to some art forms which may be inspired and influenced by the European and classical traditions, American artists (painters, sculptors, musicians, dancers and film makers) have developed their own distinctive forms of expression and traditions as the national cultural scene has expanded and evolved. Innovation, experiment, variety and reactions to earlier styles have been key determinants in this progress and the diversity of the ethnic population echoes a diversity of American artistic products.

The work of American artists has become famous overseas and cities like New York have become international centres of the arts. Innovations and new developments in very varied artistic fields have had a substantial effect on America's cultural life. This section deals with a few examples of distinctive American traditions.

American *painters* and *artists* in the early twentieth century were mainly influenced by traditional European styles. They continued, as some do today, the established realist and naturalist traditions, but often adapted these to specific American themes, locations and subject matter.

However, after the Second World War, new American painters burst on to the somewhat traditional scene with revolutionary and distinctively American concepts. Abstract expressionism, which was initially begun by New York artists such as Jackson Pollock, Willem de Kooning and Mark Rothko in the 1940s, rejected the established painting styles and subject matter and organized their work around colour, space and texture. The abstract expressionists attracted international attention and New York became increasingly a centre of world painting.

But succeeding generations reacted in their turn to abstract expressionism and moved on to new styles. Painters in the late 1950s and 1960s such as Robert Rauschenberg and Jasper Johns concentrated in their work on collage-type painting and used a variety of ordinary objects to achieve the desired effect. Other innovators, such as Andy Warhol and Roy Lichtenstein, introduced 'pop art'. This produced a range of artistic works which used everyday items of the consumer society and popular culture in order to reflect and comment on what they saw as distinctive features of modern America.

American painters and sculptors have continued to experiment with a wide range of styles and materials and have created a number of exotically named artistic movements, such as 'op art', graffiti art and performance art. The distinguishing features of such developments have been change, reaction, variety and new techniques.

But influential and interesting as some of these painting and sculptural styles have been, perhaps a more influential and commercial expression of American artistic distinctiveness in popular culture has been in *music*, particularly ragtime, blues, jazz, the musical, country and western and rock. These have been domestic American successes, but have also been exported and greatly affected a world culture.

Americans in 1994 spent some $10 billion on music. In terms of recording sales, rock accounted for 32.6 per cent, country for 17.5 per cent, pop for 11.7 per cent, urban contemporary music for 9.9 per cent, rap for 7.8 per cent, classical for 4 per cent, jazz for 3.3 per cent and other forms for 4.2 per cent. These figures illustrate the appeal of popular, urban-based and 'ethnic' music and the importance of a youth culture in the US.

The music business is consequently very lucrative and a rich source of profits for the record companies. The consumer culture has commercialized these native forms and American-produced music has consequently capitalized on its world-wide attraction and sales. Additionally, Americans attend live music shows and concerts and each form of music has its own musicians, clubs and followers.

Ragtime was an African-American music that was popular-ized by Scott Joplin and derived partly from the *blues* tradition of often melancholy and fatalistic African-American folk songs and church music which reflected the lives of poor Blacks. Bessie Smith was an early and popular exponent of the blues style and mixed the rural tradition with urban themes.

The blues also inspired *jazz* at the end of the nineteenth century. Some critics maintain that this is America's most orig-inal and native music form. It was played by Black musicians in the South; derives mainly from African and southern slave cultures; and is an improvised and rhythmic form of music. Traditionally, New Orleans was the city of jazz but it later spread to other parts of the country and was popularized by artists and band leaders like Louis Armstrong and Duke Ellington.

Reflecting an American capacity for experiment, jazz also developed many different styles and has greatly influenced later music such as pop, rock and roll and the American musical. Today, jazz is extremely popular in America and internationally; jazz concerts draw big audiences; and for some critics the best jazz is provided in New York, Chicago and Los Angeles, rather than in the South.

American *country-and-western* music has similarly become very popular in the US and world-wide. It also originated in the American South, but was based on the folk song traditions of early Scottish and English colonial settlers. It is played on the guitar, banjo or fiddle. Its frequently mournful or melancholy lyrics deal with love and poverty and reflect the disadvantaged rural life of poor Whites in the Southeast and Appalachia. Country music has also expanded beyond its origins, although Nashville, Tennessee, is still regarded as the home of country and western music.

American *folk music* has also had a lengthy and world-wide attraction, with such early figures as Woody Guthrie. It originally had a somewhat working-class, underprivileged and rural empha-sis, but later developed a wider and more commercial appeal in the 1960s through singers such as Bob Dylan and Joan Baez who also introduced social and political comment into their texts.

The modern *musical* is also of American origin (although some critics trace its origins to Italian models and the English pantomime/music hall tradition) and developed in the early twentieth century. Its combination of acting, music and dancing was often allied to escapist plots and exotic shows in glossy theatres. Some later musicals became more serious and socially aware, but the early entertainment emphasis also continued. The American musical has recently fallen on hard times and has had to compete with very successful foreign imports, particularly from Britain, which are indebted to the original American format.

Rock-and-roll music developed in the 1950s as another distinctively American form. Many of its practitioners, such as Elvis Presley and later Jimi Hendrix, Janis Joplin and Bruce Springsteen, combined the traditions of African-American blues and White country-and-western music. It proved to be a hugely popular form of music with young Americans and others world-wide and was associated with a succession of rock idols. Its sound, rhythm and style dominated the popular music scene; has since influenced other forms of pop music, whether in imitation or reaction; but has become very commercialized in recent decades. It was initially centred on live concert performances in huge stadiums or open venues but these have decreased considerably and rock generally has become confined to studio production and the issue of videos, records and compact discs (CDs).

Modern dance developed as a new distinctively American art form in the early twentieth century. Isadora Duncan, one of the first great exponents of the style, based her dances on Greek classical art and was more successful in Europe than America. But her followers, like Martha Graham in New York, began to combine modern dance more closely with developments in American music and ethnic life. They rejected the formal restrictions of classical ballet and improvised expressive dance movements. Modern (and contemporary) dance in America has continued to develop very successfully and to experiment with, and incorporate, many different elements like video, back-projection and films.

The *film industry* (and Hollywood) has been the most influential American artistic form. The film industry started on the East Coast, but later moved to Los Angeles and Hollywood became the centre of American film-making. In the early twentieth century, the motion picture (first silent, then with sound) was the most popular and dominant art form. In the classical years of Hollywood in the 1940s, the production studios were releasing some 400 films annually.

Today, however, many films are made by non-Hollywood, independent producers. Hollywood's products now include films specifically made for television in addition to those for the cinema. It is a multi-media corporate business system as well as a film industry with many associated commercial tie-ins. American themes are still examined in Hollywood films, but today Hollywood is both an American institution and a part of international popular culture.

Hollywood has always been an entertainment business concerned to sell a product. Its films were originally designed for American audiences and it has reflected American culture in its handling of themes such as the family, romance, individualism, heroism, female roles, children and patriotism. These have been used in different film genres in different periods and have reflected changing social and industrial conditions in America. But filmmakers also strove for financial profits by making film with mass appeal and repeated successful formulas such as Westerns, gangster films, comedies and musicals.

During the decades of Hollywood's golden age, films, movie stars and the architecture of cinemas were glittering and grandiose. Critics argue that the film industry sold a package, in which the cinema enthusiast was a consumer and the star was a commodity with a lifestyle and image specifically devised for public consumption and approval. Other merchandized items, such as clothes and fan clubs, were tied into this package and were also sold to the mass audience.

But the film industry and the star system have changed over the years due to various factors. They have had to adapt to changing moral, social, economic and industrial climates. The original studio structure has altered. The major companies were effectively taken over by financiers in the 1930s and eventually eight companies (Paramount, MGM, Warner Brothers, RKO, Twentieth Century-Fox, Universal, Columbia and United Artists) were formed, which varied in size. But after a prosperous period during the Second World War, the industry was split up by anti-monopolistic legislation.

The classical Hollywood of the early twentieth century with its powerful studios and business tycoons was largely finished. Fewer, but more expensive, films were made and independent production companies increased in number. Hollywood's centre of gravity was moving away from the powerful studio system and its large-scale productions. The post-Second World War period witnessed the production of increasingly different varieties and genres of film and Disney, for example, became an important source of full-length films. Disney is now the world's second-largest entertainment group after its 1995 merger with the ABC television network and has continued to develop its theme parks world-wide.

The increasing influence of television has forced the film industry to redefine itself in order to keep its market share of leisure activities. The number of television sets in the US has grown hugely from the early 1950s so that some 95.4 million homes had at least one set in 1995. Cinema audiences declined and were halved by 1953. Hollywood responded by making films for teenagers (a rapidly increasing consumer market) and Western television series such as *Gunsmoke* and *Cheyenne*. It also introduced some short-lived innovations such as Cinerama (wide-screen projection) and 3-D (dimensional) films.

Gradually, from the 1970s and 1980s, Hollywood studios were taken over by larger industrial conglomerates with diverse business interests such as Gulf and Western and there was increased competition from independent companies. As new technologies, such as video, developed, media companies and film studios were increasingly owned by multi-media conglomerates such as Time Warner Inc., which in 1989 became the world's largest media conglomerate. But Time Warner then merged with the Turner Broadcasting System (which owns the CNN cable news channel) in 1995 to become the world's largest media and entertainment group.

Hollywood has therefore changed considerably as the film, media and entertainment industries have changed. The importance of production costs has become paramount and it is difficult to find the finance to branch out into new film ideas. The audience has also changed. Young people in particular still go to the cinema both out of interest and for social reasons. But older people tend to watch television films and series, or videos in the home. In both groups, some $9.2 billion were spent on video rentals in 1994 and $4.8 billion on video games. Some 98 per cent of American households have at least one television set, 83 per cent have video-cassette recorders (VCRs) and 43 per cent have compact disc players (CDs).

Television series, or soap operas like *Dynasty* and *Dallas*, have become an important staple diet of the film production industry and studios rent their feature films to television networks. Big films are still being made in America, although more are being filmed on locations outside Hollywood and California, such as New York and Texas, in an effort to cut costs and search for new markets and ideas. However, the US continues to be the largest producer of films for a world audience.

Although the golden age is over, film is still an entertainment medium with huge domestic and international success. In 1994, Americans spent $5 billion on visits to the movies. But films can importantly also be used in business, industry, advertising and a wide range of training programmes. Hollywood and the film industry have consequently had to adapt to changing ownership structures and different social tastes and audiences in order to remain profitable and develop new markets. However, in the scramble for entertainment profits based on established themes and successful formulae, Hollywood's commercial films have recently been heavily criticized within the US for their concentration on violent, sexually explicit and action-packed films.

Sport in the US was until the mid-twentieth century relatively isolated from national and international events. It had a somewhat provincial and minority image, although it also provided many Americans with some respite from the pressures of everyday life. Now it has become a microcosm of national life and reflects the national condition. Issues such as international competition, global prestige, sex discrimination, labour–management relations, drug abuse, destructive compulsive addictions, the power of television and advertising, racism, gambling and corruption have all been associated at various times with both amateur and professional sport. The billions of dollars spent on contemporary sport and its buildings can also reflect adversely on the values of local communities, which might have prioritized their spending on other areas of social life.

US sports are very serious for some people and large commercial businesses for others. On some levels, they are obsessively involved with winning and money. But the majority of Americans probably still see sports as a wholesome and positive means of enriching their lives. They are highly involved in their sports as participants and spectators and are dedicated to the success of their particular teams.

The American sports scene is divided between the professional and amateur ranks. In terms of spectator attendances at professional events, National Football League games (with their Super Bowl finals) come top, followed by major league baseball (with its World Series), basketball, National (Ice) Hockey League games, horseracing and greyhound racing.

In terms of all sports, both professional and amateur, the four most popular spectator and participatory sports in the US are American football, baseball, basketball and ice hockey. The football season begins in early autumn; basketball is an indoor winter sport; and baseball is played in spring and summer, although these games have increasingly tended to overlap.

An interesting feature of the American sports scene is that since few other countries play baseball, basketball and American football on a professional and large-scale level, competition in them is largely restricted to the US and there is no international opposition as such. But, although these games are seen as distinctively American sports, they are increasingly being played in other countries.

However, a significant development in April 1996 was the inaugural match in Major League Soccer (MLS), which marked America's latest attempt to introduce a professional soccer league. Earlier attempts had failed, but it was hoped that the 1994 World Cup held in the US would generate new enthusiasm. Some critics suggest that the growth of soccer has been America's silent sporting revolution. There are now 20 million registered soccer players in the country and recent surveys indicate that more than 50 million Americans are 'soccer-literate'. Although soccer has long been played on college and university campuses, it is now proving to be popular with corporate sponsors, Latinos, women (40 per cent of all registered players) and affluent households (50 per cent of soccer fans are from households with an income over $50,000). It also rivals the traditional place of Little League baseball as the sport of young suburban families. While soccer may not overtake American football in popularity, it could soon be challenging ice hockey as America's fourth spectator sport.

Although some professional and college sports like professional football, ice hockey and boxing, are tough action games, American sports do not suffer from the same amount of spectator violence as some other countries' sports. Sports events, such as baseball and football, can still be family outings. They have a carnival atmosphere and a large element of show business, in which cheerleaders orchestrate the crowds and lead the cheering and marching bands provide additional entertainment.

There is an extensive, even saturating, media coverage of sports by both newspapers and television, which reflects the popularity and commercial standing of sports in the US. Sports programmes are an integral part of television and radio programming and attract huge audience figures as the networks (NBC, CBS and ABC) and other stations fight for market share. Some cable stations (like ESPN) are devoted exclusively to sports events;

report for some 24 hours a day; and attract very large audiences. The various media forms, particularly television, have not only created a profitable, audience-based industry, but have made sport accessible for many more people, who are unable either to attend or to afford live events.

The media popularization of sports has also been accompanied by increasing commercialization. The television networks and cable stations compete to obtain financially rewarding contracts from the professional sports bodies which allow the stations to televise their sports events. Advertisers are attracted by the mass audiences and pay the television stations to advertise mainly male-oriented products on their sports programmes. Advertisers benefit from the resulting sales of their products and the sports bodies receive fees and funding from their broadcasting rights contracts. Some, such as the National Football League, receive much of their revenue from the networks and cable companies. The element of big business is also reflected in the investments and assets that the owners of professional teams (who are businessmen concerned with profits) realize as players are bought and sold and some players receive very large financial contracts.

The commercialization of American professional sports can affect an athlete's career. Success and financial rewards are connected not only to the person's ability and competitive skills, but also to the marketability of the athlete, who must have agents to act on his or her behalf; take part in publicity campaigns; endorse and promote products such as sportswear; and attract sponsorship by corporate advertisers.

There is a tendency in American sports to an almost obsessive and serious competitiveness. As they have become more profit-oriented, success has become paramount and the importance of winning for participants and owners at all levels assumes considerable dimensions. Critics feel that this attitude has detracted from the traditional spirit of teamwork and playing games for fun.

An increased commercialization of college sports has also taken place. Schools and colleges provide a wide variety of sports activities for their students. Sport in educational institutions is highly organized and competitive and generally receives substantial local publicity and support. Educational institutions provide American football, basketball, baseball, tennis, wrestling, gymnastics, athletics (or track and field), soccer, swimming, volleyball, fencing and golf facilities and teams, for both boys and girls in relevant game areas, as well as practice and match facilities.

Outstanding high school athletes may receive sports scholarships to enable them to go on to college or university, where sports are an essential part of the educational programme. But college sports, which are supposed still to be amateur, has now lost much of this value, as they have become increasingly competitive and commercialized. College sports teams contribute much finance (through television rights and tickets sales) to, as well as publicity for, their individual institution and are given considerable local community support. Football and basketball are the most financially rewarding college sports and the top college teams can attract large amounts of money. But the emphasis on recruiting top high school athletes can sometimes affect the college's academic reputation, because the college sports stars have traditionally been recruited solely to play their sport and earn profits for the college and to possibly move on to the higher professional ranks, rather than to learn and gain an academic education.

Leisure

Leisure pursuits in the US can conveniently be divided into two types. First, those many individual and sometimes institutionalized physical activities outside the major sports games, which occupy at least some of Americans' leisure time as participators or observers. Second, a range of non-physical and passive pastimes such as reading, television watching and attendance at cultural events.

Participation in physical activities is widespread and varied. Interest in these areas increased greatly from the 1960s and coincided with the new popularity of health fads, dieting and exercise. In part, this was a reaction to research studies which showed that Americans smoked too many cigarettes and were becoming increasingly overweight and sedentary in their lifestyles. Fitness was promoted by the medical profession and the government, which allied physical strength and fitness to national power and vitality. Running (jogging), aerobic exercises and dancing, racquetball (an American form of squash played in a four-walled court by two or four people using a short-handed racquet), swimming, cycling, tennis, golf and fast-paced walking were encouraged and became very popular. It became increasingly fashionable for people of all ages and both sexes to be physically fit and to place an emphasis on nutrition and diet.

In 1988, according to the US Bureau of the Census, participation in the ten most popular sports or physical activities by gender among the population was:

1   Swimming: female 37 per cent, male 32 per cent
2   Walking: female 38 per cent, male 21 per cent
3   Bicycle riding: female 26 per cent, male 27 per cent
4   Camping: female 19 per cent, male 22 per cent
5   Fishing (fresh-water): female 12 per cent, male 26 per cent
6   Bowling (ten-pin): female 17 per cent, male 19 per cent
7   Equipment exercising: female 13 per cent, male 14 per cent
8   Aerobic exercising: female 19 per cent, male 3 per cent
9   Basketball: female 6 per cent, male 16 per cent
10 Running/jogging: female 9 per cent, male 13 per cent

This breakdown of activities was largely the same in 1990, according to *Sports Participation*, and has continued. The most popular physical pastime for both men and women is walking, followed by swimming, bicycle riding, camping, fresh-water fishing, bowling, exercising with equipment (such as weights), basketball, running/jogging and aerobic exercising.

Americans can become fanatical and obsessive about fitness and health. Many buy the latest expensive training equipment, clothes, books and videos on the subject. Many feel that fitness is glamorous and is connected to a general American ideal of healthy, young and lean bodies. Joggers are a frequent occurrence in the streets; aerobic exercises and weight-training are popular

TABLE 13.1   Replies to the *Time/CNN* poll on health

	Total	Men	Women
Very serious effort	37	31	43
Somewhat serious effort	45	47	43
Not very serious effort	10	12	9
Don't really try	7	10	5

Source: Time/CNN (1995)

with both men and women: health clubs have multiplied; and there are numerous public and private institutions that provide facilities for those who want to keep fit or play sports. Some of these are provided free by local communities, or by commercial businesses for their employees. Others are private clubs for those who can afford to pay for their services.

Naturally, commercial business has taken advantage of these developments and provided a wide range of stylish sporting clothes and equipment, reaping large profits. Book publishers, magazines and television programmes dealing with health and fitness concerns have also fed the expanding market. Health companies produce a wide range of supposedly beneficial products, as do food and beverage businesses. Affluent Americans spend substantial sums of money to achieve a desired slim and fit effect. Some go to extreme and even dangerous limits to produce individual fitness. However, even those who cannot afford high prices for equipment and clothes nevertheless indulge in exercise. For example, it is easy to put a basketball ring on the garage door or telegraph pole, or to run in the streets or countryside.

But, in spite of all the facilities, individual good intentions and television proclamations about diets and exercise, professional commentators report that 59 per cent of American men and 49 per cent of women are overweight. Children and the over-50s are the most obese. These figures contrast with the 1970s when only a quarter of the country's adult population was officially regarded as overweight.

TABLE 13.2 Leisure activities undertaken by Americans, 1995

Activities	Percentage
Watched a sporting event on TV	85
Read a novel for pleasure	62
Read any poetry	46
Seen a play	39
Seen a dance performance	37
Visited an art museum	36
Watched or read pornography	15

Source: Time/CNN (1995)

Opinion polls also reveal that between 80 and 90 per cent of Americans consider themselves to be overweight, unfit and lacking in exercise; some 22 per cent of them smoke; some 20 per cent suffer from high cholesterol; and some 80 per cent say that their efforts to improve their fitness and diet do not last long. This situation is made worse by the prevalence of fast-food eating among many Americans; employment stress; sedentary lifestyles; and the overeating of fatty food.

A 1995 *Time/CNN* poll reported percentage replies to the question 'How much effort are you making to eat a healthy and nutritionally balanced diet?' (See Table 13.1, p. 392.)

Outside the health and sports activities, Americans have other leisure pastimes, some of which have a surprising prominence. A 1995 *Time/CNN* opinion poll asked respondents which activity they had undertaken in the past year, with the results shown in Table 13.2.

The place of reading in this table is interesting and impressive. Book sales reached $8.5 billion in 1994. A minority of Americans spend more than $60 a year on books, a larger number spend between $48 and $60, while a slight majority spend less than $48. The highest-spending areas are California, the north East Coast and Alaska. The table also indicates the prominence of other supposedly 'high cultural' activities in Americans' leisure lives, although television watching (particularly sports) is still predominant.

EXERCISES

■ Examine and explain the following terms:

Hollywood	modern dance	tax breaks
baseball	ragtime	*Dallas*
'pop art'	banjo	college football
aerobics	racquetball	bowling

■ Write short essays on the following topics:

1 To what extent are some sports and films uniquely American?

2 Discuss the role of advertising and television in American sports, arts and leisure.

Appendix

DECLARATION OF INDEPENDENCE IN CONGRESS, 4 JULY 1776

The unanimous declaration of the thirteen United States of America

When, in the course of human events, it becomes necessary for one people to dissolve the political bonds which have connected them with another, and to assume, among the powers of the earth, the separate and equal station to which the laws of nature and of nature's God entitle them, a decent respect to the opinions of mankind requires that they should declare the causes which impel them to the separation.

We hold these truths to be self-evident: That all men are created equal; that they are endowed by their Creator with certain unalienable rights; that among these are life, liberty and the pursuit of happiness; that, to secure these rights, governments are

instituted among men, deriving their just powers from the consent of the governed; that whenever any form of government becomes destructive of these ends, it is the right of the people to alter or to abolish it, and to institute new government, laying its foundation on such principles, and organize its powers in such form, as to them shall seem most likely to effect their safety and happiness. Prudence, indeed, will dictate that government long established should not be changed for light and transient causes; and accordingly all experience hath shown that mankind are more disposed to suffer, while evils are sufferable, than to right themselves by abolishing the forms to which they are accustomed. But when a long train of abuses and usurpation, pursuing invariably the same object, evinces a design to reduce them under absolute despotism, it is their right, it is their duty, to throw off such government, and to provide new guards for their future security. Such has been the patient sufferage of these colonies; and such is now the necessity which constrains them to alter their former systems of government. The history of the present King of Great Britain is history of repeated injuries and usurpations, all having in direct object the establishment of an absolute tyranny over these states. To prove this, let facts be submitted to a candid world.

He has refused his assent to laws, the most wholesome and necessary for the public good.

He has forbidden his governors to pass laws of immediate and pressing importance, unless suspended in their operation till his assent should be obtained; and, when so suspended, he has utterly neglected to attend to them.

He has refused to pass other laws for the accommodation of large districts of people, unless those people would relinquish the right of representation in the legislature, a right inestimable to them, and formidable to tyrants only.

He has called together legislative bodies at places unusual, uncomfortable, and distant from the depository of their public records, for the sole purpose of fatiguing them into compliance with his measures.

He has dissolved representative houses repeatedly, for opposing, with manly firmness, his invasions on the rights of the people.

He has refused for a long time, after such dissolutions, to cause others to be elected; whereby the legislative powers, incapable of annihilation, have returned to the people at large for their exercise; the state remaining, in the meantime, exposed to all the dangers of invasions from without and convulsions within.

He has endeavoured to prevent the population of these states; for that purpose obstructing the laws for naturalization of foreigners; refusing to pass others to encourage their migration hither, and raising the conditions of new appropriations of lands.

He has obstructed the administration of justice, by refusing his assent to laws for establishing judiciary powers.

He has made judges dependent on his will alone, for the tenure of their offices, and the amount and payment of their salaries.

He has erected a multitude of new offices, and sent hither swarms of officers to harass our people and eat out their substance.

He has kept among us, in times of peace, standing armies, without the consent of our legislatures.

He has affected to render the military independent of, and superior to, the civil power.

He has combined with others to subject us to a jurisdiction foreign to our constitution, and unacknowledged by our laws, giving his assent to their acts of pretended legislation:

For quartering large bodies of armed troops among us;

For protecting them, by a mock trial, from punishment for any murders which they should commit on the inhabitants of these states;

For cutting off our trade with all parts of the world;

For imposing taxes on us without our consent;

For depriving us, in many cases, of the benefits of trial by jury;

For transporting us beyond seas, to be tried for pretended offences;

For abolishing the free system of English laws in a neighbouring province, establishing therein an arbitrary government, and enlarging its boundaries, so as to render it at once an example and fit instrument for introducing the same absolute rule into these colonies;

For taking away our charters, abolishing our most valuable laws, and altering fundamentally the forms of our governments;

For suspending our legislatures, and declaring themselves invested with power to legislate for us in all cases whatsoever.

He has abdicated government here, by declaring us out of his protection and waging war against us.

He has plundered our seas, ravaged our coasts, burned our towns, and destroyed the lives of our people.

He is at this time transporting large armies of foreign mercenaries to complete the works of death, desolation, and tyranny already begun with the circumstances of cruelty and perfidy scarcely paralleled in the most barbarous ages, and totally unworthy the head of a civilized nation.

He has constrained our fellow-citizens, taken captive on the high seas, to bear arms against their country, to become the executioners of their friends and brethren, or to fall themselves by their hands.

He has excited domestic insurrection among us; and has endeavoured to bring on the inhabitants of our frontiers the merciless Indian savages, whose known rule of warfare is an undistinguished destruction of all ages, sexes, and conditions.

In every stage of these oppressions we have petitioned for redress in the most humble terms; our repeated petitions have been answered only by repeated unjury. A prince, whose character is thus marked by every act which may define a tyrant, is unfit to be the ruler of a free people.

Nor have we been wanting in our attentions to our British brethren. We have warned them, from time to time, of attempts by their legislature to extend a unwarrantable jurisdiction over us. We have reminded them of the circumstances of our emigration and settlement here. We have appealed to their native justice and magnanimity; and we have conjured them, by the ties of our common kindred, to disavow these usurpations, which would inevitably interrupt our connections and correspondence. They, too, have been deaf to the voice of justice and of consanguinity.

We must, therefore, acquiesce in the necessity which denounces our separation, and hold them, as we hold the rest of mankind, enemies in war, in peace friends.

We, therefore, the representatives of the United States of America, in General Congress assembled, appealing to the Supreme Judge of the world for the recitude of our intentions, do, in the name and by the authority of the good people of these colonies, solemnly publish and declare, that these United Colonies are, and of right ought to be, FREE AND INDEPENDENT STATES; that they are absolved from all allegiance to the British Crown, and that all political connection between them and the state of Great Britain is, and ought to be, totally dissolved; and that, as free and independent states, they have full power to levy war, conclude peace, contract alliances, establish commerce, and do all other acts and things which independent states may of right do. And for the support of this declaration, with a firm reliance on the protection of Divine Providence, we mutually pledge to each other our lives, our fortunes, and our sacred honour.

John Hancock and
fifty-five others

CONSTITUTION OF THE UNITED STATES OF AMERICA AND AMENDMENTS

(Passages no longer in effect are printed in italic type). Brief identifications of the content of provisions are underlined in parentheses.

PREAMBLE   (The people establish the Constitution)

We the people of the United States, in order to form a more perfect union, establish justice, insure domestic tranquillity, provide for the common defense, promote the general welfare, and secure the blessings of liberty to ourselves and our posterity, do ordain and establish this Constitution for the United States of America.

ARTICLE 1   (Congress, the legislative branch)

Section 1 All legislative powers herein granted shall be vested in a Congress of the United States, which shall consist of a Senate and a House of Representatives. (Bicameralism)

Section 2 The House of Representatives shall be composed of members chosen every second year by the people of the several States, and the electors in each State shall have the qualifications requisite for electors of the most numerous branch of the State Legislature. (Qualifications for voters)

No person shall be a Representative who shall not have attained to the age of twenty-five years, and been seven years a citizen of the United States, and who shall not, when elected, be an inhabitant of that State in which he shall be chosen. (Qualifications for members)

Representative and direct taxes shall be apportioned among the several States which may be included within this Union, according to their respective numbers, *which shall be determined by adding to the whole number of free persons, including those bound to service for a term of years and excluding Indians not taxed, three-fifths of all other persons.* The actual enumeration shall be within three years after the first meeting of the Congress of the United States, and within every subsequent term of ten years, in such manners as they shall by law direct. The number of Representatives shall not exceed one for every thirty thousand, but each State shall have at least one Representative; *and until such enumeration shall be made, the State of New Hampshire shall be entitled to choose three, Massachusetts eight, Rhode Island and Providence Plantations one, Connecticut five, New York six, New Jersey four, Pennsylvania eight, Delaware one, Maryland six, Virginia ten, North Carolina five, South Carolina five, and Georgia three.* (Apportionment according to the census)

When vacancies happen in the representation from any State, the Executive authority thereof shall issue writs of election to fill such vacancies.

The House of Representatives shall choose their Speaker and other officers; and shall have the sole power of impeachment. (Impeachment)

Section 3 The Senate of the United States shall be composed of two Senators from each State, *chosen by the legislature thereof,* for six years; each Senator shall have one vote.

Immediately after they shall be assembled in consequence of the first election, they shall be divided as equally as may be into three classes. The seats of the Senators of the first class shall be vacated at the expiration of the second year, of the second class at the expiration of the fourth year, and of the third class at the expiration of the sixth year, so that one-third may be chosen every second year; *and if vacancies happen by resignation or otherwise, during the recess of the legislature of any State, the Executive thereof may make temporary appointments until the next meeting of the legislature, which shall then fill such vacancies.* (Staggered Senate elections)

No person shall be a Senator who shall not have attained to the age of thirty years, and been nine years a citizen of the

United States, and who shall not, when elected, be an inhabitant of that State for which he shall be chosen. (Qualifications)

The Vice-President of the United States shall be President of the Senate, but shall have no vote, unless they be equally divided.

The Senate shall choose their other officers, and also a President *pro tempore*, in the absence of the Vice-President or when he shall exercise the office of President of the United States. (President pro tempore)

The Senate shall have the sole power to try all impeachments. When sitting for that purpose, they shall be on oath or affirmation. When the President of the United States is tried, the Chief Justice shall preside; and no person shall be convicted without the concurrence of two-thirds of the members present. (Impeachment)

Judgement in cases of impeachment shall not extend further than to removal from the office, and disqualification to hold and enjoy any office of honour, trust or profit under the United States; but the party convicted shall nevertheless be liable to indictment, trial, judgement and punishment, according to law. (Judgement regulations in cases of impeachment)

Section 4   The times, places and manner of holding elections for Senators and Representatives shall be prescribed in each State by the legislature thereof; but the Congress may at any time by law make or alter such regulations, except as to the places of choosing Senators. (Rules for Congressional elections)

The Congress shall assemble at least once in every year, and such meeting *shall be on the first Monday in December, unless they shall by law appoint a different day.*

Section 5   Each house shall be the judge of the elections, returns and qualifications of its own members, and a majority of each shall constitute a quorum to do business; but a smaller number may adjourn from day to day, and may be authorized to compel attendance of absent members, in such manner, and under such penalties, as each house may provide. (Qualifications)

Each house may determine the rules of its proceedings, punish its members for disorderly behaviour, and with the concurrence of two-thirds, expel a member. (<u>Expulsion</u>)

Each house shall keep a journal of its proceedings, and from time to time publish the same, excepting such parts as may in their judgement require secrecy; and the yeas and nays of the members of either house on any question shall, at the desire of one-fifth of those present, be entered on the journal. (<u>Required congressional record</u>)

Neither house, during the session of Congress, shall, without the consent of the other, adjourn for more than three days, nor to any other place than that in which the two houses shall be sitting. (<u>Adjournment regulations</u>)

Section 6   The Senators and Representatives shall receive a compensation for their services, to be ascertained by law and paid out of the treasury of the United States. They shall in all cases except treason, felony and breach of the peace, be privileged from arrest during their attendance at the session of their respective houses, and in going to and returning from the same; and for any speech or debate in either house, they shall not be questioned in any other place. (<u>Pay and immunity</u>)

No Senator or Representative shall, during the time for which he was elected, be appointed to any civil office under the authority of the United States, which shall have been created, or emoluments whereof shall have been increased, during such time; and no person holding any office under the United States shall be a member of either house during his continuance in office. (<u>Limitation related to civil officers</u>)

Section 7   All bills for raising revenue shall originate in the House of Representatives; but the Senate may propose or concur with amendments as on other bills. (<u>The right to tax</u>)

Every bill which shall have passed the House of Representatives and the Senate, shall, before it becomes a law, be presented to the President of the United States; if he approve he shall sign it, but if not he shall return it with objections to that house in which it originated, who shall enter the objections at large on their journal, and proceed to reconsider it. If after such reconsideration two-thirds of that house shall agree to pass the bill, it shall be sent, together with the objections, to the other house, by which it shall likewise be reconsidered, and, if approved by two-thirds of that house, it shall become a law. But in all such cases the vote of both houses shall be determined by yeas and nays, and the names of the persons voting for and against the bill shall be entered on the journal of each house respectively. If any bill shall not be returned by the President within ten days (Sundays excepted) after it shall have been presented to him, the same shall be a law, in like manner as if he had signed it, unless Congress by their adjournment prevent its return, in which case it shall not be a law. (<u>Procedure of bills, veto power of the President</u>)

Every order, resolution, or vote to which the concurrence of the Senate and House of Representatives may be necessary (except on a question of adjournment) shall be presented to the President of the United States; and before the same shall take effect, shall be approved by him, or being disapproved by him, shall be repassed by two-thirds of the Senate and House of Representatives, according to the rules and limitations prescribed in the case of a bill. (<u>Presidential approval</u>)

Section 8   (Enumerated [specified] powers of Congress)
The Congress shall have power

To lay and collect taxes, duties, imposts, and excises, to pay the debts and provide for the common defense and general welfare of the United States; but all duties, imposts and excises shall be uniform throughout the United States;

To borrow money on the credit of the United States;

To regulate commerce with foreign nations, and among the several States, and with the Indian tribes;

To establish an uniform rule of naturalization, and uniform laws on the subject of bankruptcies throughout the United States;

To coin money, regulate the value thereof, and of foreign coin, and fix the standard of weights and measures;

To provide for the punishment of counterfeiting the securities and current coin of the United States:

To establish post offices and post roads;

To promote the progress of science and useful arts by securing for limited times to authors and inventors the exclusive right to their respective writings and discoveries;

To constitute tribunals inferior to the Supreme Court;

To define and punish piracies and felonies committed on the high seas and offences against the law of nations;

To declare war, grant letters of marque and reprisal, and make rules concerning captures on land and water;

To raise and support armies, but no appropriation of money to that shall be for a longer term than two years;

To provide and maintain a navy;

To make rules for the government and regulation of the land and naval forces;

To provide for calling forth the militia to execute the laws of the Union, supress insurrections, and repel invasions;

To provide for organizing, arming, and disciplining the militia, and for governing such part of them as may be employed in the service of the United States, reserving to the States respectively the appointment of the officers, and the authority of training the militia according to the discipline prescribed by Congress;

To exercise exclusive legislation in all cases whatsoever, over such district (not exceeding ten miles square) as may, by cession of particular States, and the acceptance of Congress, become the seat of government of the United States, and to exercise like authority over all places purchased by the consent of the legislature of the State, in which the same shall be, for erection of forts, magazines, arsenals, dock-yards, and other needful buildings; – and

To make all laws which shall be necessary and proper for carrying into execution the foregoing powers, and all other powers vested by this Constitution in the government of the United States, or in any department or officer thereof. (The 'necessary and proper' clause, implied powers of Congress)

405

Section 9 *The migration or importation of such persons as any of the States now existing shall think proper to admit shall not be prohibited by the Congress prior to the year 1808; but a tax or duty may be imposed on such importation, not exceeding 10 dollars for each person.* (Slave import and limited powers)

The privilege of the writ of habeas corpus shall not be suspended, unless when in cases of rebellion or invasion the public safety may require it. (Habeas corpus)

No bill of attainder or *ex post facto* shall be passed.

No capitation, or other direct, tax shall be laid, unless in proportion to the census or enumeration herein before directed to be taken.

No tax or duty shall be laid on articles exported from any State.

No preference shall be given by any regulation of commerce or revenue to the ports of one State over those of another; nor shall vessels bound to, or from, one State, be obliged to enter, clear, or pay duties in another.

No money shall be drawn from the treasury, but in consequence of appropriations made by law; and a regular statement and account of the receipts and expenditures of all public money shall be published from time to time.

No title or nobility shall be granted by the United States; and no person holding any office of profit or trust under them, shall, without consent of the Congress, accept of any present, emolument, office, or title, of any kind whatever, from any king, prince, or foreign state.

Section 10 No State shall enter into any treaty, alliance, or confederation; grant letters of marque and reprisal; coin money; emit bills of credit; make anything but gold and silver coin a tender in payment of debts; pass any bill of attainder, *ex post facto* law, or law impairing the obligation of contracts, or grant any title of nobility. (Restrictions on powers of the states)

No State shall, without the consent of Congress, lay any imposts or duties on imports or exports, except what may be absolutely necessary for executing its inspection laws; and the net produce of all duties and imposts, laid by any State on imports and exports, shall be for the use of the treasury of the United States; and all such laws shall be subject to the revision and control of the Congress.

No State shall, without the consent of Congress, lay any duty of tonnage, keep troops or ships of war in time of peace, enter into any agreement or compact with another State, or with a foreign power, or engage in war, unless actually invaded, or in such imminent danger as will not admit of delay.

ARTICLE II (The President, the executive branch)

Section 1 The executive power shall be vested in a President of the United States. He shall hold his office during the term of four years, and, together with the Vice-President, chosen for the same term, be elected as follows:

Each State shall appoint, in such manner as the legislature thereof may direct, a number of electors, equal to the whole number of Senators and Representatives to which the State may be entitled in the Congress; but no Senator or Representative, or person holding an office of trust or profit under the United States, shall be appointed an elector.

The electors shall meet in their respective States, and vote by ballot for two persons, of whom one at least shall not be an inhabitant of the same State with themselves. And they shall make a list of all the persons voted for, and of the number of votes for each; which list they shall sign and certify, and transmit sealed to the seat of government of the United States, directed to the President of the Senate. The President of the Senate shall, in the presence of the Senate and House of Representatives, open all the certificates, and the votes shall be counted. The person having the greatest number of votes shall be President, if such number be a majority of the whole number of electors appointed; and if there be more than one who have such majority, and have an equal number of votes, then the House of Representatives shall imme-diately choose by ballot one of them for President; and if no person have a majority, then from the five highest on the list said house shall in like manner choose the President. But in choosing the President the votes shall be taken by States, the representation from each State having one vote; a quorum for this purpose shall consist of member or members from two-thirds of the States, and a majority of all the States shall be necessary to a choice. In every case, after the choice of the President, the person having the greatest number of votes of the electors shall be the Vice-President. But if there should remain two or more who have equal votes, the Senate shall choose from them by ballot the Vice-President. (Electors)

The Congress may determine the time of choosing the electors and the day on which they shall give their votes; which day shall be the same throughout the United States.

No person except a natural-born citizen, *or a citizen of the United States at the time of the adoption of this Constitution,* shall be eligible to the office of President, neither shall any person be eligible to that office who shall not have attained to the age of thirty-five years, and been fourteen years a resident within the United States. (Qualifications for President)

In case of the removal of the President from office or of his death, resignation, or inability to discharge the powers and duties of the said office, the same shall devolve on the Vice-President, and the Congress may by law provide for the case of removal, death, resignation, or inability, both of the President and Vice-President, declaring what officer shall then act as President, and such officer shall act accordingly, until the disability be removed, or a President shall be elected. (Presidential succession)

The President shall, at stated times, receive for his sevices a compensation, which shall neither be increased nor diminished during the period for which he shall have been elected, and he shall not receive within that period any other emolument from the United States, or any of them. (Presidential compensation)

Before he enter on the execution of his office, he shall take the following oath or affirmation:- 'I do solemnly swear (or affirm) that I will faithfully execute the office of the President for the

United States, and will to the best of my ability preserve, protect and defend the Constitution of the United States.' (<u>Presidential oath of office</u>)

Section 2   The President shall be commander-in-chief of the army and navy of the United States, and of the militia of the several States, when called into the actual service of the United States; he may require the opinion, in writing, of the principal officer in each of the executive departments, upon any subject relating to the duties of their respective offices, and he shall have power to grant reprieves and pardons for offences against the United States, except in cases of impeachment. (<u>Powers of President</u>)

He shall have power, by and with the advice and consent of the Senate, to make treaties, provided two-thirds of the Senators present concur; and he shall nominate, and by and with the advice and consent of the Senate, shall appoint ambassadors, other public ministers and consuls, judges of the Supreme Court, and all other officers of the United States, whose appointments are not herein otherwise provided for, and which shall be established by law; but Congress may by law vest the appointment of such inferior officers, as they think proper, in the President alone, in the courts of law, or in the heads of departments.

The President shall have the power to fill up all vacancies that may happen during the recess of the Senate, by granting commissions which shall expire at the end of their next session.

Section 3   The President shall from time to time give to the Congress information of the state of the Union, and recommend to their consideration such measures as he shall judge necessary and expedient; he may, on extraordinary occasions, convene both houses, or either of them, and in case of disagreement between them, with respect to the time of adjournment, he may adjourn them to such time as he shall think proper; he shall receive ambassadors and other public ministers; he shall take care that the laws be faithfully executed, and shall commission all the officers of the United States. (<u>State of the Union message</u>)

Section 4   The President, the Vice-President and the civil officers of the United States shall be removed from office on impeachment for, and or convictions of, treason, bribery, or other high crimes and misdemeanours. (Impeachment)

ARTICLE III   (The Supreme Court, the judiciary branch)

Section 1   The judicial power of the United States shall be vested in one Supreme Court, and in such inferior courts as the Congress may from time to time ordain and establish. The judges, both of the Supreme and inferior courts, shall hold their offices during good behaviour, and shall, at stated times, receive for their services a compensation which shall not be diminished during their continuance in office.

Section 2   The judicial power shall extend to all cases, in law and equity, arising under this Constitution, the laws of the United States, and treaties made, or which shall be made, under their authority; to all cases affecting ambassadors, other public ministers and consuls; to all cases of admiralty and maritime jurisdiction; to controversies to which the United States shall be a party; to controversies between two or more States; *between a State and citizen of another State*; between citizens of different States; between citizens of the same State claiming land under grants of different States, and between a State, or the citizens thereof, and foreign states, citizens or subjects. (Jurisdiction)

In all cases affecting ambassadors, other public ministers and consuls, and those in which a State shall be party, the Supreme Court shall have original jurisdiction. In all the other cases before mentioned, the Supreme Court shall have appellate jurisdiction, both as to law and fact, with such exceptions, and under such regulations, as the Congress shall make.

The trial of all crimes, except in cases of impeachment, shall be by jury; and such trial shall be held in the State where said crimes shall have been committed; but when not committed within any State, the trial shall be at such place or places as the Congress may by law have directed. (*Jury trial*)

Section 3   Treason against the United States shall consist only in levying war against them, or in adhering to their enemies, giving them aid and comfort. No person shall be convicted of treason unless on the testimony of two witnesses to the same overt act, or on confession in open court.

The Congress shall have power to declare the punishment of treason, but no attainder of treason shall work corruption of blood, or forfeiture except during the life of the person attainted.

ARTICLE IV   (The states)

Section 1   Full faith and credit shall be given in each State to the public acts, records, and judicial proceedings of every other State. And the Congress may by general laws prescribe the manner in which such acts, records, and proceedings shall be proved, and the effect thereof.

Section 2   The citizens of each State shall be entitled to all privileges and immunities of citizens in the several States.

A person charged in any State with treason, felony, or other crime, who shall flee from justice, and be found in another State, shall on demand of the executive authority of the State from which he fled, be delivered up, to be removed to the State having jurisdiction of the crime. (*Privileges*)

No person held to serve or labour in one State, under the laws thereof, escaping into another, shall, in consequence of any law or regulation therein, be discharged from such service or labour, but shall be delivered up on claim of the party to whom such service or labour may be due. (*Fugitive slaves*)

Section 3   New States may be admitted by the Congress into this Union; but no new State shall be formed or erected within the jurisdiction of any other State; nor any State be formed by the junction of two or more States, or parts of States, without the consent of the legislatures of the States concerned as well as of the Congress. (<u>New states</u>)

The Congress shall have power to dispose of and make all needful rules and regulations respecting the territory or other property belonging to the United States; and nothing in this Constitution shall be so construed as to prejudice any claims of the United States, or of any particular State.

Section 4   The United States shall guarantee to every State in this Union a republican form of government, and shall protect each of them against invasion; and on application of the legislature, or of the executive (when the legislature cannot be convened), against domestic violence. (<u>Promises to states</u>)

ARTICLE V   <u>(Amendments)</u>

The Congress, whenever two-thirds of both houses shall deem it necessary, shall propose amendments to this Constitution, or, on the application of the legislatures of two-thirds of the several States, shall call a convention for proposing amendments, which, in either case, shall be valid to all intents and purposes, as part of this Constitution, when ratified by the legislatures of three-fourths of the several States, or by conventions in three-fourths thereof, as the one or the other mode of ratification may be proposed by the Congress; provided *that no amendments which may be made prior to the year one thousand eight hundred and eight shall in any manner affect the first and fourth clauses in the ninth section of the first article*; and that no State, without its consent, shall be deprived of its equal suffrage in the Senate. (<u>Ratification</u>)

ARTICLE VI   <u>(Effects of Constitution)</u>

All debts contracted and engagements entered into, before the adoption of this Constitution, shall be as valid against the

United States under this Constitution, as under the Confederation.

This Constitution, and the laws of the United States which shall be made in pursuance thereof; and all treaties made, or which shall be made, under the authority of the United States, shall be the supreme law of the land; and the judges in every State shall be bound thereby, anything in the Constitution or laws of any State to the contrary notwithstanding. (Supremacy clause)

The Senators and Representatives before mentioned, and the members of the several State legislatures, and all executive and judicial officers, both of the United States and of the several States, shall be bound by oath or affirmation to support this Constitution; but no religious test shall ever be required as a qualification to any office or public trust under the United States. (No religious test)

ARTICLE VII (Ratification)

The ratification of the conventions of nine States shall be sufficient for the establishment of this Constitution between the States so ratifying the same.

Done in Convention by the unanimous consent of the States present, the seventeenth day of September in the year of our Lord one thousand seven hundred and eighty-seven and of the Independence of the United States of America the twelfth. In witness whereof we have hereunto subscribed our names.

George Washington and thirty-seven others.

THE BILL OF RIGHTS
(THE FIRST TEN AMENDMENTS)

AMENDMENT I (1791)   (Basic freedoms; separation of church and state)

Congress shall make no law respecting an establishment of religion, or prohibiting the free exercise thereof; or abridging the freedom of speech, or of the press; or the right of the people peaceably to assemble, and to petition the government for a redress of grievances.

AMENDMENT II (1791)   (The right to bear arms)

A well-regulated militia being necessary to the security of a free State, the right of the people to keep and bear arms shall not be infringed.

AMENDMENT III (1791)   (Quartering of soldiers)

No soldier shall, in time of peace, be quartered in any house without the consent of the owner, nor in time of war, but in a manner to be prescribed by law.

AMENDMENT IV (1791)   (Search and seizure)

The right of the people to be secure in their persons, houses, papers, and effects, against unreasonable searches and seizures, shall not be violated, and no warrants shall issue but upon probable cause, supported by oath or affirmation, and particularly described, the place to be searched, and the persons or things to be seized.

AMENDMENT V (1791) <u>(Rights in court cases)</u>

No person shall be held to answer for a capital, or otherwise infamous crime, unless on a presentment or indictment of a grand jury, except in cases arising in the land or naval forces, or in the militia, when in actual service in time of war or public danger; nor shall any person be subject for the same offence to be twice put in jeopardy of life or limb; nor shall be compelled in any criminal case to be a witness against himself, nor be deprived of life, liberty, or property, without due process of law; nor shall private property be taken for public use without just compensation.

AMENDMENT VI (1791) <u>(Rights of the accused)</u>

In all criminal prosecutions, the accused shall enjoy the right to a speedy and public trial, by an impartial jury of the State and district wherein the crime shall have been committed, which district shall have been previously ascertained by law, and to be informed of the nature and cause of the accusation; to be confronted with the witnesses against him; to have compulsory process for obtaining witnesses in his favour, and to have the assistance of counsel for his defence.

AMENDMENT VII (1791) <u>(The right to a trial by jury)</u>

In suits at common law, where the value in controversy shall exceed twenty dollars, the right of trial by jury shall be preserved, and no fact tried by a jury shall be otherwise reexamined in any court of the United States, than according to the rules of the common law.

AMENDMENT VIII (1791) (Bail; cruel and unusual punishment)

Excessive bail shall not be required, nor excessive fines imposed, nor cruel and unusual punishment inflicted.

AMENDMENT IX (1791) (Rights retained by the people)

The enumeration in the Constitution, of certain rights, shall not be construed to deny or disparage others retained by the people.

AMENDMENT X (1791) (Reserved powers)

The powers not delegated to the United States by the Constitution, nor prohibited by it to the States, are reserved to the States respectively, or to the people.

LATER AMENDMENTS

AMENDMENT XI (1798) (Law suits against states)

The judicial power of the United States shall not be construed to extend to any suit in law or equity, commenced or prosecuted against one of the United States by a citizen of another State, or by citizens or subjects of any foreign state.

AMENDMENT XII (1804) (Electoral votes)

The electors shall meet in their respective States, and vote by ballot for President and Vice-President, one of whom, at least, shall not be an inhabitant of the same State with themselves; they shall name in their ballots the person voted for as President, and in distinct ballots the person voted for as Vice-President, and they shall make distinct lists of all persons voted for as President, and of all persons voted for as Vice-President, and of the number of votes for each, which lists they shall sign and certify, and transmit sealed to the seat of government of the United States, directed to the President of the Senate; – the President of the Senate shall, in the presence of the Senate and House of Representatives, open all the certificates and the votes shall then be counted; – the person having the greatest number of votes for President shall be the President if such number be a majority of the whole number of electors appointed, and if no person have a majority, then from the persons having the highest numbers not exceeding three on the list of those voted for as President, the House of Representatives shall choose immediately, by ballot, the President. But in choosing the President, the votes shall be taken by States, the representation from each State having one vote; a quorum for this purpose shall consist of a member or members from two-thirds of the States, and a majority of all the States shall be necessary to a choice. And if the House of Representatives shall not choose a President whenever the right of choice shall devolve upon them, before *the fourth day of March* next following, then the Vice-President shall act as President, as in the case of death or other constitutional disability of the President.

The person having the greatest number of votes as Vice-President shall be the Vice-President, if such number be a majority of the whole number of electors appointed; and if no person have a majority, then from the two highest numbers on the list the Senate shall choose the Vice-President; a quorum for the purpose shall consist of two-thirds of the whole number of Senators, and a majority of the whole number shall be necessary to a choice. But no person constitutionally ineligible to the office of President shall be eligible to that of Vice-President of the United States.

AMENDMENT XIII (1865)   (Abolition of slavery)

Section 1   Neither slavery nor involuntary servitude, except as a punishment for crime whereof the party shall have been duly convicted, shall exist within the United States, or any place subject to their jurisdiction.

Section 2   Congress shall have the power to enforce this article by appropriate legislation.

AMENDMENT XIV (1868)   (Citizenship for former slaves; due process and equal protection clauses)

Section 1   All persons born or naturalized in the United States, and subject to the jurisdiction thereof, are citizens of the United States and of the State wherein they reside. No State shall make or enforce any law which shall abridge the privileges or immunities of citizens of the United States; nor shall any State deprive any person of life, liberty, or property, without due process of law; nor deny to any person within its jurisdiction the equal protection of the laws.

Section 2   Representatives shall be appointed among the several States according to their respective numbers, counting the whole number of persons in each State, excluding Indians not taxed. But when the right to vote at any election for the choice of Electors for President and Vice-President of the United States, Representatives in Congress, the executive and judicial officers of a State, or the members of the legislature thereof, is denied to any of the male inhabitants of such State, being twenty-one years of age and citizens of the United States, or in any way abridged, except for participation in rebellion, or other crime, the basis of representation therein shall be reduced in the proportion which the number of such male citizens shall bear to the whole number of male citizens twenty-one years of age in such State. (Apportionment)

Section 3   No person shall be a Senator or Representative in Congress, or Elector of President and Vice-President, or hold any office, civil or military, under the United States, or under any State, who, having previously taken an oath, as a member of Congress, or as an officer of the United States, or as a member of any State legislature, or as an executive or judicial officer of any State, to support the Constitution of the United States, shall have engaged in insurrection or rebellion against the same, or given aid or comfort to the enemies thereof. Congress may, by a vote of two-thirds of each house, remove such disability.

Section 4   The validity of the public debt of the United States, authorized by law, including debts incurred for payment of pensions and bounties for services in suppressing insurrection or rebellion, shall not be questioned. But neither the United States nor any State shall assume or pay any debt or obligation incurred in aid of insurrection or rebellion against the United States, or any claim for the loss of emancipation of any slave; but all such debts, obligations, and claims shall be held illegal and void.

Section 5   The Congress shall have power to enforce, by appropriate legislature, the provisions of this article.

AMENDMENT XV   (1870)   (<u>Voting rights for freed male slaves</u>)

Section 1   The right of citizens of the United States to vote shall not be denied or abridged by the United States or by any State on account of race, colour, or previous condition of servitude.

Section 2   The Congress shall have power to enforce this article by appropriate legislature.

AMENDMENT XVI (1913) <u>(Federal income tax)</u>

The Congress shall have power to lay and collect taxes on incomes, from whatever source derived, without apportionment among the several States, and without regard to any census or enumeration.

AMENDMENT XVII (1913) <u>(The direct election of Senators)</u>

Section 1 The Senate of the United States shall be composed of two Senators from each State, elected by the people thereof, for six years; and each Senator shall have one vote. The electors in each State shall have the qualifications requisite for electors of (voters for) the most numerous branch of the State legislatures.

Section 2 When vacancies happen in the representation of any State in the Senate, the executive authority of such State shall issue writs of election to fill such vacancies: Provided, that the legislature of any State may empower the executive thereof to make temporary appointments until the people fill vacancies by election as the legislature may direct.

Section 3 This amendment shall not be so construed as to affect the election or term of any Senator chosen before it becomes valid as part of the Constitution.

AMENDMENT XVIII (1919, REPEALED 1933) (Prohibition)

Section 1 *After one year from the ratification of this article the manufacture, sale, or transportation of intoxicating liquors within, the importation thereof into, or the exportation thereof from the United States, and all territory subject to the jurisdiction thereof, for beverage purposes, is hereby prohibited.*

Section 2   *The Congress and the several States shall have concurrent power to enforce this article by appropriate legislation.*

Section 3   *This article shall be inoperative unless it shall have been ratified as an amendment to the Constitution by the legislatures of the several States, as provided by the Constitution, within seven years from the date of the submission thereof to the States by the Congress.*

AMENDMENT XIX   (1929)   (Voting rights for women)

Section 1   The right of citizens of the United States to vote shall not be denied or abridged by the United States or by any State on account of sex.

Section 2   The Congress shall have the power to enforce this article by appropriate legislation.

AMENDMENT XX   (1933)   (The President's term of office)

Section 1   The terms of the President and the Vice-President shall end at noon on the 20th day of January, and the terms of Senators and Representatives at noon on the 3rd day of January, of the year in which such terms would have ended if this article had not been ratified; and the terms of their successors shall then begin.

(The start of sessions of Congress)

Section 2   The Congress shall assemble at least once in every year, and such meeting shall begin at noon on the 3rd day of January, unless they shall by law appoint a different day.

(Presidential succession)

Section 3 If, at the time fixed for the beginning of the term of the President, the President-elect shall have died, the Vice-President-elect shall become President. If a President shall not have been chosen before the time fixed for the beginning of his term, or if the President-elect shall have failed to qualify, then the Vice-President-elect shall act as President until a President shall have qualified; and the Congress may by law provide for the case wherein neither a President-elect nor a Vice-President-elect shall have qualified, declaring who shall then act as President, or the manner in which one who is to act shall be selected, and such persons shall act accordingly until a President or Vice-President shall have qualified.

Section 4 The Congress may by law provide for the case of the death of any of the persons from whom the House of Representatives may choose a President whenever the right of choice shall have devolved upon them, and for the case of the death of any of the persons from whom the Senate may choose a Vice-President whenever the right of choice shall have devolved upon them.

Section 5 Sections 1 and 2 shall take effect on the 15th day of October following the ratification of this article.

Section 6 This article shall be inoperative unless it shall have been ratified as an amendment to the Constitution by the legislatures of three-fourths of the several States within seven years from the date of its submission.

AMENDMENT XXI (1933) (Repeal of prohibition)

Section 1 The eighteenth article of amendment to the Constitution of the United States is hereby repealed.

Section 2   The transportation or importation into any State, Territory, or Possession of the United States for delivery or use therein of intoxicating liquors, in violation of the laws thereof, is hereby prohibited.

Section 3   This article shall be inoperative unless it shall have been ratified as an amendment to the Constitution by conventions in the several States, as provided in the Constitution, within seven years from the date of submission thereof to the States by the Congress.

AMENDMENT XXII   (1951)   (Term limits for the President, 2 terms or 10 years)

Section 1   No person shall be elected to the office of President more than twice, and no person who has held the office of President, or acted as President, for more than two years of a term to which some other person was elected President shall be elected to the office of President more than once. But this article shall not apply to any person holding the office of President when this article was proposed by the Congress, and shall not prevent any person who may be holding the office of President, or acting as President, during the term within which this article becomes operative from holding the office of President or acting as President during the remainder of such term.

Section 2   This article shall be inoperative unless it shall have been ratified as an amendment to the Constitution by the legislatures of three-fourths of the several States within seven years from the date of its submission to the States by the Congress.

AMENDMENT XXIII (1961) (Electoral College votes for the District of Columbia)

Section 1 The District constituting the seat of Government of the United States shall appoint in such manner as the Congress may direct:

A number of electors of President and Vice-President equal to the whole number of Senators and Representatives in Congress to which the District would be entitled if it were a State, but in no event more than the least populous State; they shall be in addition to those appointed by the States, but they shall be considered for the purposes of the election of President and Vice-President, to be electors appointed by a State; and they shall meet in the District and perform such duties as provided by the twelfth article of amendment.

Section 2 The Congress shall have the power to enforce this article by appropriate legislation.

AMENDMENT XXIV (1964) (Prohibition of poll taxes)

Section 1 The right of citizens of the United States to vote in any primary or other election for President or Vice-President, for electors for President or Vice-President, or for Senator or Representative in Congress, shall not be denied or abridged by the United States or any State by reason of failure to pay any poll tax or other tax.

Section 2 The Congress shall have the power to enforce this article by appropriate legislation.

AMENDMENT XXV (1967) <u>(Presidential succession)</u>

Section 1 In the case of the removal of the President from office or of his death or resignation, the Vice-President shall become President.

Section 2 Whenever there is a vacancy in the office of the Vice-President, the President shall nominate a Vice-President who shall take office upon confirmation by a majority vote of both Houses of Congress.

Section 3 Whenever the President transmits to the President *pro tempore* of the Senate and the Speaker of the House of Representatives his written declaration that he is unable to discharge the powers and duties of this office, and until he transmits to them a written declaration to the contrary, such powers and duties shall be discharged by the Vice-President as Acting President.

Section 4 Whenever the Vice-President and a majority of either the principal officers of the executive departments or of such other body as Congress may by law provide, transmit to the President *pro tempore* of the Senate and the Speaker of the House of Representatives their written declaration that the President is unable to discharge the powers and duties of his office, the Vice-President shall immediately assume the powers and duties of the office as Acting President.

Thereafter, when the President transmits to the President *pro tempore* of the Senate and the Speaker of the House of Representatives his written declaration that no inability exists, he shall resume the powers and duties of his office unless the Vice-President and a majority of either the principal officers of the executive department(s) or of such other body as Congress may by law provide, transmit within four days to the President *pro tempore* of the Senate and the Speaker of the House of Representives their written declaration that the President is unable to discharge the powers and duties of his office. Thereupon

Congress shall decide the issue, assembling within forty-eight hours for that purpose if not in session. If the Congress, within twenty-one days after receipt of the latter written declaration, or, if Congress is not in session, within twenty-one days after Congress is required to assemble, determines by two-thirds vote of both Houses that the President is unable to discharge the powers and duties of his office, the Vice-President shall continue to discharge the same as Acting President; otherwise, the President shall resume the powers and duties of his office.

AMENDMENT XXVI (1971) (Voting rights for young people)

Section 1 The right of citizens of the United States, who are eighteen years of age or older, to vote shall not be denied or abridged by the United States or by any State on account of age.

Section 2 The Congress shall have the power to enforce this article by appropriate legislation.

AMENDMENT XXVII (1992) (Timing of congressional pay raises)

No law varying the compensation for the service of Senators and Representatives shall take effect until an election of Representatives shall have intervened.

Bibliography

American Institute of Public Opinion, occasional public opinion polls.

American Studies Newsletter, monthly.

American Symphony Orchestra League (1995) Washington, DC.

Audit Bureau of Circulations, annual, Illinois: Schaumberg.

Competitive Media Reporting and Publishers' Information Bureau (1995), New York.

Dance US (1995) Washington, DC.

Editor and Publisher International Yearbook, annual.

Electronic Industries Association Market Research Department (1995).

Gallup Organization (The), Inc., occasional and annual public opinion polls.

Gallup International Research Institute, occasional public opinion polls.

International Herald Tribune, daily newspaper, Paris.

Jowell. R, Brook. L and Dowds. L. (1993) *International Social Attitudes 1993/4*, Dartmouth: Aldershot.

National Cable Television Association, annual publications.

National Center for Health Statistics, occasional reports.

National Council of the Churches of Christ in the United States of America, *Yearbook of American and Canadian Churches*, New York, annual.

National Journal, weekly on politics and government.

National Sporting Goods Association (1990) *Sports Participation in 1990: Series 1*, Mt. Prospect, Illinois.

Newsweek, weekly magazine.

Nielsen Media Research, annual

Opera America (1995) Washington, DC.

Recording Industry Association of America (1994), New York, various publications.

Statistical Abstract of the United States, US Printing Office, annual.

The Economist, weekly magazine, London.

The *Encyclopedia Americana* (1989) Colorado: Grolier Inc.

The Roper Organization, media surveys, Washington, DC.

The Sunday Times, weekly newspaper, London.

The Times, daily newspaper, London.

The World Almanac and Book of Facts: 1996 (1995) Mahwah, New Jersey: Funk and Wagnalls Corporation.

Time, weekly magazine.

US Bureau of the Census, occasional series and reports.

US Bureau of Investigation, *Crime in the United States*, annual.

US Bureau of Investigation, *Population-at-risk Rates and Selected Crime Indicators*, annual.

US Bureau of Justice Statistics, *Criminal Victimization in the United States*, annual.

US Bureau of Labor Statistics, annual.

US Department of Commerce, annual.

US Department of Health and Human Services, annual.

US National Center for Health Statistics, *Vital Statistics of the United States*, annual.

US News and World Report, weekly magazine.

World Values Study Group, Inter-University Consortium for Political and Social Research, 1990–93, Washington, DC.

Suggested further reading

Survey books on American civilization

Breidlid, A., Brøgger, F.Chr., Gulliksen, Ø.T. and Sirevåg, T. (eds) (1996) *American Culture: An Anthology of Civilization Texts*, London: Routledge.

Bromhead, P. (1988) *Life in Modern America*, London: Longman.

Fiedler, E., Reimer, J. and Norman-Risch, M. (1990) *America in Close-Up*, London: Longman.

Luedtke, L.S. (ed.) (1992) *Making America: The Society and Culture of the United States*, Chapel Hill: The University of North Carolina Press.

Nye, D. (1993) *Contemporary American Society*, Copenhagen: Academic Press.

Sirevåg, T. (1994) *American Patterns: An Interpretation of US History and Life*, Oslo: Gyldendal Norsk Forlag.

Stevenson, D.K. (1996) *American Life and Institutions*, Stuttgart: Ernst Klett Verlag and United States Information Agency.

History and society

Bellah, R.N. *et al.* (1985) *Habits of the Heart: Individualism and Commitment in American Life*, Berkeley, CA: University of California Press.

Bloom, A. (1988) *The Closing of the American Mind*, Harmondsworth: Penguin.

Degler, C. (1984) *Out of Our Past: The Forces that Shaped Modern America*, New York: Harper.

Freeman, J. *et al.* (1992) *Who Built America?*, vol. 2, New York: Pantheon.

Hughes, R. (1993) *The Culture of Complaint: The Fraying of America*, Oxford: Oxford University Press.

Hunter, J.D. (1991) *Culture Wars: The Struggle to Define America*, New York: Basic Books.

Lasch, C. (1978) *The Culture of Narcissism: American Life in an Age of Diminishing Expectations*, New York: Norton.

Levine, B. *et al.* (1989) *Who Built America?*, vol. 1, New York: Pantheon.

Lynd, R.S. and Lynd, H.M. (1929) *Middletown: A Study in Modern American Culture*, New York: Harcourt, Brace and World.

Maidment, R. and Dawson, M. (1994) *The United States in the Twentieth Century: Key Documents*, Kent: Hodder and Stoughton/The Open University.

Mitchell, J. and Maidment, R. (1994) *The United States in the Twentieth Century: Culture*, Kent: Hodder and Stoughton/The Open University.

Norton, M.B. *et al.* (1991) *A People and a Nation: A History of the United States*, Boston: Houghton Mifflin.

O'Callaghan, B. (1990) *An Illustrated History of the USA*, London: Longman.

Samuelson, R.T. (1996) *The Good Life and Its Discontents: The American Dream in the Age of Entitlement*, New York: Times Books.

Schlesinger Jr, A. (1992) *The Disuniting of America: Reflections on a Multicultural Society*, New York: Norton.

Takaki, R. (1993) *A Different Mirror: A History of Multicultural America*, Boston: Little, Brown and Company.

Geography

Garreau, J. (1981) *The Nine Nations of North America*, New York: Avon.

Knox, P.L. *et al.* (1988) *The United States: A Contemporary Human Geography*, London: Longman.

Paterson, J.H. (1989) *North America: A Geography of the United States and Canada*, New York: Oxford University Press.

Immigration and ethnicity

Barkan, E. (1996) *And Still They Come: Immigrants and American Society, 1920 to the 1990s*, Wheeling, Illinois: Harlan Davidson, Inc.

Bodnar, J. (1987) *The Transplanted*, Bloomington: Indiana University Press.

Dinnerstein, L. and Reimers, D.M. (1988) *Ethnic Americans: A History of Immigration*, New York: Harper and Row.

D'Innocenzo, M. and Sirefman, J.P. (1992) *Immigration and Ethnicity: American Society – 'Melting Pot' or 'Salad Bowl'?*, Westport: Greenwood Press.

Glazer, N. (1983) *Ethnic Dilemmas: 1964–1982*, Cambridge, MA: Harvard University Press.

Hingham, J. (1963) *Strangers in the Land: Patterns of American Nativism 1860–1925*, New York: Atheneum.

Seller, M. (1988) *To Seek America: A History of Ethnic Life in the United States*, Englewood Cliffs, NJ: Jerome S. Ozer.

Takaki, R. (1987) *From Different Shores: Perspectives on Races and Ethnicity in America*, New York: Oxford University Press.

Thernstrom, S. (1980) *The Harvard Encyclopedia of American Ethnic Groups*, New Haven, CT: Harvard University Press.

Women and minority groups

Berry, M.F. and Blassingame, J.W. (1982) *Long Memory: The Black Experience in America*, New York: Oxford University Press.

Chafe, W. (1972) *The American Woman: Her Changing Social, Economic and Political Roles, 1920–1970*, New York: Oxford University Press.

Chan, S. (1991) *Asian Americans: An Interpretive History*, Boston: Twayne.

Chavez, J.R. (1984) *The Lost Land: The Chicano Image of the Southwest*, Albuquerque: University of New Mexico Press.

Flexner, E. (1973) *Century of Struggle: The Women's Rights Movement in the United States*, New York: Atheneum.

Fuchs, L.H. (1990) *The American Kaleidoscope: Race, Ethnicity, and the Civic Culture*, Hanover: University Press of New England.

Jennings, F. (1993) *The Founders of America*, New York: Norton.

Kerber, L.K. and Hart-Mathews, J. (1982) *Women's America: Refocusing the Past*, New York: Oxford University Press.

Norton, M. and Alexander, R. (1996) *Major problems in American Women's History*, second edition, Lexington, MA: D.C. Heath and Company.

Olson, J.S. and Wilson, R. (1984) *Native Americans in the Twentieth Century*, Urbana, IL: University of Illinois Press.

Politics

Barone, M. and Ujifusa, G. *The Almanac of American Politics*, Washington, DC: annual.

Maidment, R. and Tappin, M. (1991) *American Politics Today*, Manchester: Manchester University Press.

Welch, S. *et al.* (1995) *Understanding American Government*, St. Paul, MN: West Publishing Company.

Williams, R. (1990) *Explaining American Politics: Issues and Interpretations*, London: Routledge.

Wilson, J.Q. (1994) *American Government*, Lexington, MA: D.C. Heath and Company.

Woll, P. and Binstock, R.H. (1991) *America's Political System: A Text with Cases*, New York: McGraw-Hill.

Foreign policy

LaFeber, W. (1989) *The American Age: United States Foreign Policy at Home and Abroad since 1750*, New York: Norton.

The legal system

American Bar Association (1993) *Law and the Courts: A Handbook of Courtroom Procedures*, Chicago, IL: ABA.

Black, C.L. (1977) *The People and the Court*, Westport, CT: Greenwood Press.

Botein, S. (1983) *Early American Law and Society*, New York: Knopf.

Hofstadter, R. and Wallace, M. (1970) *American Violence: A Documentary History*, New York: Knopf.

Mayers, L. (1981) *The American Legal System*, New Haven, CT: Rothman.

Neubauer, D.W. (1991) *Judicial Process: Law, Courts and Politics in the United States*, California: Brooks/Cole Publishing Company.

Economics

Cochran, T.C. (1972) *American Business in the Twentieth Century*, Cambridge, MA: Harvard University Press.

Miller, R. (1988) *Economics Today*, New York: Harper and Row.

Robertson, J.O. (1985) *America's Business*, New York: Hill and Wang.

Sabel, C.F. (1982) *Work and Politics: The Division of Labour in Industry*, Cambridge: Cambridge University Press.

Strasser, S. (1989) *Satisfaction Guaranteed: The Making of the American Mass Market*, New York: Pantheon.

Social services

DeSario, J.P. (1989) *International Public Policy Source Book (volume 1: Health and Social Welfare)*, Westport, CT: Greenwood Press.

Dixon, J. and Scheurell R.P. (1989) *Social Welfare in Developed Market Countries*, London: Routledge.

Macarov, D. (1978) *The Design of Social Welfare*, New York: Holt, Rinehart and Winston.

Munday, B. (1989) *The Crisis in Welfare*, New York: St Martin's Press.

Patterson, J.T. (1981) *America's Struggle against Poverty*, New York: Schocken Books.

Skocpol, T. (1995) *Social Policy in the United States*, Princeton, NJ: Princeton University Press.

Education

Kozol, J. (1991) *Savage Inequalities: Children in America's Schools*, New York: HarperCollins.

Sowell, T. (1993) *Inside American Education: The Decline, The Deception, The Dogmas*, New York: Macmillan.

The media

Bagdikian, B. (1987) *The Media Monopoly*, Boston: Beacon Press.

Baker, C.E. (1994) *Advertising and a Democratic Press*, Princeton, NJ: Princeton University Press.

Barnouw, E. (1982) *The Tube of Plenty: The Evolution of American Television*, Oxford: Oxford University Press.

Becker, S. and Roberts, C. (1992) *Discovering Mass Communications*, New York: HarperCollins.

Gitlin, T. (1983) *Inside Prime Time*, New York: Pantheon.

Iyengar, S. and Kinder, D.R. (1987) *News That Matters*, Chicago, IL: University of Chicago Press.

MacDonald, J.F. (1991) *One Nation Under Television: The Rise and Decline of Network TV*, New York: Pantheon.

Tebbel, J. (1975) *The Media in America*, New York: Crowell.

Tebbel, J. (1987) *Between Covers: The Rise and Transformation of Book Publishing in America*, Oxford: Oxford University Press.

Tunstall, J. (1977) *The Media are American*, London: Macmillan.

Turow, J. (1992) *Media Systems in Society: Understanding Industries, Strategies and Power*, New York: Longman.

Religion

Ahlstrom, S. (1972) *A Religious History of the American People*, New Haven, CT: Yale University Press.

Bedell, K. (1993) *Yearbook of American and Canadian Churches: 1993*, Nashville, TN: Abingdon Press.

Carter, S. (1993) *Culture of Disbelief*, New York: Anchor Books.

Dolan, J.P. (1985) *The American Catholic Experience*, Garden City: Doubleday.

Ellwood, Jr. R.S. (1973) *Religious and Spiritual Groups in Modern America*, Englewood Cliffs, NJ: Prentice-Hall.

Fitzgerald, F. (1987) *Cities on a Hill: A Journey through Contemporary American Culture*, London: Picador.

Fowler, R.B. and Hertzke, A.D. (1995) *Religion and Politics in America*, Colorado: Westview Press Inc.

Glazer, N. (1972) *American Judaism*, Chicago, IL: University of Chicago Press.

Haddad, Y.Y. and Lummis, A.T. (1987) *Islamic Values in the United States: A Comparative Study*, Oxford: Oxford University Press.

Handy, R.T. (1974) *A Christian America: Protestant Hopes and Historical Realities*, Oxford: Oxford University Press.

Herberg, W. (1983) *Protestant, Catholic, Jew*, Chicago, IL: University of Chicago Press.

Jones, R.E. and Donald, G. (1974) *Civil Religion in America*, New York: Harper.

Marty, M.E. (1984) *Pilgrims in their Own Land: 500 years of American Religion*, New York: Little.

Olmstead, C.E. (1960) *History of Religion in the United States*, Englewood Cliffs, NJ: Prentice-Hall.

Arts, sports and leisure

Adler, P. and Adler, P. (1991) *Blackboards and Blackboards: College Athletes and Role Engulfment*, New York: Columbia University Press.

Balio, T. (1990) *Hollywood in the Age of Television*, Cambridge, MA: Unwin Hyman.

Davies, R.O. (1994) *America's Obsession: Sports and Society since 1945*, New York: Harcourt Brace College Publishers.

Maltby, R. (1989) *Dreams for Sale: Popular Culture in the Twentieth Century*, London: Harrap.

Miller Brewing Co. (1983) *The Miller Lite Report on American Attitudes Towards Sport*, Milwaukee, WI: Lite Sports Report.

Mrozek, D. (1983) *Sport and American Mentality, 1880–1910*, Nashville, TN: University of Tennessee Press.

Schatz, T. (1981) *Hollywood Genres: Formulas, Filmmaking, and the Studio System*, New York: Random House.

Seymour, H. (1971) *Baseball: The Golden Age*, New York: Oxford University Press.

Seymour, H. (1990) *Baseball: The People's Game*, New York: Oxford University Press.

Skar, R. (1975) *Movie-Made America: A Cultural History of American Movies*, New York: Random House.

Index